INTERNATIONAL POLITICAL ECONOMY SERIES

General Editor: Timothy M. Shaw, Professor of Political Science and International Development Studies, and Director of the Centre for Foreign Policy Studies, Dalhousie University, Halifax, Nova Scotia

Recent titles include:

Pradeep Agrawal, Subir V. Gokarn, Veena Mishra, Kirit S. Parikh and Kunal Sen
ECONOMIC RESTRUCTURING IN EAST ASIA AND INDIA: Perspectives on Policy Reform

Deborah Bräutigam
CHINESE AID AND AFRICAN DEVELOPMENT: Exporting Green Revolution

Steve Chan, Cal Clark and Danny Lam (*editors*)
BEYOND THE DEVELOPMENTAL STATE: East Asia's Political Economies Reconsidered

Jennifer Clapp
ADJUSTMENT AND AGRICULTURE IN AFRICA: Farmers, the State and the World Bank in Guinea

Robert W. Cox (*editor*)
THE NEW REALISM: Perspectives on Multilateralism and World Order

Ann Denholm Crosby
DILEMMAS IN DEFENCE DECISION-MAKING: Constructing Canada's Role in NORAD, 1958–96

Diane Ethier
ECONOMIC ADJUSTMENT IN NEW DEMOCRACIES: Lessons from Southern Europe

Stephen Gill (*editor*)
GLOBALIZATION, DEMOCRATIZATION AND MULTILATERALISM

Jeffrey Henderson (*editor*), assisted by Karoly Balaton and Gyorgy Lengyel
INDUSTRIAL TRANSFORMATION IN EASTERN EUROPE IN THE LIGHT OF THE EAST ASIAN EXPERIENCE

Jacques Hersh and Johannes Dragsbaek Schmidt (*editors*)
THE AFTERMATH OF 'REAL EXISTING SOCIALISM' IN EASTERN EUROPE, Volume 1: Between Western Europe and East Asia

David Hulme and Michael Edwards (*editors*)
NGOs, STATES AND DONORS: Too Close for Comfort?

Staffan Lindberg and Árni Sverrisson (*editors*)
SOCIAL MOVEMENTS IN DEVELOPMENT: The Challenge of Globalization and Democratization

Anne Lorentzen and Marianne Rostgaard (*editors*)
THE AFTERMATH OF 'REAL EXISTING SOCIALISM' IN EASTERN EUROPE, Volume 2: People and Technology in the Process of Transition

Stephen D. McDowell
GLOBALIZATION, LIBERALIZATION AND POLICY CHANGE: A Political Economy of India's Communications Sector

Juan Antonio Morales and Gary McMahon (*editors*)
ECONOMIC POLICY AND THE TRANSITION TO DEMOCRACY: The Latin American Experience

Ted Schrecker (*editor*)
SURVIVING GLOBALISM: The Social and Environmental Challenges

Ann Seidman, Robert B. Seidman and Janice Payne (*editors*)
LEGISLATIVE DRAFTING FOR MARKET REFORM: Some Lessons from China

Caroline Thomas and Peter Wilkin (*editors*)
GLOBALIZATION AND THE SOUTH

Kenneth P. Thomas
CAPITAL BEYOND BORDERS: States and Firms in the Auto Industry, 1960–94

Geoffrey R. D. Underhill (*editor*)
THE NEW WORLD ORDER IN INTERNATIONAL FINANCE

Henry Veltmeyer, James Petras and Steve Vieux
NEOLIBERALISM AND CLASS CONFLICT IN LATIN AMERICA: A Comparative Perspective on the Political Economy of Structural Adjustment

Robert Wolfe
FARM WARS: The Political Economy of Agriculture and the International Trade Regime

International Political Economy Series
Series Standing Order ISBN 0–333–71708–2 hardcover
Series Standing Order ISBN 0–333–71110–6 paperback
(*outside North America only*)

You can receive future titles in this series as they are published by placing a standing order. Please contact your bookseller or, in case of difficulty, write to us at the address below with your name and address, the title of the series and one or both of the ISBNs quoted above.

Customer Services Department, Macmillan Distribution Ltd
Houndmills, Basingstoke, Hampshire RG21 6XS, England

Economic and Political Impediments to Middle East Peace

Critical Questions and Alternative Scenarios

Edited by

J. W. Wright, Jr.
American Association for the Advancement of Science Diplomacy Fellow and Trade Policy Advisor, Office of Emerging Markets
United States Agency for International Development

and

Laura Drake
School of International Service
American University
Washington, DC

Foreword by Queen Noor of Jordan

First published in Great Britain 2000 by
MACMILLAN PRESS LTD
Houndmills, Basingstoke, Hampshire RG21 6XS and London
Companies and representatives throughout the world

A catalogue record for this book is available from the British Library.

ISBN 0–333–67899–0

First published in the United States of America 2000 by
ST. MARTIN'S PRESS, INC.,
Scholarly and Reference Division,
175 Fifth Avenue, New York, N.Y. 10010

ISBN 0–312–22577–6

Library of Congress Cataloging-in-Publication Data
Economic and political impediments to Middle East peace : critical questions and alternative scenarios / edited by J.W. Wright, Jr. and Laura Drake ; foreword by Queen Noor of Jordan.
p. cm. — (International political economy series)
Includes bibliographical references and index.
ISBN 0–312–22577–6 (cloth)
1. Middle East—Economic conditions—1979– 2. Africa, North–Economic conditions. 3. Arab–Israeli conflict—1993– —Peace.
I. Wright, J. W., Jr. II. Drake, Laura. III. Series.
HC415.15.E247 1999
330.956—dc21 99–26119
CIP

This book is printed on paper suitable for recycling and made from fully managed and sustained forest sources.

10 9 8 7 6 5 4 3 2 1
09 08 07 06 05 04 03 02 01 00

Printed and bound in Great Britain by
Antony Rowe Ltd, Chippenham, Wiltshire

To those uncounted thousands
who have sacrificed their lives or their freedom
to make the Middle East a better place

The editors and contributors to this volume wish to express their condolences to Queen Nour, the Royal Family and the people of Jordan for the loss of King Hussein. He was a great leader and a real force in the battle to achieve peace in the Middle East. We further dedicate this book to his memory.

Contents

List of Tables

List of Figures

Acknowledgments

This project has taken many turns since its inception, and at each turn a new set of people offered needed assistance. Timothy Shaw, Tim Farmiloe, Aruna Vasudevan, Keith Povey and their colleagues at the publishers have supported the project since the beginning: they deserve thanks for providing much appreciated expertise. John R. Presley and Rodney Wilson were also early supporters of the text and have our appreciation. The editors would jointly like to thank all of the contributors for their work. Likewise, the contributors want to congratulate Laura Drake on her recent marriage to John McGrane.

J.W. Wright would like to recognize a number of other individuals who have supported his work on this project. First among these are Gary Garrison and David Adams at the Council for the International Exchange of Scholars. This programme's funding of his Fulbright research award made finishing this text possible. He appreciates Drs Beverley Wolff, Davy McCall and John Presley writing on his behalf for this award. Allen M. Omoto has helped in many ways, but in this particular case he has given personal support as well as editorial commentary. Suzanne Pinckney Stetkevych continues to serve as a valued mentor, as does Salman Al-Ani, Fedwa Malit-Douglas, Allen Douglas, Harvey Hagerty and the many friends at Indiana University. Karen Pfieffer at Smith College has also been a terrific mentor. J.W. Wright also expresses thanks to Berj and Suzie Aprahamian Gene and Jerrin Bird, Tamara Duggleby, John Gideons, Omar Kader, Barbara Presley, Vicky Sawyer, Mary Schmidt, Sandra Samaan-Tammari, Kenneth Wantling and Ginger Moore Wantling, M. Valerie York, his parents J. Wayne and M. Diane Wright, and grandparents and many other friends and family who deserve credit for supporting his work over the years. We regret the loss of our friend, Jane Hallow, to cancer.

Laura Drake, likewise, would like to express her great appreciation for the personal support and encouragement offered by the faculty and colleagues at the American University School of International Service. In particular, she expresses deep and sincere thanks to Dean Louis Goodman, Dr John Richardson, Dr Abdulaziz Said, Dr Samih Farsoun, Dr Paul Wapner and Dr Fawaz Gerges, and to all her friends and colleagues in the third-year SIS doctoral cohort. The support of all of these individuals has been a continuous blessing in her current scholarly endeavours. She also takes this opportunity to recognize and express generalized thanks and appreciation to the following other individuals: Khalid Abdalla, Yaser Bushnaq, Wafa Darwazeh, Reverdy Fishel, Bill Gronos, Khaled Khalifeh, Riadh El-Khudairi, Victoria

Long, Bill Long, Munir Abu-Hassan, John McGrane, Issa Nakhleh, Nader Hussein Rabah, Carol Gallion Skeahan, Said Mahmoud Taha, Walter Wolk, Ahmed Yousef, and to her co-editor in this current project, J.W. Wright. Finally, she dedicates her work in this volume to her beloved parents, Dr William E. Drake, Jr., and Dr Margaret Drake, now deceased, but whose love and lasting influence, in both the familial and intellectual realms, will continue to transcend their own lives.

J.W. WRIGHT JR.
LAURA DRAKE

List of Abbreviations

ACDA	United States Arms Control and Disarmament Agency
AHLC	Ad Hoc Liaison Committee (Oslo Accords)
APEC	Asia–Pacific Economic Cooperation
CG	Consultative Group (Oslo Accords)
COPP	Committee for International Assistance to the Palestinian Police
DOP	Declaration of Principles (Oslo I)
EAP	Emergency Assistance Programme (Oslo Accords)
EIB	European Investment Bank
ERP	Emergency Rehabilitation Programme (Oslo Accords)
ESCWA	Economic and Social Commission for Western Asia (United Nations)
EU	European Union
FPE	Final Prediction Error
GCC	Gulf Cooperation Council
GDP	Gross Domestic Product
IAI	Israel Aircraft Industries
IDA	International Development Association
ILO	International Labour Organization
IMF	International Monetary Fund
JICA	Japan International Cooperation Agency
JLC	Joint Liaison Committee (Oslo Accords)
LACC	Local Aid Coordination Committee (Oslo Accords)
MENA	Middle East and North Africa
MMRAE	Ministry of Municipal, Rural Affairs, and the Environment (Jordan)
NAFTA	North American Free Trade Agreement
NGO	Non-Governmental Organization
NIS	New Israeli Shekel
OLS	Ordinary Least-Squares
OPEC	Organization of Petroleum Exporting Countries
OPIC	Overseas Private Investment Corporation
PA	Palestinian Authority
PECDAR	Palestinian Economic Council for Development and Reconstruction
PLO	Palestine Liberation Organization
PMA	Palestinian Monetary Authority
PPIP	Palestinian Public Investment Programme

PPP	Purchasing Power Parity
PVO	Private Voluntary Organization
SABIC	Saudi Arabian Basic Industries Corporation
SME	Small- and Medium-sized Enterprise
SWG	Sectoral Working Group (Oslo Accords)
TAP	Tripartite Action Plan (Oslo Accords)
TATF	Technical Assistance Trust Fund (Oslo Accords)
UNDP	United Nations Development Programme
UNICEF	United Nations Children's Fund
UNRWA	United Nations Relief and Works Agency
UNSCO	United Nations Special Coordinator Office
UNIDO	United Nations Industrial Development Organization
USAID	United States Agency for International Development
WHO	World Health Organization

Notes on the Contributors

Her Majesty Queen Noor In the past 20 years since her marriage to King Hussein, Queen Noor of Jordan, an Arab American by birth, has dedicated herself to promoting international exchange and understanding. She travels extensively to lecture at universities, world affairs organizations, and international conferences on global issues and Middle East politics. She is actively involved with the United Nations and other international organizations working in the fields of health, education, women's issues, the environment, human rights and development.

Barbara Balaj is a consultant with the World Bank's Middle East Department, and completed her graduate work at George Washington University. She is a former Guest Scholar at the French Institute for International Relations, and Fulbright Scholar of the German Society for International Affairs, and she has published works on European–Middle East relations. Her other professional interests include research on study of the role of non-governmental organizations in the West Bank and Gaza Strip, and the Middle East Multilateral Working Groups.

Rex Brynen is an Associate Professor of Political Science at McGill University, and a faculty member in the Inter-University Consortium for Arab Studies. He is the author of *Sanctuary and Survival: The Palestine Liberation Organization in Lebanon*, and the editor of four collections on the contemporary Middle East.

Ishac Diwan was born in Lebanon, and earned his PhD in economics from the University of California, Berkeley. He is an economist with the World Bank's Economic Development Institute, where he supervises research projects on the region and other developing areas. His publications are mainly in the areas of economic development and international trade. He also writes on Middle East economic issues, including articles on labour mobility in the Middle East and North Africa, the Levantine economic triangle, and external factors in reconstruction policies in Lebanon.

Peter L. Doan is an Associate Professor of Urban and Regional Planning at Florida State University, Tallahassee. He teaches in the Planning for Developing Areas specialisation of the Department of Urban and Regional Planning. Dr Doan is also a visiting Senior Fulbright Scholar at the Population Studies Department at the University of Jordan in Amman, where he received a Fulbright serial research grant for 1995–97. His primary research interests include regional development, decentralization strategies, and relationships between infrastructure and economic development.

Laura Drake is a Middle East academic and international consultant specializing in the region's political-military and strategic affairs. She teaches international relations and Middle East politics at the American University in Washington DC, where she received her PhD. Her recent research includes analyses of the military and political aspects of the Arab–Israeli conflict, the results of United States containment strategies against Iraq and Iran, and the issue of unconventional weapons proliferation in the area.

Mohamed A. El-Erian is Deputy Director of the Middle Eastern Department of the International Monetary Fund. He holds a doctorate and a master's degree in economics from Oxford University, having earned his undergraduate degree from Cambridge University. He is widely published in the fields of regional and macroeconomics, international finance and economic development. His most recent publications have been on the Middle East and North Africa, including several essays on the peace process.

Michael Field is a leading writer, business journalist and financial analyst on economics in the Middle East. His most recent book, *Inside the Arab World*, was published in 1995. He is also the author of *A Hundred Million Dollars a Day: Inside the World of Middle East Money*, and *The Merchants – The Big Business Families of Arabia*. Mr Field manages his own consulting firm, which specialises in business and commercial development in the Middle East.

Stanley Fischer has served as the First Deputy Managing Director of the International Monetary Fund since September 1994. Prior to taking this position, he was Killian Professor and Head of the Department of Economics at the Massachusetts Institute of Technology. He has also taught at the University of Chicago. From 1988–90 he served as Vice-President for Development Economics and as Chief Economist at the World Bank. Dr Fischer has also held positions at Hebrew University and the Hoover Institution at Stanford University.

Peter Gubser has been president of the American Near East Refugee Aid (ANERA) since 1977, an international non-profit organization based in Washington with offices in Jerusalem and Gaza. Prior to that appointment he was Assistant Representative for the Ford Foundation in Beirut and Amman. He is also a Professor at Georgetown University's School of Foreign Service. Dr Gubser received his DPhil in social studies and politics from Oxford University, St Antony's College, his MA in Middle Eastern Studies from the American University of Beirut, and his BA in Political Science from Yale University. His books include *Jordan, Crossroads of Middle Eastern Events*, and *Politics and Change in Al-Karak, Jordan*.

Robert E. Looney is Professor of National Security Affairs at the Naval Postgraduate School in Monterey, California. Prior to this he served as a development economist at the Stanford Research Institute as well as a faculty member at the University of California at Davis. He has also been an advisor to the governments of Iran, Saudi Arabia, Panama, Jamaica and Mexico, and he has written over 20 books on various aspects of economic development, the latest of which is *The Economics of Third World Defense Expenditures* (1995). He has a forthcoming book on Saudi Arabia.

Emma C. Murphy is a political-economist and Director of the Centre for Middle Eastern and Islamic Studies at the University of Durham, England, where she has also served as a British Academy Postdoctoral Fellow. One of her major interests is the economic impacts of diplomatic and legal efforts in the Middle East region, about which she has recently published several essays on the potential economic rewards of peace. In addition to work on Palestine and Israel, Dr Murphy writes about Tunisia's role in the pan-Arab economy. (She will soon publish *Economic and Political Change in Tunisia*, (1999), on the role of the Middle East region in the new world order.

Volker Perthes is a researcher at the Stiftung Wissenschaft und Politik in Ebenhausen, Germany, specializing primarily in the politics and economies of the Middle East, particularly in contemporary Syria. His published works include *The Political Economy of Syria Under Asad* (1995) and *Scenarios for Syria: Socio-economic and Political Choiceas* (1998) as well as articles on similar topics in the *Middle East Journal*, the *International Journal of Middle East Studies* and *Current History*.

Bernard Philippe holds a doctorate in economics and is an official with the European Union. In the course of a two-year secondment he represented the European Union at the World Bank in Washington, where he was charged with coordinating economic assistance to the West Bank and Gaza Strip. His publications deal principally with international exchange and questions of development. Since his return to Brussels he has been active in working on the European Union's Mediterranean Initiatives.

William Stoltzfus was born in Beirut, Lebanon in 1924 of missionary parents, and lived in Lebanon and Syria for 40 years. He entered the US State Department's Foreign Service after graduating from Princeton University in

1949. His diplomatic postings allowed him to serve in Aden, Egypt, Ethiopia, Libya and the former North Yemen, before being named the concurrent Ambassador of the United States to Bahrain, Kuwait, Oman, Qatar and the United Arab Emirates. After retiring from the Foreign Service, Ambassador Stoltzfus began a 17-year career in international banking and global finance.

Elias H. Tuma, Professor Emeritus of Economics at the University of California, Davis, has written ten books and a prolific range of articles on the Middle East and other areas and topics. Among his books are *Peacemaking and the Immoral War, Arabs and Jews in the Middle East* (1972), *The Economic Case for Palestine*, with Haim Darin-Drabkin (1978), *Economic and Political Change in the Middle East* (1987), and *The Persistence of Economic Discrimination: Race, Ethnicity, and Gender: A Comparative Study* (1995).

Rodney Wilson is Reader in Economics at the University of Durham in England and has over 25 years of experience working on Arab issues. He recently published *Economic Development in the Middle East*, *Politics and the Economy of Jordan*, and *Islamic Financial Markets*, all in 1995. He is also the author of *Banking and Finance in the Arab Middle East* (1983), *The Economies of the Middle East* (1979), and *Trade and Investment in the Middle East* (1977). Dr Wilson is an active advisor to the European Commission on the Arab–Israeli peace process.

J.W. Wright, Jr. holds an American Association for the Advancement of Science Diplomacy Fellowship and serves as a Trade Advisor in the Emerging Markets Office at the US Agency for International Development. Before that he worked at the Dubai Chamber of Commerce and Industry, and was a Fulbright Scholar at the Juma Al Majid Centre in the United Arab Emirates. His publications include *Muslim Attitudes Toward Islamic Finance* (1999), *The Political Economy of Middle East Peace: The Impact of Competing Trade Agendas*, (1999), *Business and Economic Development in Saudi Arabia* (1996), *Saudi Arabia: Tradition and Transition*, (1993), and *Structural Flaws in the Middle East Peace Process* (1999)

Foreword: The Face of Daunting Challenges

Most countries in the Middle East and North Africa (MENA) region have begun to emerge from the grip of the Arab–Israeli conflict and petroleum-linked economic surpluses and distortions. All of them face daunting political, social and economic challenges that must be addressed simultaneously if they are to be dealt with effectively. It is also becoming self-evident, though, that diplomatic efforts and political–economic reforms can only succeed if other sectoral challenges are met – in fields such as the environment, demography, information, social policy and the interaction between nationalism, religion, governance and personal identity.

As the chapters in this book confirm yet again – with a most useful combination of statistics, cross-sectoral analysis and fresh urgency – the MENA region suffers from low regional integration and lacks linkages needed to enter global trade. Many of the political and economic causes of this situation are well-documented in this book and are complemented by a wide range of possible remedial suggestions. While I neither endorse nor reject any of the specific policy recommendations or historical information provided in this book, I am confident that the peoples and nations of the Middle East and North Africa can only benefit from such earnest analyses of how to resolve their pressing political, economic and social challenges.

To do so, though, perhaps we should transcend the traditional parameters of political economy and dare to appreciate other factors that impact on nation- and economy-building in our region. Some of these other factors include transnational and often primordial forces such as religion, ethnicity, Arabism and tribalism. In other words, we should try to see and understand the societies of the Middle East and North Africa through the eyes of their own people. Through elections, political activism, civil society expansion, freeing the press and other means, the peoples of the region have expressed themselves vigorously on three main concerns in recent decades – politics, economics and the great issues of personal, social and national identity. All these areas of concern need to be addressed with equal seriousness in the MENA region, which suffers from pressures in the following broad areas:

Population/natural resource imbalances and environmental stress. The high annual rate of net population increase in most parts of MENA and the relatively low age of the population means that the total regional population will triple before it begins to stabilize. The World Bank estimates that the Arab population alone will increase from 200 million in 1990 to 450 million by the year 2025, and will only stabilize when it reaches over 700 million people. The population of the entire region (the Arab states, Iran, Turkey and Israel) is projected to stabilize only after it reaches approximately one billion people, around the year 2040.

The Arab population increased by 45 per cent in the period 1980–93, but total Arab gross national product grew by just 15 per cent, and thus total Arab GNP per capita declined in that period from $3283 to $2116. In the period 1980–94, the annual food gap of the Arab states alone remained stubbornly consistent, at an average of some $11 per year, while total annual food imports averaged $23 billion. Most states of the Middle East suffer water deficits, and most are over-pumping their naturally replenishable underground aquifers.

Debt, economic adjustment and social stress. By 1993 the Arab states had an "official" foreign public debt of $153 billion, but the actual total public debt was more realistically thought to be well over $200 billion. Annual foreign debt service payments nearly doubled in the decade after 1983, from around $8 billion to around $16 billion per year; as a percentage of exports they increased from around 26 per cent in 1985 to 32 per cent in 1992. Public expenditures as a percentage of gross domestic product for the period 1985–93 fluctuated within the very high range of 38–49 per cent; Arab defence and security expenditures in that period accounted for an average 27 per cent of total public current expenditures.

Consequently, economic structural adjustment programmes have been widely instituted in the MENA region. These programmes, which usually require lower government spending and a greater reliance on the private sector, generally aggravate the socio-economic conditions of the middle and lower income classes, especially among unemployed urban men. The rapid pace of urbanization, at an average of 4.1 per cent in the Middle East and North Africa region for the period 1980–93, compounds the destabilizing problems of unemployment, poverty, social alienation and economic distress.

Political culture and good governance. Most MENA states, with only a few exceptions, remain challenged to formulate satisfactory political cultures and fair governance systems which both respond to indigenous cultural identities and also reflect the widespread popular desire for democratic principles such as participation, accountability, pluralism and human rights. The crucial strategic relationship between good governance, the confidence of domestic and foreign investors and the prospects for sustained economic expansion must be widely activated in the Middle East in order to achieve stability and progress.

Community, state, nation and identity. The question of political governance is closely linked to a larger strategic issue that still challenges many peoples and lands in the Middle East – personal social, ethnic, religious and national identity and the configuration of statehood. It is noteworthy that among the enduring political or national sentiments that have been expressed by the peoples of the Middle East in recent decades, Islam, Arabism and tribalism are transnational forces that explicitly express the relevance of regional identities alongside state and local identities. If people instinctively assert such identities and forces as a means of coping with current economic stress, political discontent or cultural change, it seems appropriate somehow to include these elements in our common drive to promote stability, economic progress and regional integration.

Militarization. The Middle East has the world's highest regional ratio of military spending to gross national product (8.7 per cent on average, and obviously higher in several countries), as well as the highest increase in absolute terms in military spending. These high rates are not surprising, given the region's legacy of foreign control and fragmentation and the consequences of the Arab–Israeli conflict, economic distress, political discontent and social tensions.

The intense focus on the need of the MENA region for policy reforms, regionalization, globalization, privatization and other changes is likely to increase social and economic pressures on the majority of people in the short term; this, in turn, may heighten the search for relief and protection on a mass scale across national borders.

This should prompt us to explore more rigorously the precise points and nature of the interaction between political economy and identity in the MENA cultures. Our economic structural adjustment experience in Jordan since 1988 is often held up to others in the developing world as exemplary, because of the combination of sustained economic progress combined with political and social stability. Our own analysis suggests that this is primarily due to two reasons: (1) the steady expansion of political participation, liberalization and democratization alongside economic adjustment; and (2) a gradualist approach to socio-economic change that respects social traditions and cultural values. This is true at both the national level and the village or community level. The challenge to modernize while also safeguarding one's cultural identity requires a balanced commitment to economic, political and human identity values; the commitment becomes more powerful and effective if it includes a steady pace of change, a clear strategic goal and a meaningful, open process of political consultation and consensus-building.

We are all well aware of the various policy changes required to place the MENA region on a collective course of sustainable development and economic expansion. We must strike an appropriate balance between politics, economics, social issues and human identity factors, and we must learn how to expand successful project-based dynamics at local levels to nationwide systems and values. Less clear is the mechanism by which we can implement economic policy changes while simultaneously safeguarding social safety nets, economic equity, political participation and hope for a better quality of life in the future – the essential elements that comprise what we might simply call "human dignity". If transformations in the political economy are to succeed and to last, they must be measured by the dual criteria of technical efficiency and human dignity. This duality can be achieved and sustained if the target beneficiary population is sent the following message: you must make significant changes in your traditional economic system in order to shift from dependency to productivity, but such changes will only be made through a process in which you will participate actively and at all levels, and change will occur in accordance with your community's social values and cultural traditions.

Community development projects that we have implemented through the Noor Al-Hussein Foundation, at village and neighbourhood levels in urban and rural Jordan, have achieved noteworthy and quantifiable results. They have increased family and community productivity, raised family incomes and living standards, lowered dependence on the central government, promoted the participation of women in economies and decision-making processes, integrated local productive ventures into the national and even the global economy, and enhanced maternal and child health as measured by fertility, education and mortality rates. We know that the reasons for this success include: participation by men and women in all aspects of project decision-making; a commitment to gender equity and the education of women; the use of training in an ongoing rather than an occasional manner; and the adoption of a gradual pace of change that does not precipitously shock social sensibilities or traditional values.

The lessons we have learned from community-level development are relevant to our desire to promote MENA-wide domestic policy reforms, regional economic integration and global trading linkages. Perhaps the key developmental lesson of recent decades is that political inclusion and gender equity are essential for meaningful and sustainable economic reform. Every society interprets these principles according to its own values, religious ethics, environmental conditions and cultural traditions, especially *vis-à-vis* the nature of political participation and the role of women in public life and the economy.

The MENA region presents perhaps a more daunting challenge than other regions of the world in terms of promoting long-term, sustained economic development, because of the sharp strategic distortions it has experienced due to oil, the Arab–Israeli conflict and other factors. The need to resume long-term, balanced economic growth in this region demands that we shed the constraining influences of the past and look to a future in which the peoples, resources and cultures of the MENA region once again contribute their share to the common saga of human civilization. We have done so many times in the past, in moments of equally historic global transformation, and we are certainly well on our way to doing so again.

HER MAJESTY QUEEN NOOR OF JORDAN

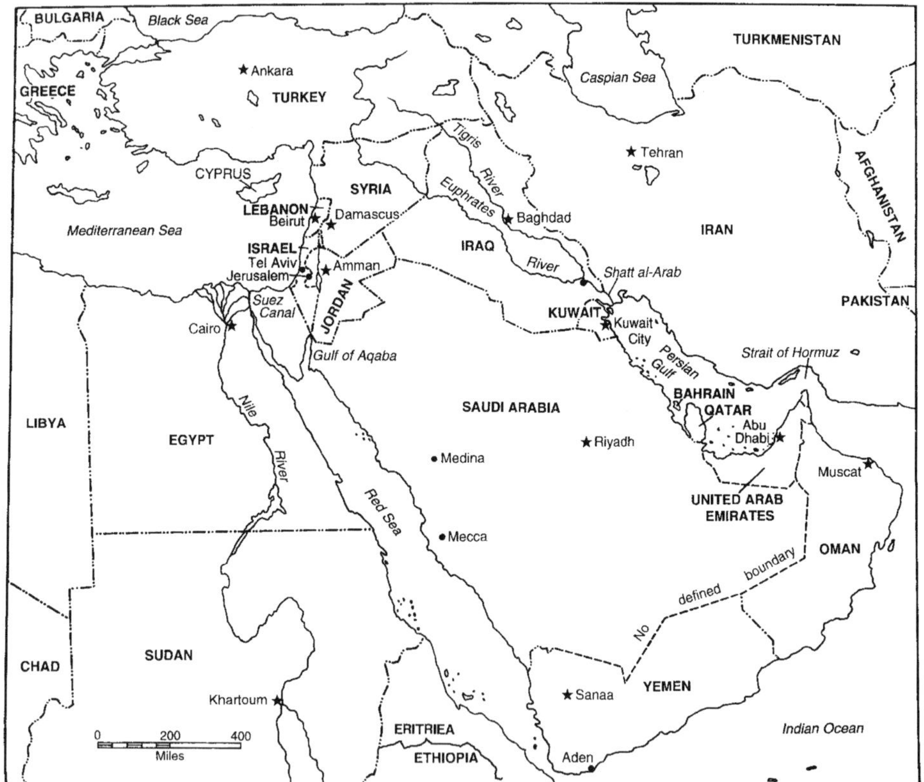

Source: Congressional Quarterly, *The Middle East*, 8th edn (Washington DC: 1994). Reprinted with permission.

Introduction: Economic and Political Impediments to Middle East Peace

J.W. Wright, Jr.

On 4 March 1996 Jordan's Queen Noor, Arab American Lisa Halaby, was honoured at the Kennedy Center for her contributions to world peace and philanthropy. An eloquent speaker, she characteristically maintained the fine balance between her role as an Arab advocate and her position as an unofficial international diplomat. However, unlike many of her speeches about Jordan's cultural wealth, in this address Queen Noor added a clear economics theme to her repertoire. She spoke of the occupational inequities in the occupied territories which fueled the *Intifada* as well as occasional civil strife among Palestinians. She spoke of the high density of refugees in the Levant and the influence of their abject poverty on questions of regional stability. She discussed the Arab governments' inordinately high budgetary expenditures for military equipment, and she mentioned the role international aid plays in the region. Her husband's people, she said, care more about employment stability than radical politics, and she asserted that investment leading to job creation is an essential factor in promoting peace. In sum, Queen Noor argued that many of the remaining critical questions facing Arab and Israeli negotiators concern economic inequities. I believe these inequities create political turmoil too.

Few regional specialists have been willing to admit this is the case, preferring instead to focus only on political rhetoric surrounding development issues, or, at best, focusing on the political implications of aid distribution structures. With the exception of the Peace Media Programme,[1] this lack of notice is in some cases due to the over-supply of journalists in the region unable to recognize economic trends, or unwilling to analyse commercial agreements. In fairness to these reporters, the pace of events surrounding Arab– Israeli peace talks has left the world, its diplomats, and the people who write about them working at breakneck pace. Reporting on the more visible political events in Israel and Palestine has kept the international press busy enough. Benjamin Netanyahu's tenure as Prime Minister in Israel – including an address to both houses of the United States Congress – and his seemingly constant and changing announcements of new strategies for attaining regional peace feed into dramatic political coverage.

However, the rise in dramatic political events and the reactions they have generated from both supporters and opponents of the peace process lead us to believe that no sustainable solutions will come to pass without considerable costs. Moreover, we are now clearly in the midst of an expensive payback period for the long-standing undervaluation of Palestinian security requirements in comparison to those of the Israelis.[2] As we enter a new millennium, we must ask some critical questions. What is the new price for peace? If the worsening economic situation of the Palestinians under occupation was a major impetus to the *Intifada*, what does the closure in the occupied territories mean to our current chances for peace? How is investment to occur under such circumstances, and what will be the outcome of a protracted situation of massive unemployment among Palestinians in the West Bank and Gaza Strip? What better result can we expect than the inevitable upsurges in violence? If the lack of cooperation between Arab and Israeli institutions was a key problem before, how can either side trust the other now?

The focus of this collection surrounds the economic and political impediments to Middle East peace, especially those aspects that make the vision of a peace dividend via economic cooperation difficult to envision. Indeed, rhetoric about the economic separation of Israel and Palestine may sound sweet when tasted alongside the bitter history of the Israeli occupation. But no matter how strong the perceived motives for separating these peoples may be, Queen Noor is correct to point out that closing the door on economic opportunities in Israel will not help the Palestinians. Dr Sari Nusseibeh states this position more clearly: "Even if a genuinely independent Palestinian state is established, political and economic separation will not be possible in the future…it is unworkable."[3] Queen Noor's and Dr Nusseibeh's claims are both realistic and simple: while the politics of separation is popular, the economics of state-building make cooperation essential.

Fortunately, there seems to be room for cooperation. In a survey of attitudes towards economic cooperation (195 Palestinian business owners and 372 Israeli business owners), Hazboun and Bahiri found both Arabs and Israelis willing to increase trading alliances. Among the Arabs surveyed, 76 per cent were interested in cooperating with Israeli firms. Among the Israelis, 85 per cent were interested in cooperating with Palestinian firms. Fifty-three per cent of the Palestinian firms already had subcontracting relationships with Israelis, and 51 per cent of the Israelis surveyed believed it was necessary to maintain subcontracting relationships with Palestinian suppliers. Ninety-two per cent of Palestinian firms and 96 per cent of Israeli firms felt the Declaration of Principles (on trading activities) would facilitate economic growth.[4] It is these sorts of cooperative arrangements that could lift the Palestinian labour market out of the despair it has faced since the end of the *Intifada* and since the beginning of the Gulf War.[5]

However, willingness notwithstanding, the institutional and legal impediments to commercial cooperation are immense. The 30-year-old Israeli occupation of the West Bank and Gaza Strip has left the Palestinians with a dilapidated business sector and an economy wherein as much as 80 per cent of their internal trade takes place in informal markets. As Ford and Peterson put it, "a principal cause of this situation is the labyrinth of regulations established during the occupation that were aimed at controlling virtually every aspect of the Palestinian economy."[6] There is almost no working financial system in the occupied territories, even still – and the state of even basic infrastructure cannot support industrial-grade development in Gaza and elsewhere.

Almost no formal banking system existed in the West Bank and Gaza Strip when the Declaration of Principles was signed in 1993. Since 1967 the Palestinians have not been allowed to develop financial institutions, leaving them dependent on Israeli banks for financial services. After the money confiscations that took place in the West Bank town of Beit Sahour, Palestinian investors were left with no financial institutions that could be trusted to protect their savings.[7] By the end of the *Intifada*, the few financial services providers that were operating in the occupied territories had withdrawn.[8] While the Paris Protocol of 1994 sets forth initiatives aimed at giving the Palestinian Authority a theoretically freer hand in setting its own trade agendas and creating fair regulations,[9] the familiar Israeli economic strictures – in addition to the new ones associated with closures – cannot be underestimated as an inhibiting influence on Palestinian commercial trade.[10]

Under Israeli occupation, obtaining economic or commercial licenses became a complex of policy games and procedures. In most cases Palestinians have been required to apply for "special licenses" for tasks like buying raw materials, hiring employees and even shipping goods to other Arab firms. Business expansion licenses have been nearly impossible for Arabs to obtain.[11] New firms in the West Bank must pass the scrutiny of the Knesset's "strategic investments" committee, which verifies that the firm supports Israel's interests. Foreign investors have usually been required to have a Jewish partner, and all non-Israeli foreign investors have been required to sign a document supporting Zionism.[12] In addition, Arab exporters have had to hire Israeli agents and pay the Israeli government a "special tax" that has made it difficult for Palestinians to remain price competitive.[13]

In addition, the less than stable money supply in Israel has made the prospect of recycling any Palestinian deposits unlikely, inside or outside the Green Line.[14] Shifting alliances between Jordan and its neighbours, and changes in Jordanian land policies also make it difficult to see incentives for bank managers to reinvest funds in Palestine.[15] There are also few facilities available to middle-class professionals in fields like medicine that help them mobilize human or financial capital in Palestinian society.[16] These situations have led to capital-hoarding in the informal sector, severely limiting productivity. Wealthy Palestinians have been compelled to transfer their money to other economies, such as those in Europe or the United States, and, just as often, much in the way of Palestinian overseas earnings never entered the West Bank or Gaza as financial remittances. This latter phenomenon has limited remittance spending to squanderables instead of having these monies recycled into businesses and capital investments that would create jobs.

There is also little in the way of efficient infrastructure in the West Bank or Gaza. Services such as power, water and other utilities in Gaza are among the worst in the world. Because of the occupation, the territories have fallen far behind Egypt, Jordan and their other Arab neighbours in terms of infrastructure construction, communications technologies and in the number of facilities providing human services. Even in the post-Paris Protocol state of affairs, and even after the Wye Accords, too little attention is focused on the institutions needed to transfer international aid commitments into productive projects.[17] There is also a large community, comprising Arabs and foreigners alike, who enjoy the lack of institutional formality because a more informal milieu provides greater opportunities to create wasteful yet wealth-accumulating systems via biased aid-distribution programmes.

For example, a key assumption of negotiators is that Palestinians will trade most with Jordan.[18] In practice, trade between the West Bank, Gaza and Jordan has not exceeded more than 10 per cent of Palestinian trade during any time under Israeli occupation. This means there are fewer marketing contacts and established trading lines between Palestinians and Jordanians than one might expect. Moreover, the 50 per cent decline in Jordan's GNP since the Gulf War has only weakened the ability of Palestinians to enhance their commercial positions with Jordanian buyers or suppliers.[19]

Another trade impediment has been the erosion of the Palestinian production base. Not only are the manufacturing bases and financial structures in the West Bank and Gaza weaker today than they were a few years ago, the Israeli occupation so "weakened the Palestinian economy and made it increasingly dependent on the Israeli economy that it can hardly recover".[20] Examination of economic data reveals that the dominant sources in Palestinian economic growth come from income generated via transfers made outside the occupied territories, such as employment in Israel or labour exportation to the Gulf States. While it can be said that the *Intifada* led to an increase in Palestinian self-reliance in numerous markets, the following are still true: (1) the Palestinian labour force is largely dependent on Israeli employment; (2) Palestinians have been left with a poor and crumbling infrastructure; (3) Israel's attempts to disenfranchize the territories' formal sector financial structure have succeeded; and (4) the aforementioned "strategic investment policy" severely limits the availability of investment from the Palestinian diaspora.

Moreover, these strategies are part of the Israeli policy of "communal stagnation", as the Deputy Mayor of Jerusalem Meron Benvenisti phrased it, which was used to justify Israel's expropriation of at least 67 per cent of usable land in the West Bank and 40 per cent of the usable land in the Gaza Strip, as well as its almost complete control over the Palestinian water supply, 68 per cent of which has been transferred to Israeli settlers. As a result, the contribution of agriculture to the Palestinian gross domestic product (GDP) fell from 36 per cent in 1972 to 23 per cent in 1987.[21] More striking is the fact that the contributions of agriculture and industry to Palestinian GDP was less in 1980 than it was during the British Mandate. Then, industry was 9 per cent of GDP, but 45 years later industry's share was only 6 per cent.[22]

Israeli strictures creating situations like these, especially in areas where climate and topography make only 10.4 per cent of the land productive and, even then, only with access to intensive irrigation, make it difficult for Arabs to produce anything.[23] And too often, even productive Arab firms have existed only as subservient subcontractors to Israeli firms.[24]

Clearly, then, critical obstacles which must be removed in order to facilitate the Middle East peace process are the economic impediments to political stability. It is these economic and political issues the contributors to this volume wish to address. On the one hand, we hope the chapters that follow will demonstrate the fragility of Palestinian economic and political institutions, as well as identify the reasons their structures may not support regional economic growth or a full-fledged political peace. We have tried to enhance our discussion of these points by presenting a variety of analytical methods and by offering a series of conclusions, some of which are conflicting. On the other hand, we do not want our chapters to be entirely negative. Therefore, we go beyond analysis of the weaknesses by offering alternative scenarios and potential solutions to the economic and to a lesser degree the political problems that confront regional and international decision-makers.

By design, the chapters move from least to most-specific approaches to the topic. For example, Her Majesty Queen Noor's prologue to the collection introduces the general state of affairs faced by diplomats in the region for several decades. This is followed by this introductory section by the volume's co-editor, J.W. Wright, Jr, which provides a broad outline of the reasons why economic factors in the West Bank and Gaza Strip must be considered if lasting peace is to be reached by Arabs and Israelis. Chapter 1, authored by the volume's other co-editor, Laura Drake, identifies and examines Israeli Prime Minister Benjamin Netanyahu's political and economic agenda, strategy and worldview, assessing the prospects for their implementation given the current Middle Eastern and international realities.

One of the key questions being raised about the peace process is whether or not it will bring about regional integration and economic growth. The next four chapters address the question of regional integration, though with different conclusions. Michael Field offers his views in Chapter 2 as to whether or not the Middle Eastern economies can be modernized in such a way that they can participate in a regionally integrated economy. Emma C. Murphy in Chapter 3 begins by asking questions about globalization that should be considered by negotiators in the Middle East peace process. She claims it is a mistake to consider only the national interests of stakeholders in the peace process because doing so might isolate much of the Middle East region from world commercial markets and international political alliances.

In contrast, Mohamed A. El-Erian and Stanley Fischer in Chapter 4 challenge the notion that Middle East and North Africa (MENA) is a region, economically speaking. Their chapter analyses the scope and implications of economic integration in the region, such as it can be defined. However, they, too, see increasing participation in international commercial markets as the key to meeting MENA's economic goals. In Chapter 5, Elias H. Tuma questions the value of a peacetime trade dividend from a process where "economic complementarity" has not been considered alongside the educational, institutional, psychological and social dimensions of trade relations.

Few people have investigated the relative worth of incentives for maintaining peace, or have recognized that they vary greatly for stakeholders in the peace process. Certainly arms dealers and military officials are among these players. Chapter 6, by Robert E. Looney, examines the budgetary consequences of economic efforts aimed at reducing military expenditures. He points out that the Israelis and Saudis, and the Americans and Europeans, are unlikely to fully support proposals that weaken regional arms sales markets. However, Jordan and especially Syria will potentially benefit from transferring military expenditures towards more productive economic development.

On the subject of finance, co-editor J.W. Wright, Jr chronicles in Chapter 7 the demise of Palestinian banking and sees the introduction of Islamic finance as an alternative solution. In Chapter 8, Rodney Wilson asks readers to consider whether or not the peace process will encourage portfolio investments into Israel and the Arab cordon states. He envisions an increasingly vicious circle developing wherein private capital illiquidity will lead to increased aid dependency in Israel and in the occupied West Bank and Gaza Strip. The primary solution is left to Israel, but is Israel willing to reduce its commercial and military dominance over the territories in return for trade cooperation? Peter L. Doan takes a different perspective in Chapter 9 by assuming that increased portfolio investment will take place in Jordan as a result of its peace treaty with Israel. However, he questions the ability of administrators to properly plan for these investments.

These chapters on the implications of peace on investment lead to discussions about financing development through aid and foreign direct investment. Barbara Balaj, Ishac Diwan and Bernard Philippe note in Chapter 10 that an immediate issue facing negotiators is the fight over who gets which pieces of the international aid pie. Thus far, aid payments to the West Bank and Gaza are behind schedule and disbursements have not significantly raised production or income. Cash transfers create other problem. The trio asks the key question about foreign aid funding to the Palestinians: "What went wrong?" Rex Brynen's Chapter 11 inquires into why the Middle Eastern economies are so very political, and he finds that competition over foreign aid is one of the reasons. The author poses questions about the economics of peace which we should now be better able to answer – if we choose to use the data we have. At the same time, Jordan, Syria and the Palestinians want more international aid, leading to discussions about financing development through aid and foreign investment. Much of this aid has been distributed through civil service organizations, many of which do not yet have established regional networks. Peter Gubser looks at this socio-economic dimension of funding civil society groups in Chapter 12.

The last analytical chapter in the book examines the politics of economic integration in two competing states, Syria and Israel. Syrian leaders worry that they risk becoming a backyard state if Israel is allowed to successfully integrate itself into the regional economy. Volker Perthes investigates this risk in Chapter 13. Finally, Ambassador William Stoltzfus provides an Epilogue that leaves readers considering the relative value of American national interests and policies in the Middle East region. His summary illustrates why effectively answering the remaining economic questions faced by diplomats is imperative to creating a sustainable Middle East peace.[25]

We hope you learn from this volume, and that you enjoy reading our contributions. We also hope it will impact policy decisions toward the region. Whether it will or not is a question we cannot answer yet.

Notes

1. The reader is referred to the Peace Economics project, a quarterly publication series that is supported by the European Union's *Peace Media* programme, edited by Valerie York and produced by the Economist Intelligence Unit in London.
2. Ahmad S. Khalidi, "Security in a Final Middle East Settlement: Some Components of Palestinian National Security", *International Affairs* 71(1) (January 1995), pp. 1–18.
3. Daoud Kuttab, "The Peace Process and the Palestinian Interest: An Interview with Sari Nusseibeh", *Palestine–Israel Journal of Politics, Economics and Culture* 1(4) (Autumn 1994), pp. 69–73.
4. Samir Hazboun and Simcha Bahiri, "Palestinian Industrial Development and Israeli–Palestinian Attitudes to Cooperation", *Palestine–Israel Journal of Politics, Economics and Culture* 1(4) (Autumn 1994), pp. 74–81.
5. Gil Feiler, "Palestinian Employment Prospects", *Middle East Journal* 47(4) (Autumn 1993), pp. 633–51.

6. Kent Ford and Doyle Peterson, "Conducting Business in the West Bank and Gaza", *Developing Alternatives* 5(2) (Fall 1995/Winter 1996), pp. 1–6.
7. Norman Finkelstein, "Bayt Sahur in Year II of the Intifada: A Personal Account", *Journal of Palestine Studies* 19(2) (Winter 1990), pp. 62–74; Anne Grace, "The Tax Resistance at Bayt Sahur", *Journal of Palestine Studies* 19(2) (Winter 1990), pp. 99–107.
8. Philip Levine, "The Intifada and its Impact on the Banking System in the State of Israel", *The American Economist* 37(1) (Spring 1993), pp. 68–71.
9. "Developing the Palestinian Economy: An Interview with George T. Abed", *Journal of Palestine Studies* 23(4) (Summer 1994), pp. 41–51.
10. Elia Zureik, Fouad Moughrabi and Vincent F. Sacco, "Perceptions of Legal Inequality in Deeply Divided Societies: the case of Israel", *International Journal of Middle East Studies* 25(3) (August 1993), pp. 423–42.
11. *Ibid*.
12. Emma C. Murphy, "Structural Inhibitions to Economic Liberalization in Israel", Proceedings of the British Society for Middle East Studies Conference on Democracy in the Middle East, St Andrews University, St Andrews, Scotland, 1992.
13. Ford and Peterson, *op. cit.*, pp. 2–3.
14. Avraham Ben-Basset and Arie Marom, "Is the Demand for Money in Israel Stable? (1965–1983)", *Bank of Israel Economic Review* 60 (January 1988), pp. 52–71; Rafi Melnik, "Two Aspects of the Demand for Money in Israel, 1970–1981", *Bank of Israel Economic Review* 60 (January 1988), pp. 36–51; Rafi Melnik, "Financial Services, Co-Integration, and the Demand for Money in Israel", *Journal of Money, Credit, and Banking* 27(1) (February 1995), pp. 140–53.
15. Laurie A. Brand, "The Economics of Shifting Alliances: Jordan's Relations with Syria and Iraq, 1975–1981", *International Journal of Middle East Studies* 26(3) (August 1994), pp. 393–413; Michael R. Fischbach, "The Implications of Jordanian Land Policy for the West Bank", *Middle East Journal* 48(3) (Summer 1994), pp. 492–509.
16. Glenn E. Robinson, "The Role of The Professional Middle Class in the Mobilization of Palestinian Society: The Medical and Agricultural Committees", *International Journal of Middle East Studies* 25(2) (May 1993), pp. 301–26.
17. "Interview with George T. Abed", *Journal of Palestine Studies*, *op. cit.*, p. 49.
18. See Chapters 4, 5 and 8 in this volume for specific information about the feasibility of this claim.
19. Sara Roy, "The Political Economy of Despair: Changing Political and Economic Realities in the Gaza Strip", *Journal of Palestine Studies* 20(3) (Spring 1991), pp. 58–69.
20. Fadle M. Naquib, "The Economics of the Israeli Occupation of the West Bank and Gaza Strip", Address to the Middle East Studies Association, Washington DC, 1995. The author notes that this paper draws on a contribution made to a study prepared by UNCTAD entitled: "A Quantitative Framework for the Future Prospects of the Palestinian Economy".
21. Fadle Naquib quoting the Report of the United Nations Secretary General on Assistance to the Palestinian People in the Light of the Cartagena Decision, UNCTAD TD/B/39(1)/4 20, August 1992.
22. Unfortunately, there has not been a rise in new industries, causing the agriculture and manufacturing percentages to fall. These figures represent total economic decline.

23. Fawzi Asadi, "How Viable will the Agricultural Economy be in the New State of Palestine?", *GeoJournal*, Special Issue on Some Geographical Aspects of the Israeli–Palestinian Conflict 21(4) (1990), pp. 375–83. See also Naquib, *op. cit.*, p. 4l; and Jacob Meltzer, "The Arab Economies in Mandatory Palestine and in the Administered Territories", *Economic Development and Cultural Change* (1992), pp. 844–65.
24. George T. Abed, *The Palestinian Economy: Studies in Development under Prolonged Occupation* (London: Routledge, 1988), p. 165.
25. J.W. Wright, Jr has used similar quotes from Amb. William Stoltzfus in two recently published texts. See J.W. Wright, Jr (ed.), *The Political-Economy of Middle East Peace: the Impact of Competing Trade Agendas* (London: Routledge, 1999), and *Competing Trade Agendas in the Middle East Peace Process* (Abu Dhabi: Emirates Centre for Strategic Studies and Research, 1998).

1 Implementing Netanyahu's Political and Economic Programme: What are Israel's Strategic Objectives for the Current Historical Phase?

Laura Drake[1]

INTRODUCTION

The history of the Middle East, and especially in Arab–Israeli affairs, has never been a straight line, nor does it move at constant speed: it is a tight, winding road with sharp, quick turns about once every five years. In May 1996, history once again threw a curve ball, installing one Benjamin Netanyahu into the driver's seat for its current segment. This happened just as the peace process seemed to be constructing the foundational elements of predictability long absent from the Middle Eastern political scene. Looking at this politician in his individual dimension, and forgetting about the immediate context that brought him to power, the pitch could be detected almost as it departed the plate. During the earlier part of 1988, buried beneath several layers of Israel's government structure, the image of Israel's future leader appeared clearly, standing out in stark contrast to the rather ordinary surroundings of the Israeli political landscape. Here was a mid-level politician (an ambassador to the United Nations) with a set of ideas and strategies all his own, combined with an extraordinary sense of human agency, a strong element of dynamic energy, and a telegenic appearance befitting a Ronald Reagan.

Indeed, Netanyahu surpassed expectations in his rush to the forefront of Middle East politics. Leapfrogging over one generation of Likud leaders and part of a second, Benjamin Netanyahu brought the future into intersection with the present by arriving at the summit a number of years earlier than anticipated.[2] Motti Morell, who has reportedly known Netanyahu for nearly 20 years and who directed his electoral advertizing campaign, explains it in these terms: "He's made out of different material [than] other Israeli politicians. From the beginning he didn't run along the regular route but overtook everyone on the ladder to reach the top. He knows exactly what he wants and goes straight there."[3] Though dismissed as "artificial" by significant segments of elite opinion in Israel, the United States and the Arab world – and whether he wins his next election or not – Netanyahu represents a major phenomenon on the Israeli political landscape.

What does the Israeli Prime Minister believe in, and what might he do in the coming years? Embedded in his voluminous writings and numerous press interviews dating back to the 1980s are the contours of Netanyahu's basic political thought, along with detailed discussions of his programmatic objectives for Israel. These spring from what he sees as Israel's current historical position and capabilities and which he understands as being in a state of continuous change. By subjecting the documentation to close analysis, Netanyahu's conceptions of possible and impossible can be separated out in general terms, understanding, however, that such boundaries are never fixed within the mind of a dynamic individual such as Netanyahu, that they exist only on a provisional basis. By nature such individuals are always watching out for small changes in circumstance, as they are aware that even incremental fluctuations can open up huge, if temporally limited, windows of opportunity. More generally, it becomes possible to derive the relevant conceptual frameworks and broad parameters within which the Israeli Prime Minister is expected to function in winding his way through this segment of historical time and the current challenges he faces.

The discussion follows a strategic blueprint. It begins with perceptions, the prerequisite to all ends–means formulations. From there it addresses Netanyahu's concrete objectives and his specific capabilities, all of which are formulated within the context of the programme itself – Netanyahu's peace.

NETANYAHU'S "GIVENS"

To Netanyahu, the term "Palestine" and its adjectival derivative, "Palestinian", are geographical designations, much resembling our understanding of the term "Middle East". They apply to territory and not to people; they are not understood by him in any political sense. When Netanyahu says "Palestine" he means the precise area that fell under the original British colonial Mandate, an area encompassing present-day Israel, Jordan and the occupied territories. Within that geographical region, there are two peoples: Palestinian Arabs and Palestinian Jews. For just as "Palestine" refers to present-day Israel, Jordan and the occupied territories, the term "Palestinian Arabs", or "Arabs of Palestine", means the people which most of us understand as the Palestinians *and Jordanians*: "Clearly, in eastern and western Palestine there are only two peoples, the Arabs and the Jews."[4]

To the Arabs of Palestine, the Israeli Prime Minister has made his concession. He made it involuntarily, a quarter of a century before he was even born. As a political descendant of Vladimir Ze'ev Jabotinsky, Netanyahu believes that the British had promised the entirety of these combined areas to the Jews as their national home in the Balfour Declaration of 1917. The unilateral severance of Transjordan from Palestine by the British back in 1922 is an event which Netanyahu termed, in 1993, "The Betrayal". He wrote:

> What had been regarded as obvious moral truths and obligations before the British had formally received the Mandate were now quickly discarded as policies unsuited to the moment. Britain tore off Transjordan from the Jewish National Home in 1922: With one stroke of the pen, it lopped off nearly 80 percent of the land promised the Jewish people, *closing this area to Jews to this day*.[5]

What remains of Israel, as he understands it, is but a "pittance",[6] a rump remnant of what he believes the Jewish state could and should have been. This little remnant, "only forty miles wide",[7] is *inclusive* of the areas Netanyahu calls Judea, Samaria and Gaza. And it should be apparent that an individual who is just barely able, more than 60 years later, to come to terms with what he would consider to be a concession made that long ago, is very unlikely to contemplate making any more significant concessions to those which he considers to be *one and the same people*.

Behind these perceptions and webs of meaning resides the origin of Netanyahu's de-legitimation of the Palestinian self-determination principle, which he has shortened to the disparaging "Palestinian principle". That principle, in Netanyahu's lexicon, is the proposition by which a people constituting a national "minority" within a sovereign state demand self-determination within the border region in which they live and abutting the national state they already have – which, of course, for him is Jordan.[8] From this "Palestinian principle" it is but a short logical step to consider the Palestinians as foreigners in their own country. Indeed, to Netanyahu, in echoes of Golda Meir, "Palestinians" are, from the very beginning, a "phantom nation".[9]

Nor is any of this new to either branch of political Zionism. The adjectival form of "Israel" is more accurately "Jewish", not "Israeli". While the latter may be used to denote possessions of the Jewish people, or to indicate inanimate objects that fall under their collective sovereignty, the term entirely lacks political content when used in reference to the people themselves.

What is new is that Netanyahu extends the Palestinian-as-foreigner concept to the territories occupied by Israel in 1967. Netanyahu has integrated the 1967 lands fully and completely into his definition of Israel, not as a future goal but as a conceptual starting point. Yet he has not incorporated the people into that definition, people who cannot stand in the air but only on the land. Of course the potential for violence inherent in this distortion of physical spatiality is enormous. The Palestinians of the West Bank in particular are already de-humanized as the unwanted byproducts of the soil from which they spring, while the soil is itself humanized as Israel's "heartland",[10] worshipped underneath the feet of living, breathing, human beings.

Netanyahu announced early on that he was against the separation of Rabin; he went on record denouncing its prescription for "sealed entities that do not live and breathe and interact with one another".[11] This attempt to preserve conceptual separation while renouncing physical separation, however, is a logical impossibility; if it emerges as a *status quo*, it will be a transitional one. For once the possibility of the territorially contiguous Palestinian state is closed off in a factual sense, as Netanyahu intends through the forcible appropriation of more West Bank land for Israel; followed by a final round of rapid settlement construction, the potential alternatives for the area will be reduced from three down to two – expulsion of the population, or the re-establishment of Israel/Palestine as a binational state.[12] Unpalatable as it may be, the facts on the ground do not lie.

The Israeli Prime Minister is a practical man. Having ruled out the statehood or third option as a result of his historical and situational "givens", he will realise that, given a binary situation, the extreme right is the preferable choice for him, but he understands this is not possible in the current circumstances. Thus, he implants himself into what he perceives to be the practical centre-ground[13] and refuses to budge, until and unless circumstances change in such a way as to allow him to move away from it. That centre-ground is the one we have come to know as permanent occupation, now restructured to include the policy of constriction of Palestinians – the closure of Palestinian life – which Netanyahu has inherited from Rabin and Peres.

NETANYAHU'S PROGRAMME: THE "BLUEPRINT FOR PEACE"

Inside Israel

In assessing Netanyahu's objectives, we begin, where Netanyahu does, from within Israeli society. This politician, unlike his predecessor, seeks to strengthen Israel from the inside out rather than vice versa: "The first and foremost peace that must be reached is peace among us [Israelis]....Peace begins at home, but it has to be continued abroad."[14] While Prime Minister

Shimon Peres sought to use the external Arab world as a source of Israeli power, Netanyahu looks instead to the Israeli people as the source of that power. One of his first priorities will therefore be to create many more Israelis. In 1993 his goal was explicitly to have a total of eight million Jews in Israel within 20 years, thereby doubling the Jewish population.[15] Obviously some of that will occur through natural reproduction; the rest will be through a heightened attention to stimulating a new wave of immigration:

> The Government will put immigration and absorption at the top of its priorities...[I]t will initiate a strategic long-term program to tap the immigration potential from various countries, estimated at one million immigrants in the coming decade.[16]

The second, and complementary aspect of Netanyahu's economic programme is to dismantle the Israeli socialist bureaucracy and put an end to big government. As he told the United States Congress:

> We are committed to turning Israel's economy into a free market of goods and ideas....This means free enterprise, privatization, open capital markets, an end to cartels, lower taxes, deregulation.[17]

The new Prime Minister fully intended to be the author of an Israeli *perestroika*, but on a scale much larger than what the doomed Soviet leader Gorbachev had ever conceived. Netanyahu's intention is to project Israel out into the world as a dynamic independent, and growing force in the global economy. A week after his election he told a foreign reporter: "I would like to see Israel move very rapidly from a position of a dependent nation...to become a significant economic power in the world." For this, "the potential is enormous".[18] The potential is much more than simple economics would suggest: Netanyahu believes this economic privatization will be the catalyst to attract that wave of new immigrants he seeks. As he wrote in 1993:

> The restructuring of Israel's economy into a vibrant and prosperous free market would empty the former Soviet Union of many of its Jews and draw hundreds of thousands of Jewish immigrants from other lands....Israel is now poised before another such opportunity to dramatically increase its Jewish population, if it only chooses to partake of it....[19]

Thus, economic liberalization and immigration are interactively reinforcing, an ongoing dynamic engine with the potential to dramatically increase Israeli power in the strategic sense: "An Israel boasting eight million Jews in the early decades of the next century, with double the economic output per person, could be a substantial force on the world scene."[20] Because Israel will become "so much stronger" as a result, the Arabs would make their peace with it.[21] He did not elaborate on the question of peace on whose terms. Immediately upon taking office, the new Prime Minister wasted no time getting started on his plans for economic restructuring: a mere month after the election, Finance Minister Dan Meridor was busily working on major cutbacks in the Israeli budget.[22] This resulted in loud rumblings of protest on the part of those who have been accustomed to relaxing under the shelter of Israel's massive socialist entitlements, or enjoying the patronage of the unwieldy socialist bureaucracy.[23]

Towards the Palestinians

Now, in the midst of this new immigration and economic expansion, one might inquire what is to become of the Palestinians? Will they not be affected by all this new Israeli growth, in economy, in population, in its overall level of power? Indeed, Netanyahu has already laid out a blueprint delineating their fate in some great detail.[24] The first aspect that appears in his discourse is the functional separation of what he calls the "Judean Arabs" and the "Samarian Arabs"[25] from the "Arabs of Gaza". The proposed solutions for them are slightly different; they seem to occur on two different tracks – Gaza and the West Bank are, Netanyahu once said, "two separate issues".[26]

To the "Arabs of Gaza" Netanyahu promises the "fullest possible autonomy" in a "self-contained authority under the rubric of Israeli sovereignty". If during an interim period of "at least a decade", they have demonstrated their ability to run a non-belligerent and stable government, then Israel might "consider" offering them "an even greater degree of self-rule".[27] Israel will continue to maintain control of all border, security, and foreign relations functions, and it is quite unlikely that Netanyahu – who describes post-Oslo Gaza as a "free-terror zone" and "a lair of some of the most rabid Jew-haters in the world" – would ever be willing to give those up.[28]

For the "Arabs of Judea and Samaria", a significantly more complex enterprise, the Prime Minister would like to create "four self-managing counties", or tiny autonomous regions centred on the cities of Jenin, Nablus, Ramallah and Hebron and accompanied by their surrounding villages.[29] Bethlehem, Jericho, Tulkarem and Qalqilya are left out; one can only assume that they would have been fully incorporated into Israel but for Oslo. The critical issue for Netanyahu is the need to balance Israel's security requirements with the Palestinians' desire to conduct their own affairs:

> Such a balance can be achieved by a peace plan that would designate the areas of dense Palestinian population as autonomous areas, and the open (and largely unpopulated) land as Israeli security zones....Israel would

> retain direct control of the strategic terrain so vital for its defense against terrorism and invasion from the east.[30]

Within these dense enclosures the Palestinians will be allowed to "manage" many areas of their communal and "daily lives" under a civilian governance; whether it be under local notables or the PA makes little difference. For whether it be the PLO or the PA or a municipal authority by any other name, Netanyahu will allow for some Palestinian institution capable of maintaining the basic requirements for the subsistence of individual Palestinians, and keeping order among them, so that the Israelis will not have to be burdened with it. However, the Israelis will always have permanent control over land and water, and other vital resources, to grant or withhold these from the population at their discretion, while their military forces and *mukhabarat* (security services) will continue to encircle the "autonomous" municipalities, retaining the right to enter them if need be, at least as a fall-back option in times of crisis. In the final analysis, Netanyahu's solution is not too far from the general pattern of the A-areas allocated to the Palestinians under Oslo II, but without irrevocably surrendering control over the internal counter-insurgency functions; for Netanyahu this was one of the major faults in the Rabin/Peres plan.[31] With minor adjustments, Netanyahu's plan can be easily adapted to fit realities on the ground. Indeed, the current situation in the West Bank and Gaza – born of a political process which was suddenly frozen in mid-stream, in a partially unfolded state with little control over economic and security mechanisms – is a complex hybrid containing elements of both the Rabin/Peres plan (removal of Palestinians from Israeli life by way of enclosure, known as separation) and the Shamir/Begin municipal autonomy plan (autonomy for the larger Palestinian cities as part of a Greater Israel, or integration into an apartheid-like situation).

With that in mind, then, we proceed to Netanyahu's version of final status. If the Palestinians continue to behave themselves through the interim period, he says, then they will advance to the final status, into which the self-managing counties (municipalities) will be incorporated. Netanyahu would like the final status talks to include questions such as "whether to grant Israeli citizenship to the residents of the counties". That is, "if these Arabs demonstrate clearly that they had adopted a genuine peacetime footing", then "at the end of a cooling-off period of twenty years", Israel "could consider" offering them Israeli citizenship. This is contingent upon their agreement to proclaim their loyalty and offer their service to the state. If not, then they will retain their individual rights as citizens of their Palestinian state on the East Bank. These Palestinians will then be allowed to live in the West Bank as "resident foreign nationals…much as millions of residents of the United States who hold green cards".[32] This solution, Netanyahu tells us, will allow Arabs and Jews to "develop mutual trust" and "adjust themselves to changing circumstances".[33] For any peace, he says, must be built on "foundations of security, justice, and above all, truth".[34]

Benjamin Netanyahu's "truth" is that those areas which do not contain dense concentrations of Palestinians are considered empty and ripe for Jewish settlement. Most importantly, they are not to be seen as a potential solution to the problem of the more than one million Palestine refugees of 1948 and 1967 awaiting return home from neighbouring states, especially those several hundreds of thousands in Lebanon who are now openly unwelcome in that country. This is a potential of which Netanyahu is well aware, which he openly fears, and explicitly tries to rule out,[35] despite his own admission that the area already settled by Israelis amounts to *only 5 per cent of the territory*.[36] As his political-strategic advisor Dore Gold explains, to allow the Palestinian refugees to return, even to the West Bank and not to Israel proper, would interfere with Israel's "demographic security". He states:

> We do not want to find ourselves in a situation where the Palestinian Authority floods Judea and Samaria with refugees; after all, the demographic balance in Judea and Samaria will also influence the situation within the Green Line....This is, after all, one of the fundamental differences between an independent Palestinian state and self-rule, which is less than a state. An independent Palestinian state can allow itself full control over immigration policy....One cannot rule out the possibility that Lebanon may decide to deport Palestinian Arabs. Where will they be transferred? If the Palestinians have exclusive control over border crossings, as is the case in all countries, this gives the option of letting them enter.[37]

Yet this very option remains perhaps the last possible humane and politically decent opportunity to put an end to the long tragedy of the large proportion of the Palestinian population still in exile – especially those in the economically deprived camps – and it is rapidly evaporating.

Netanyahu's plan for the "open" lands of the West Bank is quite simple; it is essentially a 1990s variation of the original Zionist ideological formulation of "a land for a people for a people without a land". The densely populated regions consist solely of the four urban areas slated for autonomy; "the rest remains in large part vacant".[38] In any case, Netanyahu asserts, "the simple fact is that most of it [the West Bank] was not taken from anyone. It was simply empty public land....It is to this land, virtually as barren and lifeless as it was...a century ago, that Israel is now bringing to life."[39] Any notion that Israel's progressive expansion into Arab lands is the primary cause of war in the area is called a "reversal of causality", essentially, a distortion of truth.[40] For it was the Arabs who caused the original Jewish diaspora, Netanyahu tells us; it was the Arabs who usurped the land from the Jews and uprooted them from it, and not the other way around.[41]

Much of Netanyahu's discourse regarding his plans for the West Bank land is replete with "living space" arguments, though he does not call them that. These are supplemented with the more familiar security reasons. Netanyahu uses American terms to talk about Israel's cities in Jerusalem and Tel Aviv, which he believes will die of suffocation without their "suburbs" – his name for settlements, which are of course located in the West Bank:

> [T]he great majority of the 250,000 Jews living in what are being called "settlements" are for the most part suburbanites, living in much the same way that New York City commuters, whose homes are in New Jersey or Long Island live. Without its suburbs, a city would become overcrowded, living conditions would decline, and industry would be forced to relocate. The ultimate result of constraining the development of suburban areas is the strangulation of any metropolis and its eventual decay.[42]

The Palestinian, it will be remembered, is perceived as alien to the Land of Israel; therefore it does not matter what happens to Palestinians within the State of Israel. Israel is "already squeezed" within its present boundaries, *even inclusive of the occupied territories as part of Israel*, and if "Judea and Samaria" were lopped off, he contends, the army would not be able to function effectively.[43] Furthermore, Netanyahu believes it is likely that a Palestinian state in the West Bank would eventually topple Hashemite Jordan and incorporate the East Bank into its domain as well, thus destroying the security buffer. This enlarged Palestinian state would then conclude alliances with its friends in Iran and Iraq, thus leading to the full reintegration of the eastern front – a fear bolstered by King Hussein's death.[44]

If the local Palestinians are unhappy with their lot under the urban autonomy, if life is that unbearable for them, if their livelihoods are too thin, he seems to believe that they might simply cross the river to what he considers to be their existing Palestinian state on the East Bank. As for the refugees in exile, Netanyahu says, the Western countries could absorb them, or their existing camps in the Arab world could be converted into towns.[45] Agreeing to forget about the West Bank and submit it forever to Israeli rule, this is called a "microscopic one-time concession" on the part of Palestinian and other Arabs, enabling Israel to live. If they do not agree to it, he believes, "it is hard to make the case that they are in fact ready for peace".[46]

Netanyahu's strategy towards the Palestinians, and especially towards the Palestinian Authority, is to broaden the definition of terrorism so as to include *all forms of opposition to the Arab–Israeli status quo that require the use of force*, while simultaneously containing the Palestinians' *political* demands for a state.[47] The Palestinians do not start out well-suited to face this kind of strategy, because they have allowed their political organization uniting all the Palestinian people, inside and outside, to become operationally defunct. The political umbrella organization of the Palestinian people has gone through a very rapid transition over the past several years – from PLO, through the midway point of the PNA, to an entity which has now come to be known simply as the PA, a much smaller umbrella with many holes and little economic leverage, gradually shedding the "N" for National and nominally covering only one-third of the Palestinian people. Now even that is uncertain, as is the fate of Arafat himself. Netanyahu feels no obligation to even speak with him except at his own leisure.[48]

The first item on the Netanyahu government's agenda towards the PA, as towards Syria and even the United States, is provision of security against terrorism. For, as Netanyahu is fond of saying, peace cannot coexist with terrorism. The Authority, to be in compliance with Oslo, will be expected to "conduct a continuous, unconditional, and unchanging struggle against terrorism". This means, among other things, "disarming" and even "dismantling" Hamas.[49] In the event the PA complies with Oslo, Israel too will comply, hence "reciprocity". One important PA official, Marwan Kanafani, stretched credulity with his comment after the initial Gold–Arafat meeting that, regardless of its content, "the meeting itself was a positive sign". Oslo negotiator Hassan Asfour added that "the initiative came from the Israeli side".[50]

Towards the Arab States (and Iran)

Addressing the broader Arab world, Netanyahu's concept of peace contains the following "three pillars": security, reciprocity, and the strengthening of democracy.[51] It is impossible, however, to understand these Netanyahu positions without being aware of the larger paradigm within which he interacts at the international level, for his entire concept of peace is built around it.

Netanyahu's world is self-consciously a Kantian one, made up of two kinds of entities: democracies and dictatorships. It then follows that there are two kinds of peace: the "peace of democracies" and the "peace of deterrence". The peace of democracies is of the kind that has existed among European states since the end of World War II, a peace determined by the participation of ordinary people in the decisions of government. These checks tend to preclude government from initiating rash stampedes to war, especially if one's own side is bound to lose, or if a military counterstrike by the designated enemy would cause great damage to the initiating state. The peace of deterrence, in Netanyahu's thought, is the kind of peace which prevails between a democratic state and an undemocratic state,[52] or, for that matter, between two or more undemocratic states. The evidence for this view, Netanyahu believes, is provided by the course of world history during the twentieth century, through the interaction of the free world with the two great totalitarian powers – Germany and the Soviet Union. When concessions are made to a totalitarian adversary, which is called "appeasement", Netanyahu says, the enemy takes it as a sign of weakness rather than as a sign of goodwill, *by virtue of its totalitarianism*. Thus, for him, *it is the nature of the adversary and not the nature of the conflict that is the determining factor*.

Switching from a wide-angle focus to the zoom lens, as Netanyahu has done (perhaps he has done it in reverse, we do not know), we arrive at the following equation: the Arab Republic of _______ (fill in the blank) is either Germany of the early 1930s or the Soviet Union of the early 1950s. Which it is depends on what the democracy does, what the Arabs become depends on what strategy *Israel* chooses. To offer concessions towards those Arab states that are "strongly anti-democratic", to compromise with those "unreconstructed dictatorships whose governmental creed is based on tyranny and intimidation",[53] will only make them warlike. Deterrence will make them peace-like, but only as long as deterrence continues. Therefore, deterrence is a strategy of historic rather than interim proportions.

By extension, then, a peace of historic length is achievable only through deterrence; therefore *any peace agreements with the Arabs in their current state must be based on deterrence and not on concessions*. One might even say that the US–USSR detente, held in place by a complex treaty relationship, was little more than deterrence waged by other means, or what one might call "managed deterrence". Netanyahu himself declares explicitly: "a durable peace in the Middle East must be based on deterrence".[54] His perspective ultimately led directly to a Middle Eastern application of "peace through strength".[55] He finally adopted it explicitly, as a kind of post-election slogan, but it was long in coming, for the pieces were in place years before.

Netanyahu's worldview therefore implies that the Arabs, including the Palestinians, can do nothing short of changing their political natures to meet the requirements for a real peace, a peace of substantive compromises, a peace of democracies. Barring a profound change in *internal* Arab relations, the peace of deterrence in Arab–Israeli politics, a peace in which Israel refuses to budge from the proverbial front-line, will remain as Netanyahu's general strategic posture. Running these conceptual data through an Arab computer, however, yields an impasse. The Arab perception, which has attached its own distinct set of meanings to the same historical processes that have formed their interaction with Israel, brings up a different set of perceptions and, thereby, a different set of priorities regarding the criteria of peaceful intentions. For the Arabs it is Israel's *international* behaviour, not its internal behaviour, that is important. And for the Arabs, therefore, there are also two kinds of peace: the peace of justice and the peace of the *status quo*. And viewed through this particular lens, the two kinds of Netanyahu peace distill down into only one: the peace of the *status quo* – the peace of the *fait accompli*. It is not only George Orwell who understands that even a single person can see either four or five of a given object, depending on his mindset, his situation, and the environment in which he must exist – in short, his perspective.

In gaining Arab acquiescence to his own perspective, in a few cases even tacit support, Netanyahu had several successes in his pocket before even leaving the proverbial starting gate, courtesy of his opponent Shimon Peres. The most important is obviously Jordan. "He wanted me to be among the first to be contacted", offered King Hussein after the Netanyahu victory; "I was very touched by that."[56] The others are Tunisia and Qatar,[57] and maybe Oman, for which normalization in principle seems to have been something other than provisional. Indications are that these states will simply leave things in place and intact, awaiting the day when it becomes politically possible to resume their forward movement on economy fronts. Qatar is more forward than the others – they have more gas and oil to sell – but this is essentially the state of affairs and it is likely to stay that way. And other Arab states wishing to join them in establishing such trade for recognition relations with Israel are deemed welcome by Netanyahu to do so, either now or in the future; the familiar Likud slogan "peace for peace" should be understood in this light. What is important to remember is that the grand-historic sense, now or ten years from now will make little difference; one does not get the sense that Netanyahu sees peace as a closing window, but rather as one that Israel is gradually forcing open, over a very long period of time.

This line of thinking is most consequential in the case of Syria, a point made clearly in Chapter 13. Initially finding himself unable to convince the United States to isolate and punish Syria, which he calls the "classic terrorist state",[58] Netanyahu stands ready to continue negotiations with Damascus "without preconditions" while simultaneously planning for war, as is the case with any strategy based on active deterrence. Again, Netanyahu is in no hurry. And even if peace with a strong Syria is not likely to come today, peace with a much weaker Syria might come tomorrow and, in any case, any peace that might be reached today is still only a peace of deterrence. It is reasonable to suppose that Netanyahu might simply be content with waiting out President Assad and deferring peace with Syria into the indefinite future. It seems to be the most likely outcome, since as far as "land for peace" is concerned, Netanyahu, like Begin and Shamir before him, rejects it for Syria as he does for the Palestinians, on the grounds that Israel complied with UN Security Council Resolution 242 when it completed its withdrawal from Egyptian territory in 1982.[59]

What would Netanyahu want to negotiate with the Syrians about, if not the Golan Heights, given the chance? Basically, the answer is normalization, or as Shimon Peres would have called it, mutual cooperation. Subjects for discussion would include such areas as joint efforts on water and the environment, arms reductions,[60] and the establishment of confidence-building measures.[61] It was later clarified that the meaning of "building confidence" is, first and foremost, for Syria to disable the Lebanese resistance campaign against Israel's army in Lebanon, which Netanyahu considers "terrorism".[62] Israel's first item on the agenda of any talks with Syria will be to achieve tranquility, to pacify the borders with the Syrian-controlled territory, to gain a cessation of violence,[63] an end to terrorism – all of which add up to "a dismantling of Hezbollah's capability".[64] In other words, Netanyahu wants to negotiate over Syria's negotiating cards to trump them into a backwater state of diplomacy. If Syria is not interested, then the prime minister, taking a page from the US–USSR cooperation in managing their deterrence relationship, would be willing to discuss concrete steps to reduce the threat of war between the two countries. Either way, Damascus will have to give up "this obsessive unilateral focus on having Israel return to indefensible lines".[65]

NETANYAHU'S STRATEGY AND CAPABILITIES

Sceptics might ask: so what if Netanyahu had a blueprint? And so what if he has repeated the same points ever since? *Mein Kampf* notwithstanding, politicians write down much in the way of rhetoric before they take high office, it is said, but once they get there they are forced to change course in deference to the realities on the ground. The answer to this objection is as follows: it only holds true insofar as the designer of the blueprint believes that the conditions on the ground are antagonistic to a peace plan rather than conducive to a peace programme's implementation. This is not so in the case of Benjamin Netanyahu. The world he sees is one of unprecedented opportunities for Israel to further its agenda.

With length of time, Netanyahu achieves a better sense of the political constraints Israel faces in the current phase. However, that does not mean he will abandon his programme; that is an illusion. For Netanyahu's programme is much older than the 1996 election campaign; it has evolved gradually over the course of two decades. It is born out of the substance of Netanyahu's life experience, political education, and his own analysis of the situation he perceives around him.[66] His basic political outlook has familial roots going back two generations: his paternal grandfather was a devoted Zionist, and his father, Benzion Netanyahu, was a direct exponent of Jabotinsky with whom he worked before taking up life as historian and scholar. For a time the elder Netanyahu served as editor of the right-wing daily *Yarden* (Jordan);[67] Jabotinsky has even been categorized as Benzion's "mentor".[68] Some of the initial assessments, both in America and in the Arab world, that Benjamin Netanyahu would suddenly appear as someone he has never been, belong in the category that psychologists call "denial"; it seems most of the players have since been stripped of their illusions by Netanyahu's candour and are now content to simply wait him out. They are hoping that the Labour party will return to power in fairly short order and, more importantly, that the Labour proposals will not have been rendered obsolete by Netanyahu's term(s) in office.

Netanyahu, like anyone else, will see obstacles in his path; there will be constraints. He adapts to the constraints, and tends to make political capital of them. For what is important is not that he reach every precise goal that he has set for Israel. The specifics – will he or will he not withdraw from Hebron tomorrow, or the difference between four and six cantons as part of the autonomy – these are unimportant. Netanyahu can camouflage the far-right in his cabinet, pull out of Hebron or, as he has repeatedly done, change his mind and meet with Arafat, or fly to Washington or elsewhere. But in and of themselves, any one of these decisions or even all of them together will mean little. For Washington, they are test cases, or rather trip wires not to be stepped on. Netanyahu knows where they are, and he will beware of them.

Much more important is the issue of *directionality*: whatever historical force Netanyahu exerts in international and Middle East politics will be projected *in the direction of his original programme* and not in the direction of Palestinian independence, not towards putting an end to Israeli occupation. It will be projected into the gradual, steady, incremental appropriation of West Bank land by force always, but with actual violence only where necessary. The aim is to build up a Jewish majority in the territory as an evolutionary process by confiscating land from Palestinians in a strategic manner, with the use of maps as one would in a military combat operation – sometimes destroying Palestinian homes where they stand – making life unbearable for Palestinians and gradually clearing room for more settlers. Netanyahu's objective for the West Bank closely parallels the policy of his predecessors in Labour to bring about the gradual and forcible transformation of East Jerusalem from an Arab city into a Jewish city, as it also parallels the methods used during late 1947 and early 1948 just prior to the formal establishment of Israel and the inception of war with the surrounding Arab states. Netanyahu will strive to incorporate the West Bank into Israel in much the same manner but with minimal fanfare, in a gradual and steady operation that will not trigger the international tripwires: quietly, one settlement-house at a time.

Netanyahu is the kind of individual who endeavors to find a way to satisfy the American and Arab requirements for symbols of progress; this he does in order to eliminate them as obstacles to the implementation of his programme, which is how he seems to conceive them. For he knows that as long as he keeps saying "peace process" he will be given ample maneuvering room, in Washington and maybe even in the Arab world, to move in his own direction. All the while, he is formulating the term "reciprocity" in such a way as to render the Labour version of the peace process an anachronism.

This is the same process on which the PLO had staked all its hopes, indeed its existence – even the continuation of the Palestinian people as an historic unit. Netanyahu and his advisors can be expected to increasingly ignore this process as a strategy to defeat its relevance, stressing if need be the supposed Palestinian "violations" of Oslo, thereby allowing Israel to delay implementation of its own meagre obligations to whatever extent it desires. As Dore Gold told his Israeli interviewer: "I have a whole file of issues which I do not wish to open now".[69]

In understanding Netanyahu's strategic moves, it is important to understand that he is first and foremost an *optimist*, unlike Israel's Holocaust-inspired pessimists that have characterized the past. Born in 1949 in Tel Aviv of Lithuanian parentage, Netanyahu operates from a post-1967 Israeli political framework and a Western–Ashkenazi civilizational perspective.[70] This has been heavily supplemented by very strong American influences resulting from his extended stay in the United States. Netanyahu reflects that American "can-do" attitude. He believes that he can make the Palestinians accept his terms – which amount to terms of existence – when it becomes clear that Israel will not agree to a Palestinian state.[71] The Arab states, he believes, are "adjusting rapidly" to his government, and to Israel's choice for what he calls a "strong peace". Based on "contacts with the Arab world" Netanyahu is "optimistic" not only in regard to the old peace partners but also towards the possibility of eventually adding new ones.[72] And once it is clear that Israel "steadfastly refuses" the establishment of a Palestinian state, he believes, "important Arab parties preferring autonomy to statehood will undoubtedly emerge."[73] Netanyahu does not even fear the "demographic demon" – he claims the so-called demographic threat, much touted by Labour and the parties to its left, "is not a product of the 'facts'...but a hobgoblin in the minds of people who have lost their nerve."[74] His view of the future is such that Jewish immigration and Palestinian Arab emigration from the West Bank will prevent the problem from emerging, as he contends it has done thus far.[75] Netanyahu well understands that a slight adjustment of tactics will be required to fulfill the strategy. At the same time, he has no intention of abandoning the strategy itself, for he sees no reason to do so.

Netanyahu is not only an optimist but also an *opportunist*. An opportunist is one who treats fleeting potentialities, the proverbial "windows' of time, as bridges to cross from one side of history to another. Since these bridges often appear suddenly and remain only temporarily, the opportunist will often move boldly to cross them before they crash into the quantum abyss. One example of Netanyahu's propensity in this direction – that is, an example other than the path of his swift rise to power – appears in a statement he made in 1989, in the aftermath of the Tiannenmen Square Crisis in China:

> Israel should have exploited the repression of the demonstrations in China, when world attention focused on that country, to carry out mass

> expulsions among the Arabs of the territories. Regrettably, there was no support for this policy, which I put forward then and still recommend.[76]

Though in this political climate Netanyahu claims to be against transfer, it is clear that he is really for it; only he recognizes that the current structural constraints do not now allow for it to be formulated as a near-term objective. If circumstances change, however, or if he finds a way to push them incrementally in that direction, the objective will come back over Netanyahu's strategic horizon in full colour.

For Netanyahu is also a *strategist*, one with an extraordinary sense of the power of individual human agency. "Israel's future", he wrote, "is not a deterministic problem in Newtonian physics, but a question of which policies it will choose – and of the energy and intelligence with which it will pursue them over time."[77] Such persons do not see all obstacles as impossibilities, they see some of them as challenges to be overcome, as mazes to find one's way out of by way of shrewd maneuvering around the corners of history. He recognizes: "We cannot forge, at once overnight, a new reality by simply willing it. There are things we can will. There are directions we can establish."[78] Though the strategist is indeed an opportunist, he is also on the lookout for ways in which to *create* opportunities out of nothing, to shape the raw material in a way that suits him. For such persons as Netanyahu, not all circumstances are automatically given. Some of them are, but many of them are not.

While some other players may see themselves as receiving a hand of cards from the deck and playing them as they come due, in a passive, almost robotic fashion, the strategist focuses his attention on how to accumulate more cards, *and on how to actually play as few of them as possible*. Thereby he is participating not only in the game itself, but in shaping the conditions by which the game is played, thus placing the opponent inside his private goldfish-bowl. The opponent's sphere of action thus becomes limited, though the actor may not be fully aware of those limitations, or indeed of the possibility that he might be capable of finding a way to overcome them; rather, his actions within that limited sphere thus become highly transparent and predictable.

This type of assessment, of Netanyahu's possessing such capabilities obviously runs entirely counter to the highly popularized imagery of Netanyahu as artificial, as media-savvy, what one commentator referred to as the "Bibi is a lightweight" campaign.[79] But conventional wisdom is often mistaken. Netanyahu's abilities and dynamism are unique. As Moshe Arens, his professional mentor, acknowledged after the election:

> Today the public has seen what others knew all along. Bibi is an intelligent, quick-witted person, with an analytical mind, outstanding organizational and communication skills and the stamina to suffer crises and setbacks and come out on top.[80]

Arens is the official who gave Netanyahu his first important assignment, selecting him in 1982 to be his deputy at the Israeli embassy in Washington where he was serving as ambassador. Why Netanyahu? According to Arens, "I saw in him abilities which I believed would take him far". He also characterized him as the "best U.N. ambassador we've had".[81]

CONCLUSION: IMPLICATIONS FOR NETANYAHU'S ADVERSARIES

Netanyahu himself is well aware of the tendency of people to underestimate his abilities. Rather than being insulted, he is quite happy about it; he sees it as a formidable strategic advantage. He said: "I've had the great fortune of being the recipient of the greatest favor that any politician can have – and that is the systematic underestimation by one's opponents...I doubt very much I'd be here today if I didn't enjoy that benefit."[82] This applies to both his domestic and his Arab adversaries. The one thing that may really get in Netanyahu's way, however, is his inexperience as a politician; strategic gaps could emerge within his "root-directory" as a result. After all, his involvement in politics constitutes only a short historical moment, as compared to other Israeli leaders. But, judging from the past, he will probably adapt and fine-tune his position gradually unless some huge single mistake irrevocably sinks him.

Finally, it is important to remember that while Netanyahu operates within the framework of his worldview, he is and has been a realist in the sense of being a *pragmatist*. His words are not rhetoric. They are situational assessments and strategic objectives for the future. Netanyahu tends to take the long view; his understanding of changing political and situational constraints, both present and future, are already structured into the observations, lending him a sense of tactical flexibility. Netanyahu the pragmatist has dropped the quotation marks from the term "Palestinian"; he now generally uses the term in place of his own "Palestinian Arab" to foreign audiences. That does not mean that he actually sees "Palestinians" the way others see Palestinians.[83] He still sees "Palestinian Arabs", a term by which he means Arabs originating from Eretz Israel, from the geographical area of Palestine which is still present-day Israel, Jordan and the occupied territories. And imagine that Netanyahu agrees to meet again and again with Arafat in recognition of political realities, or, alternatively, imagine that he were to withdraw from the Arab parts of Hebron and turns the rest over to Arafat as a canton. But what of it? He may decide to hold a hundred meetings with Arafat to please Washington or Arab leaders, but if he does not seriously talk with him about a Palestinian state, then what does it matter? And as for the Palestinian (Arab) canton in Hebron, it will be remembered it was part of Netanyahu's own programme as embodied in his blueprint. And so what if Arafat gets millions from Wye. Can he implement programs with the money anyway? In other words, what is important is not the positions themselves, but the nature of the substance that resides within them at any given point in time.

Netanyahu's writings are essentially recommendations to future policy-makers, the first of which just so happened to be himself, though it might not necessarily have turned out that way. If the recommendations were not realistic then they would not be relevant to the individual sitting in the prime minister's chair. And Netanyahu wants nothing more than to be relevant. For his Arab adversaries, any kind of reactive or static "wait and see" or "business as usual" attitude was then and will be no match for a dynamic adversary who is keenly aware of the capacity of human agency to gradually re-shape constraining economic, political, and social structures over time.

Notes

1. Laura Drake's prediction of Netanyahu's eventual rise to power dates back to the early spring of 1988; she has closely followed his political writings and statements since that time. An earlier summary of her observations and analysis of Netanyahu immediately after the 1996 elections was published in "Netanyahu: A Primer", *Journal of Palestine Studies* 26(1) (Autumn 1996), pp. 58–69, and presented at a lecture entitled "Netanyahu's Peace", held at the Center for Policy Analysis on Palestine, Washington DC, 18 July 1996.
2. The individuals who were overtaken by the racing Netanyahu include the Likud "princes" such as Ehud Olmert, Dan Meridor, and especially Ze'ev Benjamin Begin, son of Menachem Begin. The latter two are now serving in Netanyahu's cabinet. Netanyahu has been categorized by one expert along with the young Begin as the most "hawkish" among the princes, Olmert was categorized as the most moderate, while Dan Meridor was thought to reside somewhere in between. See Elfi Pallis, "The Likud Party: A Primer", *Journal of Palestine Studies* 21(2) (Winter 1992), pp. 41–60. The Likud coalition "heavyweights" now serving Netanyahu in various capacities include Israeli military generals Ariel Sharon, Yitzhak Mordechai and Rafael Eitan; and on the civilian side, the irrepressible David Levy, Netanyahu's foreign minister, who allegedly resorted to blackmail against him in the familiar "Bibigate" scandal of 1993, to prevent him from climbing the next to the last rung of the ladder to power.
3. Quoted in Liat Collins, "From A to Bibi: A Guide to Netanyahu", *Jerusalem Post*, 7 June 1996, p. 9.
4. Benjamin Netanyahu, *A Place Among the Nations: Israel and the World* (New York: Bantam Books, 1993), p. 148.
5. Emphasis added. *Ibid.*, p. 50. Two maps are attached to that text. The first stands under the heading "1920: The Jewish National Home under British Administration", encompassing present day Israel, occupied territories and Jordan, without frontiers, with the label "Palestine" across the centre. The second map, under the heading "1922: The Jewish National Home After Creation of Transjordan", shows only a dashed line where today's Jordanian border with Israel and the West Bank now stands. *Ibid.*, p. 267.

6. *Ibid*., p. 75.
7. *Ibid*., p. 348.
8. *Ibid*., pp. 149–50.
9. *Ibid*., p. 42.
10. Interview with Benjamin Netanyahu on *Larry King Live*, Cable News Network, 3 July 1996.
11. David Makovsky and Bill Hutman, "Netanyahu backs away from separation idea", *Jerusalem Post*, Internet edition, 3 July 1996. Rabin first initiated closure in 1992, soon after taking office. At a briefing before Arab ambassadors and journalists Netanyahu repeated his opposition to Rabin's "separation", adding that "we do not believe in the closure as a principle; we believe in openness, if anything, as a principle." Benjamin Netanyahu, Remarks at the symposium of the *Middle East Insight*, Willard Hotel, Washington, 10 July 1996. In practice, however, Netanyahu has embraced the (en)closure of Palestinians within small areas as a useful instrument of pacification and has continued its implementation on the ground; the closure over five consecutive years has frozen all normal Palestinian life, constricting it almost to the point of suffocation. However, he does not use the closure as an instrument of separation, which he opposes.
12. The Labour party has made a not insignificant contribution to this outcome through its relentless construction of the bypass roads for the Israeli settlers and the virtual containers of human enclosure in which it has encased the Palestinian population. The destruction of territorial contiguity and freedom of movement that has accompanied these recent structural changes is also destructive of the concept of separation in the long run, since separation cannot exist in the absence of a spatial *dis*continuity between the elements being separated. Instead of having Palestinians mixed in between Israelis as individuals, Labour had inadvertently mixed them in as clusters. Rabin's work on the ground, that is, gradually transforming what used to be open Palestinian cities and villages into small, heavily-guarded enclosures, was the physical manifestation of a desire to have it both ways – political inclusion and exclusion of Palestinians – at one and the same time.
13. For Netanyahu's claim to represent the centre, and for his definition of the left and right extremes, see *A Place Among the Nations*, *op. cit*., p. 295.
14. Benjamin Netanyahu, Address to Supporters, 2 June 1996, broadcast live on CNN News.
15. Netanyahu, *A Place Among the Nations*, *op. cit*., p. 308.
16. *Guidelines of the Government of Israel* (initial draft), communicated by Prime Minister-Elect Netanyahu's bureau, Jerusalem, 17 June 1996, p. 4.
17. Address of Israeli Prime Minister Benjamin Netanyahu to the Joint Session of Congress, Washington, 10 July 1996.
18. Glenn Frankel, "Netanyahu Sketches Upbeat View of Israel", *Washington Post*, 5 July 1996, p. A17.
19. Netanyahu, *A Place Among the Nations*, *op. cit*., pp. 319–20.
20. *Ibid*., p. 320.
21. *Ibid*., p. 328.
22. The target figure is 4.9 billion NIS annually. David Harris, "Cabinet to Okay Budget Cuts Today", *Jerusalem Post*, Internet edition, 7 July 1996.
23. Michal Yudelman, "400,000 to Strike in Protest of Government's Economic Proposals", *Jerusalem Post*, Internet edition, 1 July 1996. Also see Michal Yudelman, "Histadrut to Launch Battle Against Economic Decrees", *Jerusalem Post*, Internet edition, 7 July 1996.

24. That "blueprint" for the Palestinians appears in the chapter entitled "A durable peace", *A Place Among the Nations, op. cit.,* pp. 329–57.
25. *Ibid.*, p. 345.
26. Interview with Benjamin Netanyahu, *Evans and Novak*, 8 May 1993.
27. Netanyahu, *A Place Among the Nations, op. cit.*, p. 351.
28. The quotation is taken from Benjamin Netanyahu, *Fighting Terrorism: How Democracies Can Defeat Domestic and International Terrorists* (New York: Farrar Straus Giroux, 1995), p. 103. Netanyahu considers today's Gazan "mini-state" as similar in form, indeed a "replica" of the "PLO mini-state in Lebanon of the 1970s", when the PLO was powerful there. See *ibid.*, p. 105.
29. Netanyahu, *A Place Among the Nations*, *op. cit*., p. 352. Note that these differ from those cities which elsewhere in his book he calls the "main cities" of the Palestinian Arabs – namely, Nablus, Ramallah, Hebron and Bethlehem. See *ibid.*, p. 172.
30. Benjamin Netanyahu, "A Real Peace Plan for Israel," *Wall Street Journal*, 7 December 1993, p. A16.
31. Benjamin Netanyahu, *Fighting Terrorism*, *op. cit.*, p. 111.
32. Netanyahu, *A Place Among the Nations*, *op. cit.*, p. 353.
33. *Ibid.*, p. 354.
34. *Ibid.*, p. 329.
35. See, for example, Benjamin Netanyahu, "Peace in our Time?" *New York Times*, 5 September 1993, section IV, p. 11; Benjamin Netanyahu, "The Alternative is Autonomy", *Jerusalem Post*, 8 April 1994, p. A4; and Hillel Kuttler, "Clinton to Seek Specifics from Netanyahu", *Jerusalem Post*, Internet edition, 9 July 1996.
36. Netanyahu, "Peace in our Time?" *op. cit.*
37. As Israel well knows, given its own immigration policies of bringing Jews in from all over the world. See Interview with Netanyahu advisor Dore Gold, *Yediot Aharanot*, 4 June 1996, pp. 2–4.
38. Netanyahu, *A Place Among the Nations*, *op. cit*., p. 172. If these areas are not vacant now, one must imagine that Netanyahu's policies will eventually make them so. Extensive appropriation of land belonging to Palestinians who were able to remain in Israel after its establishment brought about a large-scale migration of individual Palestinians to the cities in search of menial labour. As an agricultural people, the seizure of their land meant the stripping away of their normal livelihood, as well as the destruction of much of their communal life which is based on the villages. There is no reason to believe that this same pattern will not eventually be repeated in the West Bank's approximately 400 villages; after a certain threshold of land confiscation has been reached, Palestinians will have no means of livelihood in the villages. This is especially true given the prohibitions on ordinary Palestinian movement that have been in effect in various forms since 1992; these have effectively eliminated the ability of Palestinians to "commute" to the cities and still return home at the end of the day. For one early indication that Israeli officials are expecting such a migration at some point in the future, see the passing comment in the *Washington Post*, 9 December 1996. Such an event would, of course, further intensify the enclosure of Palestinians by concentrating their living pattern, while leaving their village lands available for future Israeli settlement.
39. *Ibid.*, p. 174.
40. See the chapter entitled "The Reversal of Causality", in *ibid.*, pp. 130–83.
41. To execute their "policy of armed settlement", the Arabs "poured in a steady stream of colonists" and relied on the "regular expropriation of land, houses, and Jewish labor", *ibid.*, p. 25.

42. *Ibid*., p. 178.
43. *Ibid*., p. 213.
44. Netanyahu, "The Alternative is Autonomy", *op. cit.*
45. Netanyahu, *A Place Among the Nations*, *op. cit*., pp. 354–5.
46. *Ibid*., p. 348.
47. Netanyahu does not define terrorism that way in principle, but he does so in practice by neglecting to distinguish between attacks on Israeli military and civilian targets – both of which, to him, are equally "terrorist". For his theoretical definitions, see Benjamin Netanyahu (ed.), *Terrorism: How the West Can Win* (New York: Farrar, Straus and Giroux, 1986): pp. 7–15; and Netanyahu, *Fighting Terrorism*, *op. cit.*, p. 8.
48. Netanyahu's policy is to speak to Arafat at his own discretion, not as a result of any kind of obligation to him or to the people he represented in the negotiations. Prior to the first meeting, he said: "If it is in the interest of the security of Israel, then I will think about it." See "Netanyahu: Defining Peace", *Washington Post*, 30 June 1996, p. C2. Also see Edward Cody, "Netanyahu Unyielding in Christopher Talks", *Washington Post*, 26 July 1996, p. A23.
49. Press Conference of President Clinton and Prime Minister Benjamin Netanyahu, The White House, Washington, 9 July 1996. It is widely understood in Palestinian circles that such a move is beyond the PA's capabilities and could trigger a Palestinian civil war.
50. These quotations are from David Makovsky and Jon Immanuel, "Begin Rebuked for Criticizing Arafat–Gold Meeting", *Jerusalem Post*, Internet edition, 30 June 1996.
51. Benjamin Netanyahu, Address to the Joint Session of Congress, 10 July 1996.
52. Benjamin Netanyahu, "There are Two Kinds of Peace", *Jerusalem Post*, 28 May 1993.
53. Netanyahu, Address to Congress, *op. cit.*
54. Netanyahu, "Two Kinds of Peace", *op. cit.*
55. Netanyahu, *Larry King Live*, 3 July 1996.
56. John Lancaster, "Hussein Endorses Netanyahu", *Washington Post*, 2 June 1996, p. A25.
57. "Assad, Mubarak Gloomy about Bibi", *Mideast Mirror* 10(106), 3 June 1996.
58. Netanyahu, *Fighting Terrorism*, *op. cit*., p. 77.
59. Netanyahu, *A Place Among the Nations*, *op. cit*., p. 291. Netanyahu believes this to have been a "generous" move on the part of Israel, which "renounced every one of the Jewish historical, strategic, and economic claims to land where the Jewish people had received the Law of Moses and become a nation." *Ibid*, pp. 288, 348.
60. Netanyahu has termed the Syrian army "one of the largest and best equipped in the world", Netanyahu, *ibid*., pp. 288–9. These terms seem reminiscent of the United States characterization of Iraq in the run-up to the Gulf War as a fearful million-man army, the "fourth largest in the world."
61. Netanyahu, *Evans and Novak*, 8 May 1993.
62. David Makovsky, "Netanyahu Makes No Concessions to Clinton", *Jerusalem Post*, Internet edition, 10 July 1996.
63. Netanyahu, *Larry King Live*, 3 July 1996; and Press Conference of President Clinton and Prime Minister Benjamin Netanyahu, The White House, Washington, 9 July 1996.
64. Netanyahu, symposium of the *Middle East Insight*, 10 July 1996.
65. Netanyahu, *Evans and Novak*, 8 May 1993.

66. Netanyahu's focus on "fighting terrorism", which one commentator called an "obsession", derives from the death of his brother Jonathan during the raid against the PFLP unit that hijacked the Air France airliner to Entebbe in 1976. Netanyahu himself was injured during the counterstrike against the PLO-hijacked Sabena plane in 1972 and was also involved in the Israeli destruction of the Lebanese civilian air fleet at Beirut airport in 1968. See Collins, "From A to Bibi", *op. cit.*
67. Pallis, "The Likud Party: A Primer", *op. cit.,* p. 43.
68. Collins, "From A to Bibi", *op. cit.*
69. Interview with Netanyahu advisor Dore Gold, *Yediot Aharanot*, *op. cit.* The list is potentially infinite; it is as long as Israel desires it to be at any particular time, just as the American list on Iraqi violations of UN resolutions. Netanyahu himself, originally cited the PA refusal to dismantle Hamas "terrorists", to fully abrogate the Palestinian charter, and its conduct of political activity in Jerusalem. Interview with Netanyahu on *Larry King Live*, *op. cit.* Later he added another item, which is that the PA stop releasing "perpetrators of terrorist acts" and indicated there were still "a few other things"; the number is unspecified. Benjamin Netanyahu, White House Press Conference, 9 July 1996.
70. His grandfather, born in Lithuania, was one Natan Mileikowsky. After directing a Jewish school in Poland, he departed for Tel Aviv in 1920 and changed the family name. Collins, "From A to Bibi", *op. cit.*
71. Netanyahu, "The Alternative is Autonomy", *op. cit.*
72. Netanyahu, *Larry King Live*, 3 July 1996.
73. These "Arab parties" are identified by name as Egypt, Syria and Saudi Arabia, in addition to the obvious case of Jordan. Netanyahu, "The Alternative is Autonomy", *op. cit.*
74. Netanyahu, *A Place Among the Nations*, *op. cit*., p. 327.
75. Netanyahu's battle against the demographic monster takes place in the chapter of his book entitled "The Demographic Demon", in *ibid*., pp. 294–328.
76. This quotation of Benjamin Netanyahu appeared in the Hebrew newspaper *Hotam*, 24 November 1989. Cited in Pallis, "The Likud Party: A Primer", *op. cit.,* p. 57.
77. Netanyahu, *A Place Among the Nations*, *op. cit*., p. 318.
78. Netanyahu, symposium of the *Middle East Insight*, 10 July 1996.
79. Collins, "From A to Bibi", *op. cit.*
80. *Ibid*.
81. *Ibid*. Netanyahu as Israel's UN Ambassador is generally credited with, among other things, achieving the renunciation of the Zionism is racism resolution, passed by the UN General Assembly in 1975.
82. Quoted in Glenn Frankel, "Israelis Trying to Sort Out New Leader", *Washington Post*, 9 July 1996, p. A10.
83. When asked outright in an Arab forum if he recognized the Palestinians as a nation, he tactfully dodged the question, saying: "I don't get into the discussions of defining nationhood." Netanyahu, symposium of the *Middle East Insight*, 10 July 1996.

2 What are the Prospects for Modernizing the Middle East Economies?[1]

Michael Field

INTRODUCTION

Fifteen to twenty years ago the Middle East was an area of prime economic interest to governments and businesses throughout the developed world. The industrialized countries were heavily dependent on Gulf and North African oil and were constantly worried about the possibility of those supplies being cut off. The region was nearly as important as a market for industrial exports. It was rich – by far the richest market in the developing world. At one point in the late 1970s there was as much construction activity under way in Saudi Arabia as in the United States. People in both the Middle East and the Western world believed that government spending on development projects, both in the oil states and in countries receiving aid and remittance-based income from those states, would create fast growing and increasingly modern and sophisticated economies. According to a widespread belief, there was in progress an important transfer of economic power from the West to raw materials producers in Asia, Africa and Latin America.

Now the Middle East has become something of an economic backwater. Part of the reason is simply that demand for its oil has decreased, while supply has increased, causing oil prices to fall. In real terms Arab governments' revenues per barrel are now reckoned to be roughly what they were in November 1973. There is another, less obvious problem. It is that for all the money spent on them – or perhaps because of their money – the Middle East economies and societies have failed to develop. They have changed much less in the last 15–20 years than the countries of the Far East and South East Asia, which have developed through human ingenuity and hard work.

It has been striking how at the economic summit conferences – when Arabs, Israelis, Americans and Europeans gathered to discuss the region's development – the emphasis in delegates' speeches was on how out of date the region has become. Shortly before the first of these meetings, one of the most successful of the Gulf bankers summed up his feelings on the region in a private conversation. He suggested that after the great ideological conflicts of the twentieth century, the early decades of the next century – perhaps the whole century – would be a period of mostly economic change. In itself this was not a controversial or even original analysis. What would have alarmed the governments in his region was his assessment of the Arab world's prospects. "Will the Arabs be among the leaders of this change?" he asked:

> Will they participate at all? In the early stages I honestly think not. The problem is partly one of governments. They do not allow their people sufficient freedom to criticise, demand change and take economic initiatives. The possible exceptions are the UAE, Qatar, and Oman, whose governments are pursuing economic liberalization. But even here there are not sufficient competition policies and conflict of interest laws. The result is that too many businesspersons are corrupt, selfish, very short term minded and too prone to grovelling to their governments – looking to the governments, not the markets or society, for their incomes.

CAUSES OF WEAKNESS

The basic manifestations of the Arab world's economic failure are its low growth, which applies throughout the region, and the fact that in the major oil producing countries most economic activity remains dependent on government spending of oil revenues. The richest states in the region – especially Saudi Arabia and Kuwait – have recently added high budget deficits to their problems. These deficits ran to an average of 9 per cent of their gross domestic products. Saudi Arabia has built up a debt – mainly domestic – that is equivalent to about $100 billion. Much of the high government spending in both Saudi Arabia and Kuwait stems from the Iraqi invasion of 1990, the military response that followed and the work to repair the damage done by the occupiers. Another important cause of the difficulties in the southern Gulf is that in all of these countries the populations are increasing as fast as it seems possible for human populations to reproduce themselves. Workforce growth in Saudi is 5.17 percent – leaving governments with growing social spending commitments and the need to build new infrastructure, particularly power stations and sea-water desalination plants, on which all the populations, even in the Saudi cities inland, depend for their drinking water. They also have to maintain the aging infrastructure built in the 1970s.

The poorer countries – all the Middle Eastern states outside the Arabian peninsula, including several that are significant oil exporters – have failed to generate growth that is in any way self-sustaining. Their economies are very inefficient and unproductive. Egypt, which has the largest Arab population with more than 60 million people, has visible and invisible exports of only some $5 billion – made up of oil revenues, Suez Canal dues and tourist spending. In spite of more than 40 years of "development" as the government's main objective – ever since President Nasser's coup in 1952 – the country's industrial exports today are negligible. In all the poorer Arab countries there is high unemployment, generally estimated at 15 per cent or more of the workforce. Every country is saddled with a large foreign debt, though thanks to austerity measures imposed on the governments in recent years the debts are for the most part declining as a proportion of GDP.

The rich and poor Arab states are more similar than one might suppose. Since the oil price explosion of 1973–74, the poor have received a great deal of money from the rich – in aid, worker remittances and investments – and this has led their governments and peoples to adopt some of the habits of the rich. The governments pay subsidies on basic foodstuffs. The middle classes – most conspicuously in Jordan, where there is much private capital that has been earned in the Gulf – have a standard of living that is well above what they might achieve from the resources inherent in their own economies. Property prices are high. Investors look for big short-term profits. And, as we saw in the Karak riots in Jordan, supply shortages and threats to the standard of living turn political very quickly.

Rich and poor are influenced by the same social and political ideas. All the Arab peoples are preoccupied with the idea of national independence, and this has led governments to encourage import substitution industries which have often been very inefficient. It has also led to an obsession with preventing foreigners from "exploiting Arab wealth". This idea applies particularly strongly in the oil states, where the popular belief is that oil is a God-given Arab birthright which the outside world is intent on stealing. Most Arabs have a greatly exaggerated idea of the importance of their oil to the world economy. Their protective attitude extends to land and all the other productive parts of their economies. Behind it is a very simplistic view of what wealth is and how it is created. People see wealth not as something dynamic that is created by human activity, but as something static, like a pile of gold. On this analogy, the more they allow others to take the less there is for themselves.

These ideas have been much reinforced in the last 50 years by the conflict with Israel. This has strengthened nationalist sentiment and made the Arabs feel that they have been confronting the whole world, because they have been very aware that until recently popular sentiment in the industrialized countries was generally pro-Israeli. This has made the struggle for economic independence seem even more important. It has also served to justify authoritarian government; those in power have been able to argue that while they are in a state of war normal freedoms have to be suspended. It seemed natural to regimes that they should control all aspects of their people's lives.

In most Arab countries – Egypt, Iraq, Syria, Yemen, Sudan, Libya, Tunisia and Algeria – the governments that emerged in the 1950s and 1960s were Arab socialist republics. Their leaders believed in control on ideological as well as practical grounds. Nowadays the governments that run these states remain republican, but they no longer have any ideologies. They stand for no principles other than the maintenance of their own power and the preservation of regime security against threats from real and imagined enemies. In two of these Arab republics – Syria and Iraq – the leaders have even been moving towards making the presidency hereditary in their own families.

The combination of nationalist, authoritarian and socialist ideas has led Arab governments to take over much of their economies. In the socialist states private assets were nationalized in the 1960s. Elsewhere the governments took the lead in investing in big projects – mines, strategic industries, even big hotels – because they felt their private sectors lacked sufficient capital or they felt entrepreneurs and their foreign partners could not be trusted with important parts of their economies. A side effect of state control is that very little intra-regional trade has developed. The governments have hedged about their economies with tariffs, import licensing systems and bureaucratic regulation designed to protect their weak industrial sectors. Much of what regional trade and investment there is takes place in the context of inter-government protocols, often related to single projects.

Foreigners have been largely excluded from the Arab economies. In the socialist countries foreign companies were nationalized in the 1960s, and it is only in the last five–ten years that the more moderate states – such as Egypt and recently the UAE, Qatar and Oman, that are reforming – have been making efforts to invite them back. In Saudi Arabia and the other Gulf states much of the oil industry and some of the foreign banks have been nationalized, but the main factor working against a foreign presence has been the desire of these governments to reserve the most profitable activities for their own nationals. Only citizens of these states are allowed to own real estate or equity shares in local companies and import agencies, and in most other types of business, particularly contracting, foreign companies are required to have local sponsors or partners. The latter may contribute to the capital cost of a venture, or they may just take a share of its profits. In the latter case, this serves as an informal tax that, if paid not to the government is paid to a limited citizenry, adds significantly to the cost of doing business.

One result of the limited foreign presence in the oil states is that local business practices have remained unsophisticated, very slow moving and, in some ways, uncompetitive. Many businesspersons have little grasp of how Western markets operate, and partly as a result of there being no formal taxes in their own economies, have primitive ideas about accounting. Most still think of income not as the annual percentage yield on an investment, but in terms of the number of years (fewer than five, they hope) it will take them to recover their capital, before they can move into the happy realm where their revenues become virtually "pure profit" as they put it. Few see the benefit of giving themselves "unnecessary costs" by investing in the proper maintenance of their assets or paying good salaries to attract able managers.

The Middle East is receiving little of the massive international flow of investment capital that has developed in the last ten years (as Wilson points out below). This is partly because foreign companies find it difficult to invest in the region, but also because its lack of sophistication and slow growth have given it rather low demand for capital. Given that many bankers believe the world will face a capital shortage in the next ten years, brought about by continued high demand in the newly-industrializing economies and the recovery of demand in the developed world, the region may receive even smaller sums in the future (also see Chapter 3 in this volume).

Subsidies have increased the backwardness and isolation of the Arab economies. In Saudi Arabia, and even more in the southern Gulf emirates, governments traditionally have seen their main business as being the enrichment of their citizens. This they have done by charging them virtually no tax, subsidizing basic foodstuffs, water and energy, and providing industrial and agricultural investors with free land, cheap or interest free loans, and grants. It goes without saying that education and medical services are provided free, with free overseas university education and highly-specialized medical treatment where necessary. Citizens have been virtually guaranteed employment. Families receive allowances for every child. In Kuwait the rate is about $200 per child per month. Approximately 85 per cent of the Kuwaiti government's oil revenues is spent on wages, benefits and subsidies. The remainder of government spending is financed by minor amounts of tax and tariff revenue and the income (and sometimes principal) of foreign investments.

This system of "absolute welfare", as it has been called, makes Saudi and other southern Gulf citizens secure and comfortable. What makes many of them extremely rich is the privileged opportunities they have for making money in importing, contracting and real estate development, together with various devices the governments have for pushing capital into their hands. These devices, which vary from state to state, are normally based on land gifts and land purchase. The system is most formally organized in Abu Dhabi, UAE. Here most of the land in urban areas has been bought by the government. Compensation has been paid to every Abu Dhabian family on the basis that everybody at some point had grazing rights to an area of land, and every family has been given a new plot of land on which it can build a house using the compensation money. Every seven years the compensation is augmented to reflect the rising value of land. Payments are normally in the range of $100 000–200 000. To provide some further income, the Buildings and Social Services Committee allocates to individuals or families plots of land zoned for the construction of office, retail and apartment buildings – the last to be let to foreigners. The "owners" chose between several artists' impressions of what their buildings might look like, and then the Committee pays for the construction of the building, leases it and maintains it, retaining 80 per cent of the revenues to cover its costs and giving the "owner" 20 per cent. This extraordinarily generous system has the effect of spreading income more evenly than in Saudi Arabia or Kuwait, and capital makes Abu Dhabi better planned and more attractive than its neighbours.

The Kuwaiti authorities have spent even more on land purchase than the UAE, and they regularly compensate their citizens for commercial losses by buying loss-making companies from private investors. In the late 1970s and 1980s the state supported the stock exchange on such a scale that it came to own large majorities in every public company.

The poorer Arab countries have not been able to enrich their citizens, but they have provided them with jobs and subsidized them in other ways. The government of President Gamal Abdel Nasser in the early 1960s, for example, guaranteed jobs to all Egyptian university graduates, partly so it could build itself a constituency of middle-class supporters. Later the system was extended, unofficially, to high school graduates – and copied in other poor Arab countries. President Nasser began subsidizing basic foodstuffs for his people; subsidies were greatly increased and extended to some industrial products by President Sadat in the 1970s. Again, the same policies were adopted by other Arab countries. The subsidies grew fastest in the late 1970s and early 1980s when governments were tightening internal security and further restricting the freedom of their people. They were afraid of their societies being affected by the chaos in Lebanon and the Iranian revolution, and they saw subsidies as a means of compensating their people for the repression.

The whole framework of subsidies, state enrichment programmes, and state jobs has had a weakening effect. It has produced inefficiency and uncompetitive attitudes. In the rich countries people have very inflated ideas of what is a reasonable profit on a business, and little notion of how much knowledge and hard work is required for a company to make a profit when it is facing a normal amount of competition. One of the results of this is that many Gulf citizens investing in the West find themselves drawn to dubious middlemen who promise them returns that would seem normal in their own countries but would most likely be obtained by fraud in Europe or America.

In all Arab countries the availability of jobs (until recently) in the bureaucracies and state companies has given large parts of the middle classes and others the feeling that a government post and a state salary is their right. It has eroded the link in people's minds between their performance in their jobs and what they are paid. Many have come to see their jobs as being for life and their salaries as a means of their governments' looking after them in a material sense. These attitudes have led to the employees of state companies having no concept of their being obliged to provide the best possible service to the public, let alone having to improve their service because some other organization is competing with them. The hallmarks of state organizations throughout the Arab world are second-rate goods and smiling service provided by people who have no idea of how poor a job they are doing.

REFORM

Most of the poorer Arab countries were forced to begin to reform their economies in the late 1980s, when their foreign debts rose above 100 per cent of their GDPs and debt-service consumed two-thirds or more of their foreign exchange income. The governments had to reschedule their debts, and the International Monetary Fund, imposed reforms on them. In a few cases governments organized the refinancing of their debts themselves and had no need of IMF mediation, but they still implemented the same types of reforms and quietly sought IMF advice.

The reforms were designed mainly to control government budget deficits, which in some countries were around 10 per cent of GDP. It was the deficits that had led to excessive foreign borrowing. A secondary objective was to bring the countries' external current accounts into balance. The IMF insisted that currencies be devalued and exchange controls dismantled, with the ultimate purpose of making the currencies fully convertible. Multiple exchange rates, designed to provide invisible subsidies to certain types of imports and exports, were abolished. The devaluations and removal of multiple rates helped make visible to governments and their peoples just how much they were living beyond their means. Then, direct subsidies were reduced as far as possible, which in most countries has meant that they have been removed from energy products altogether and are now given on a reduced scale on just three or four essential food items. Government spending was further cut by reducing the hiring of new employees. In Egypt the government had already begun to economize by delaying the employment of graduates for several years after they had finished their courses, in the hope that they would go abroad or find work in the private sector. In most countries the tax systems were made more efficient, with income tax rates being lowered (to make people more willing to pay) and the burden of revenue-raising shifted from direct to indirect taxation. As a means of controlling inflation, discouraging consumption and encouraging saving, the IMF insisted that the banks should pay interest rates that were positive in real terms (see Chapter 10).

Where these financial reforms have been applied thoroughly – which to date has been in Morocco, Tunisia, Egypt and Jordan – they have been remarkably successful. Debt-service ratios have been reduced to tolerable levels, helped in the Egyptian and Moroccan cases by some debt-forgiveness; in addition, budget deficits have been cut to around 2–4 per cent of GDP. Inflation has been curbed and private saving encouraged. Even committed reformers, though, have not been able to bring themselves to implement every detail of the IMF prescription. Morocco, which has been reforming for the longest and has certainly been the most successful, has yet to make its currency fully convertible. Egypt, which implemented financial reform with surprising zeal in 1991 and 1992, has recently begun again to set (slightly unrealistic) rates for its currency, rather than allowing it to float freely.

A second phase of reforms, which has generally been supervised by the World Bank, was labelled "structural change". This has involved removing import licensing systems and lowering tariffs, with the purpose of making domestic industries more competitive. Those countries that had domestic price controls have reduced their scope. Foreign investment has been permitted and/or encouraged. Banking systems have been switched from socialist models, which used to prevail even in non-socialist states, to modern systems of prudential controls and Cooke ratios. The banks are no longer being told how much to lend to each sector and what rates to charge to each type of borrower; they are being allowed to operate more like banks in the West. State industries are being privatized and, so that shares in newly-floated companies can be traded, stock exchanges are being revived.

Even more than with financial reform, however, there are hesitations about the rate of privatization. Most countries have retained quite high tariffs on a large number of items. Foreign investment is encouraged in some sectors but restricted or banned in others. Jordan and Egypt are being particularly cautious. The Jordanians, for example, have discussed a privatization programme but decided that a safe first step would be "commercialization", which means turning state enterprises into independent companies and having them run at a profit for three years before a decision is taken on whether they should be sold. Worry about increasing unemployment is most responsible for the delays in privatization programmes.

The other important causes of official nervousness are the governments' fear of losing "control" of their economies and populations, and bureaucratic resistance. Government management of economies has provided jobs and a sense of self-worth for an army of civil servants. Company presidencies in Egypt have made dignified posts, with salaries, for retired generals. The system pays badly but offers such benefits as housing, cars and pensions, together with opportunities for petty corruption and power through abilities to create jobs for friends and family. The prospect of this world being swept away has alarmed officials, and regime leaders have taken note of their views. They fear that if they lose the confidence of their middle classes they will be undermined from within and left vulnerable to pressures from the bottom of society.

In the rich Arab countries, governments now seem to see the necessity of reform since they realized that their budget deficits are temporary but structural. This has been the accepted wisdom since 1993. Financial reform in these countries has been a matter of cutting spending. This might seem simple on paper, but in any country it is fraught with practical problems.

Moreover, privatization in the rich countries has begun even if it is moving slowly. It is only in the last two or three years that the Kuwaiti government has sold some of the shares it acquired in its stockmarket support operations. Qatar, Oman and the United Arab Emirates have privatized some of their utilities, and several banks have gone public. All the governments in the region are talking to consultants about more expensive privatization programmes. Potentials in the Gulf for privatization are enhanced by the fact that there are proper stock exchanges, and governments that are less worried about privatization making large numbers of nationals redundant.

The forces that work against reform are the usual instinct for "control" and the fact that most government enterprises, being vehicles for the payment of subsidies to the people, will not be able to pay dividends to shareholders without considerable financial reorganization. Also, traditionally the Arabian Peninsula governments, while presiding over basically capitalist economies, have had little faith in their private sectors as responsible long-term investors. They know how chaotic are the annual general meetings of most public companies. They have been careful in licensing even quite small industrial operations; not for environmental planning reasons but in order to avoid large numbers of bankruptcies, they have wanted only the more professional businesspersons to invest. They are nervous about relinquishing control of utilities, national airlines and major gas-based industries such as petrochemicals, let alone selling shares in their national oil companies.

The idea of liberalizing the foreign investment regime is equally sensitive. It is not too difficult for these governments to allow foreign companies to invest in utilities, provided they can negotiate satisfactory pricing and profit regimes. What is much more difficult is the opening to foreigners of those parts of their economies where the private sectors have made their fortunes. Real estate, stock markets and the importing business remain largely closed. Small recent changes have included Oman's opening of its stockmarket to foreign mutual funds, which may own up to 49 per cent of listed companies, and the Bahraini decision to give permission to foreigners resident on their island for three years to own up to 1 per cent of a company. The Dubai government has considered the licensing of a big property development in which foreign companies operating in the emirate would be allowed to buy leases, which would exempt them from the normal sponsorship rules.

INVITING BACK THE OIL COMPANIES

Rather separate, in Arab eyes, from the main body of foreign investment rules is foreign investment in oil and gas industries. This is a highly sensitive and important area in which Arab state policies are beginning to change.

The Arab producers, like the other members of the Organization of Petroleum Exporting Countries (OPEC), took control of their oil industries in the 1970s. The Western concessionaire companies were either nationalized outright or obliged to sell majority shares in their operations to the national governments. In some cases, even where 100 per cent of their assets were confiscated by the state, the companies kept an important role behind the scenes as advisors, operations managers and preferred purchasers of crude oil. This was what happened in Dubai, where the government took control in only a nominal sense, and in Saudi Arabia, where they retained equity shares or managerial roles the companies continued to have access to crude on advantageous terms. In other countries the takeover of the concessionaires involved the price of the crude they bought – if they wished to continue buying – being raised to international market levels.

At the time of the takeovers, the fact that Gulf oil was being made less attractive to the companies did not seem to matter, because the world was becoming increasingly dependent on it. However, since the late 1970s the picture has changed. Energy conservation in the industrialized world, the development of new oil resources and the exploitation of alternative sources of energy, particularly gas and nuclear power, have destroyed OPEC's hold on the market. OPEC output fell steadily from the beginning of the 1980s until the autumn of 1985. Then Saudi Arabia, which had borne the brunt of the fall, began selling its oil at open market prices – much reduced since the beginning of the decade – thus precipitating the collapse of OPEC's price structure in February 1986. This caused OPEC output to slowly recover. It climbed from 16 million barrels per day in 1985 to 25 million barrels per day in 1992 – which was still some 7 million barrels per day below the peak level of 1977 – and according to the more conservative forecasts it is expected to stay flat through the year 2000.

Opinions are divided on whether beyond 2000 the global supply pattern is going to change. World oil demand is growing by between 1–1.5 million barrels per day every year, with the growth being generated entirely by the newly-industrializing countries. It was once believed that this demand could only be met by the Gulf, and there are still some forecasts that suggest this. The International Energy Agency predicted early in 1995 that world oil demand was set to rise from about 68 million barrels per day in 1996 to between 92 million barrels per day and 102 million barrels per day by 2010, with almost the entire increment coming from OPEC and principally from the Gulf. But other forecasters are suggesting that non-OPEC output will continue to expand under the influence of new technology. The conventional wisdom at the time of the first oil crisis in 1973–74 was that there was little new production to be had outside OPEC and the North Sea, yet since that date non-OPEC production has grown by 15 million barrels per day to its current level of 42 million barrels per day. If non-OPEC output continues to grow at this rate, less than half of the new demand up to 2010 will be met by OPEC, and. presumably, a smaller proportion by the Gulf.

If the Gulf states start to believe that their oil production is going to either remain static or increase slowly, and if they continue to require higher revenues, as they are bound to do, they will want to gain access to the markets by having a larger oil company presence on their territories. Already Oman, Qatar and Kuwait have agreed to production-sharing arrangements on new acreage or for fields which need to be redeveloped. Iraq will invite back foreign oil companies once United Nations sanctions are lifted, and Iran is anxiously involving foreign companies in the development of its gas reserves and might apply the same policy to its oil fields were it not so nationalistic. Algeria is leasing new acreage and old proven fields to foreign companies. The two countries in the Gulf that will probably be last to change their policies are Saudi Arabia and UAE – Saudi Arabia because it still has a close relationship with the old Aramco shareholders (Exxon, Texaco, Chevron and Mobil), and UAE because its concessionaires have retained 40 per cent equity stakes in its operations.

POLITICAL OBSTACLES

Open economies, such as some Arab governments feel they ought to create, generally go with open or reforming political systems. This is important to foreign investors. European, American and Far Eastern companies want to feel that the region is stable for the long term and has the same political and economic ethos as newly-industrializing countries with which they are familiar elsewhere in the world.

There are also indigenous pressures for political reform within the Arab world. There is a feeling among the Arab intelligentsia, and much of the rest of the population, that the authoritarian regimes the region has endured for the last 30 or 40 years are morally bankrupt. They have failed to give their people free civil societies, economic prosperity, or military security. The sense of the need for change is strengthened by the fact that many of the rulers – both monarchs and republican leaders – are old and have been in power for many years. King Hussein of Jordan has died and the world hopes the new King, Abdullah, will pursue political liberalization. Others, including King Hassan of Morocco and even the Emir of Qatar and Sultan of Oman, show interest in developing democratic institutions or at least more participatory parliamentary processes, which can play greater roles in running their countries after their deaths.

Stronger pressure for change has come from economic reform. When governments have had to tell people that budgets have to be balanced and subsidies reduced, and that they can no longer guarantee jobs, they have felt obliged to propose some form of political liberalization in exchange – especially as many of the subsidies were instituted in the 1980s to compensate for a gradual loss of political freedom at that time. Economic reform has also brought proposals from the business community that it be consulted in the drafting of new financial legislation. In Morocco a dialogue has already begun.

In the late 1980s several Arab governments embarked on cautious reform. In 1989 King Hussein recalled his parliament after a sharp cut in subsidies early in the year led to riots in a part of the country normally considered most loyal. Throughout the late 1980s and the first years of the 1990s there were slow changes in Egypt. The press and judiciary became steadily freer, and opposition parties were legalized. The same reforms were begun in Tunisia, and from 1993 in Morocco. The most radical reforms, economic and political, were introduced in Algeria, where overnight in 1989 the country was given a free press, legalization of opposition parties, and the promise of free elections. Of course, regime backsliding in all of these countries has significantly hampered progress in the late 1990s. During this period Qatar, and then Oman have made the most progress toward political liberalization.

Still, the paradoxes caused by elections in the region should not go unnoticed. It was events in Algeria, where the elections were cancelled in January 1992 when it seemed the Islamists might win, that brought the reform process virtually to a halt. King Hussein has continued to allow his parliament to function and hold elections but he simultaneously and seriously limited the freedom of the press; King Hassan of Morocco had the confidence to begin reforms after the Algerian debacle but did not permit them to go very far. In Egypt and Tunisia the presidents have been so frightened by what they saw in 1991–92 and by the civil war that erupted in Algeria in 1993, as well as what they have seen in the Sudan, that they have stopped reform and even put the process into reverse. Other Arab leaders who may have been contemplating modest reform programmes were also deterred by Maghrebi developments. Both Hosni Mubarak in Egypt and Zine El-Abidine Ben Ali in Tunisia, as well as some of the others, are worn by the cares of office, unimaginative and preoccupied with "control".

The general lack of freedom in the area prevents innovation and integration (see Chapter 4 in this volume). Because people in these societies do not believe their governments will allow change – and anyway are restricted in their freedom of speech – they do not discuss new ideas. There is not the flow of controversial ideas in books, newspaper articles and conference proceedings that exists in free societies. This is bound to have an impact on business. It hinders the adoption of new business practices and the formation of new companies to provide new services and make new products. It makes it more difficult for governments to understand how they might tackle the problems produced by economic reform. It slows the introduction of new commercial legislation, and stifles efforts in anti-corruption and judicial reform.

A force which should work in the opposite direction, accelerating economic change, is the gradual move towards peace in the Middle East. In theory, at least, peace will remove the justification for authoritarian rule usually given in Arab countries and should eventually lead to a cut in defence spending. It should also lead the Arabs to make comparisons between their own slow-growing economies and the remarkably dynamic economy of Israel. The Israelis, with a population of well over five million, have a GDP of some $70 billion. This compares with the Jordanian GDP of only $5 billion, produced by a population of about four million, and an Egyptian GDP of little more than $50 billion, produced by 60 million. (The Egyptian figure excludes the country's large black-market economy.)

Some Arabs fear that if they open their doors to Israel their economies will quickly be taken over by their former enemy, and certainly many Israelis imagine that across their borders there is an "Arab economy" with a strong flow of trade and investment among the Arab states. They talk of integrating their country into the Arab economy, tapping its labour force (through investing in Arab countries) and its markets, and building projects which would use Israeli technology. In short, they see themselves exploiting their position in a potentially rich area of the world which has hitherto been closed to them. Few of them realise that there is very little inter-Arab trade and little inter-Arab investment outside the real-estate sector. Most likely in the years to come, many Israeli businesspersons and foreign policy officials will be disappointed, and Arab fears of their being overwhelmed by the Israelis will fade.

As well as having the fragmentation of the Arab world working against them, the Israelis will be hampered by the fact that it will take much longer for the Arabs to accept them than for them to accept the Arabs. Israel has said repeatedly, especially in the context of its talks with the Syrians, that it wants its peace with the Arabs to be a real one, leading to the whole range of contacts that exist between friendly neighbours. It wants to be accepted as a natural part of the Middle East. Most of the Arabs feel differently. They are prepared for peace with Israel, but not for friendship. The different attitudes of the two sides are reflected in the figures for tourist and business visits between Egypt and Israel since the signing of their peace treaty in 1979. In the past 15 years approximately half a million Israelis have been to Egypt, but only about 4000 Egyptians have travelled in the opposite direction.

The prospect for the next few years, therefore, is for Arab–Israeli economic contacts to be composed mainly of projects encouraged by the governments, such as the Israeli–Egyptian oil refinery in Alexandria and the Israeli–Jordanian Dead Sea bromine plant, both of which have been announced in the recent past. What would change the picture would be a final settlement between the Palestinians and Israelis, resolving the vexing issues of borders, the status of East Jerusalem, the settlements in the West Bank and Gaza Strip, and the Palestinian right of return. Palestinian and Israeli businesspersons know each other well; if political conditions permitted there would be major flows of trade in both directions, including Israeli investment in a future Palestinian state.

CONCLUSION

Arab feelings of wariness towards Israel are echoed, in a small way, in their attitudes towards the rest of the world. The Arab–Israeli conflict, in which the Arabs have suffered nearly 50 years of humiliation, has left its scars. The Arabs feel that much of the rest of the world has been hostile to them during this period. They are also separate from most other peoples and countries in that the great majority of them are Muslim; this religious aspect in their thinking is important. This is not only because God tells Muslims through the *Qur'an* that they are special as the recipients of His final message to mankind, but also because Islam at present is undergoing a revival – a revival which is stimulated by the economic failure and political unhappiness of much of the Muslim world. Therefore, even if their economies do begin to modernize, many Arabs are unlikely to suddenly embrace the materialist, secular, global culture of successful newly-industrializing countries elsewhere.

Their view of themselves was well-illustrated at two conferences on economic development in Southeast Asia, which were sponsored by Cairo University and the newspaper *Al-Ahram*. At the meetings businesspersons and government officials from several Asian states spoke about their countries' extraordinary economic success, and Westerners in the audience imagined that Arab participants – who, significantly, were mainly middle-aged academics and journalists rather than businesspersons – would ask the speakers how their methods might be applied in their own country. But their reaction was completely different than expected. What most questioners wanted to know was not how southeast Asia had been able to modernize, but how it had managed to keep its cultural identity.

Note

1. This chapter is adapted from an article which appeared in January 1996 in the German publication *Friedrich Ebert Stiftung*, with the permission of its editors. The author extends his thanks to them, and for allowing this article to be updated and reprinted in this volume.

3 The Arab–Israeli Peace Process: Can the Region Benefit from the Economics of Globalization?

Emma C. Murphy

INTRODUCTION

When the then-US President, George Bush, announced the arrival of a New World Order in March 1991[1] he also redefined American policy goals in the Middle East region. With the principal aim of securing a stable Persian Gulf, the United States would henceforth direct its energies towards four component paths: regional disarmament, security, economic development and revitalization of the Arab–Israeli peace process. These last two were considered by most observers to be closely related and interdependent. They merged well with the general ethos of economic globalization expected of the New World Order; that moulds of international confrontation should be broken and new paths of dialogue, political reform and economic integration based on market liberalization should be pursued. It was assumed by many that creating economic linkages between countries would underpin efforts at peacemaking, while regional peace would itself promote greater economic development (or at least remove existing obstacles to it).

This analysis was not confined to the Middle East region. Born of the World Trade Organization, the new economics of globalization[2] demands that political obstructions to the free movement of capital be removed and, furthermore, that the various regions of the globe begin to respond to the wider challenges by developing common and mutually advantageous trade regimes. There was no consensus over the regionalization of the global economy; some analysts viewed the United States as the hegemonic representative of triumphant capitalism, while others anticipated a multipolar world with competition taking place among regional economic entities such as Europe, Asia-Pacific, the Americas and, possibly, the Middle East.

What this meant in practice for the Middle East was that exponents of the liberal market view of economics, who predominated in the world's financial centres and institutions, considered that regional economic development on the basis of cooperation and even integration would not only underpin developing political structures in the peace process, but were in themselves an essential programme for Middle Eastern economies. The peace process would become a facilitator for a more fundamental process to take place: the integration of the region's economies into the global capitalist system in a way that would allow them to maximize any existing or potential comparative advantage.

We have thus seen since the Oslo Accord the emphasis in the peace negotiations being laid on advances in the economic realm. It would be unfair to deny the existence of economic imperatives leading the parties to peace independently of the globalization process; they are discussed briefly in this chapter. The main argument, however, concerns the concept of a developing regional economy in the Middle East as a "fruit" of the peace process. The chapter argues that, while Arab analysts and politicians tend to take a regional approach to the economics of peace, the Israelis have taken a far more advanced global approach. By concentrating on the internal economic dynamics of a Middle East region, the Arab states are in danger of "missing the boat", of watching Israel move onto the fast-track of developed-nation status while they themselves become part of an increasingly fragmented and marginalized economic region of the world. In this context, it would be wise for Arab and Israeli negotiators to consider the economics of globalization in the protocols they establish and the treaties they sign.

ECONOMIC DYNAMICS FOR PEACE

There can be little dispute over the economic logic which contributed to the decisions of Arabs and Israelis to participate in then-President George Bush's renewal of efforts to achieve Middle East peace. To summarize, the Kuwait crisis – the cutting-off of Arab Gulf funds to the PLO and the subsequent expulsion of many Palestinians from the southern Gulf states – left the PLO coffers empty at a time when its Islamist competitors in the occupied territories were benefiting from Islamic source-derived funds. Participation in the Madrid Conference and the subsequent bilateral and multilateral negotiations offered an opening to dialogue with the Arab world as much as with Israel, and it also provided a mechanism whereby the PLO could regain the initiative from both Hamas and the secular leadership of the *Intifada*.

For the intransigent Israeli Prime Minister, Yitzhak Shamir, the Madrid conference and the subsequent negotiations were an extremely unwelcome precondition to receiving American loan guarantees to support the settlement of the latest wave of Soviet immigrants to Israel. With Bush set on achieving at least that breakthrough, even existing US aid levels appeared to be on the line at a time when Israel's own resources were being fully stretched. Egypt and Syria were rewarded directly for their contributions to the Gulf war coalition with debt write-offs and aid from the United States and/or Arab Gulf states, and they were assured that participation in the peace process would result in both direct and indirect forms needed at critical times. For Egypt this meant helping it to bear the costs of a traumatic structural adjustment experience, and for Syria providing it with some relief from the difficulties resulting from the Soviet "withdrawal".

At a very specific level, the economic deterioration of the West Bank and Gaza under Israeli control had reached a critical level that not only engendered political chaos but also transformed the territories from being an Israeli economic asset to being a potentially disastrous liability. The very visible impoverishment of the Palestinians was drawing intense international criticism against Israel, which sought to restructure the occupation in a way that would allow for some relief of that impoverishment without drawing upon Israeli resources.[3]

On a broader level, the collapse of the Soviet Union was interpreted by many as evidence of the obsolescence of the socialist alternative for economic development and the triumph of the neo-liberal school of economic thought. The so-called Washington Consensus, shared by major international financial institutions such as the IMF and the World Bank, as well as leading Western economists and governments, asserted that the free market was the most efficient mechanism for matching demand and supply and creating the overall wealth which, through a trickle-down effect, would benefit rich and poor alike as it promoted economic growth. Such theories denied the culpability of the international trade and financial systems in being structurally flawed in favour of developed countries, and asserted that, with socialism on the retreat, a new phase in the global spread of capitalism was becoming possible. Areas previously closed, geographically and politically, to the influences and activities of capitalism, were now falling within its grasp as international linkages in trade and finance widened and intensified economic globalization.

During the 1980s, the international debt crisis and the conditions attached to new loan programmes to help developing countries had forced the majority to abandon central planning or state-led development in favour of economic liberalization and full-scale re-engagement in the international economy. They also thus fell to the wave of capitalist expansion that has been sweeping the globe.[4] Analysts such as Harry Magdoff have termed this the "globalization of capital", pointing out that, while capital has always contained within it the need to expand, it has since the 1980s been able to "globalize" this expansion in a way which threatens the character of the nation-state itself. Samir Amin has argued that it is not the nation-state itself that is under threat, since capitalism has a social and political dimension which is, so far, organized or represented by the state. Rather the economic efficiency of the state is undermined and its economic functions thus deteriorate, an argument Kenechi Ohmae also makes repeatedly.[5]

As capital seeks to expand across borders, the political conflicts between states become transformed into economic policy obstacles that hinder a more dynamic and irresistible process. International security and a reduction in the political efficacy of national borders become essential if capital is to move, foreign investment to take place and operate most efficiently. Thus, in George Bush's New World Order, the global phenomenon of economic growth through liberalization of production and distribution (both national and international) required the resolution of regional disputes and the establishment of regional political security if it were to take effect.

This argument can to some extent be reversed and yet still hold true. It is also the case that where mutually beneficial economic ties have been established between countries, their political disputes are more likely to be resolved peacefully through negotiation than through direct conflict. In the case of the negotiations for peace with Syria, the former Israeli Prime Minister, Shimon Peres, like his predecessors, was adamant that peace must include "normalization" of relations, both economic and political. This included but was not limited to economic and cultural-social ties underpinning paper agreements, as has been the case with Egypt to a degree, though much more so with Jordan. Over time, it was believed, the interaction of peoples and their collaboration in wealth generation and distribution would bind them together through mutual interest and thus preserve security.[6]

Some economists argue that as the world becomes more economically open, states will seek regional alliances to maximize their comparative market advantages: J.W. Wright, Jr., for example, does so often. Regional markets enable states to take advantage of a certain level of protection from raw international competition, yet still derive the benefits of the internal competitive market. Thus, they argue, we see the world dividing into regional economic groupings around the United States, Japan and Europe.

It is necessary to distinguish clearly between a number of concepts: the notion of regional economies assumes that a certain commonly-attained level of economic development already exists among states, enabling them to interact and to some degree integrate on mutually beneficial terms. This is not the same as regional economic development, which means exactly what it says. Nation-states may cooperate in plans and projects to further mutually beneficial development across the region without surrendering the organization of their economies to a regional market or network of organizations. The notion of integration is applicable to regional economies but not necessarily to regional economic development. In discussions of the economics of the current peace process there has been a great deal of confusion between these concepts. They carry with them political preconditions and implications which will become evident from the following discussion.

ECONOMIC ELEMENTS OF THE PEACE AGREEMENTS

When the Oslo Accords were signed, one of their most distinctive features was the importance attached to economic issues and commitments. Four of the 17 articles in the Declaration of Principles of September 1993 referred directly to economic arrangements, as did Annex II, the Protocol on Israeli–Palestinian Cooperation in Economic and Development Programmes and the Protocol on Israeli–Palestinian Cooperation Concerning Regional Development Programmes. Two levels of economic activity were to result from the agreement. At the immediate level the Oslo agreement provided for some economic functions to pass to a Palestinian Interim Self-Governing Authority, while others would be exercised by that institution in cooperation with, and ultimately under the direction of, the Israeli government.[7] At the second level, the PLO/PA and Israel would work together to engineer a new era in regional economic cooperation from which both could benefit.

Discussion of the first of these is beyond the remit of this chapter, although there is one issue which should be raised. The final economic arrangements agreed upon in the Paris Protocol of April 1994 established a customs union between the Palestinian Authority and Israel. The inequality between the levels of development of the respective economic areas, and the dictating of the conditions of that customs union by Israel according to its own national interests, have meant that the basic economic structures of occupation remain intact. The Palestinians have little produce of their own, other than some agricultural goods, to sell to Israel, but they are prevented from acting as a conduit to channel cheap imports from third parties into Israel. The Israelis set the common customs tariffs to protect their own producers, who still benefit from some (although decreasing) subsidization. Free trade within the customs union works to the benefit of the more developed economy, which can still dump its manufactured goods on the less-developed economy.[8] Practical constraints – in addition to the devastation caused by the general closure – have been imposed upon Palestinian trade by the Israelis, including extensive and ruinous delays on agricultural exports, seizures of imported technology on "security" grounds, and much more.[9]

A thornier issue still in this "free" market of the future between Israel and the Palestinians is that of labour. The agreement states that the Israelis will not seek to impose a ceiling on the number of Palestinian workers travelling to Israel. Employment in Israel provides around 30 per cent of Palestinian national income, and development planners agree that at least 100 000 Palestinians must be allowed to work in Israel if the Palestinian economy is to have any chance of growing. In practice, Israel has not only imposed quantitative restrictions unilaterally (fewer than 30 000 last year), but it has also sought to replace Palestinian workers with foreign workers from Eastern Europe, Turkey and the Far East and/or increased Jewish immigration.[10] Another tactic has been to offer wage subsidies to new immigrants to take the manual labour themselves. Despite promises of international aid (much of which remains unfulfilled[11] and which in any case carries its own risks for the Palestinian economy, not to mention the fact that much of it has resulted in contracts for foreign contractors rather than for Palestinians),[12] the Palestinian economy is faring quite a bit worse today than before the Oslo Accords were signed. Israel, by contrast, has made the conditions of its domination over the smaller economy both legitimate in international eyes and free, in terms of having passed the responsibility for economic rehabilitation to the international donors and the Palestinians themselves.

The second aspect, that of regional economic development, is more interesting for our purposes. The intent of the Declaration of Principles was that the Palestinians would now effectively "vouch" for Israel's credibility as a trading partner in the Middle East, leading to the dismantlement of the Arab boycott. In return, the Palestinian economy would also be allowed to benefit from a new openness to the neighbouring Arab economies. This theme was echoed in Israel's peace treaty with Jordan, which likewise contained a heavy economic content and reiterated the theme of mutually-beneficial regional economic development. The Casablanca economic summit in November 1994 and the Amman summit in October 1995, both of which included substantial Israeli contingents and participation, appeared to herald a new era of economic cooperation and dialogue between Arabs and Israelis as a result of the new economic respectability of Israel following its two additional peace agreements.

The Israelis have been most vocal in expressing their vision of a new regional economy. At Casablanca the Israelis produced a confident glossy brochure outlining their vision for future economic cooperation. It stated that Israeli's goal would be "the creation of a regional community of nations, with a common market and elected centralized bodies, modelled on the European Community."[13] This would have three stages of bilateral or multilateral projects, international consortia and regional community policy. The Netanyahu government has taken a slightly different tack towards the negotiations, but in fact the "regional community model" has always been integral to the Israeli strategy, regardless of its head of government.

This idea is based on the belief that peace will provide the opportunity for all Middle Eastern states to divert resources from their military budgets towards human and economic development (see Chapter 6 in this volume). It is thought that the resulting newfound and shared prosperity will underpin the peace itself, while providing opportunities for the resolution of shared regional problems such as water shortages and environmental degradation.

Critics of the vision point out that a true common market requires compatible national political systems, social systems that are not in conflict, levels of democracy not yet seen in the Middle East and general perceptions that a common market will be mutually beneficial.

While the Israelis may perceive the future in terms of a common market and regional economy, Arab states are more hesitant and remain committed at present only to cooperation and joint projects. They fear that the relative strength of the Israeli economy in any attempt at more intensive interlinkage will result in Israeli regional economic domination. Together the Arab world represents a market of over 240 million potential customers, compared to only five million in Israel. While Israel can provide the high-tech, high-quality consumer goods that people in the wealthy Gulf states may want to buy, according to the Israeli professor Eliyahu Kanovsky, there is little for sale in the Arab world that the Israelis may want to purchase.[14] This is not entirely true because Jordanians and Palestinians can often produce these products more cheaply, though Kanovsky's point is true for many segments of the economy. Energy might be an exception, although it will inevitably be the energy-wealthy Arab states that benefit from this (for example, the $5 billion deal for Qatar to supply Israel with liquefied natural gas).

In addition, Arab governments are aware of the domestic unpopularity of visible relations with Israel, a nervousness which often extends into the business community and is reflected in a certain distaste at the idea of rushing headlong into economic relations with the enemy of 50 years. Even though the Palestinians themselves, or at least the PLO, have sanctioned such moves by taking the initiative via Oslo, old habits die hard, especially when they are founded on genuine economic concerns. The Peres government's bombings in Lebanon and Netanyahu's harsh rhetoric and hard-line ideology, not to mention his own military interventions, have not led the general Arab populace to trust Israel, either economically or politically.

ASSESSING ADVANCES IN ARAB–ISRAELI TRADE AND COOPERATION SINCE OSLO

One can divide the Arab response to Israeli economic overtures into four categories:

1. *Arab states accepting formal normalization.*
   This category currently includes only Egypt, Jordan and the Palestinian Authority at present. Egypt's post-1979 peace agreement experience was actually rather negative; as Samir Abdullah has pointed out:

   > ...the Camp David peace agreement is a startling example of how nominal political peace cannot act as a catalyst to regional economic

> co-operation if it excludes all the main players. Egyptian trade with Israel, apart from oil export, has remained negligible despite this agreement and even joint tourism ventures – possibly one of the most potentially rewarding co-operative initiatives – is still only in the planning stages.[15]

Predictions for trade between the two countries proved to be grossly over-optimistic. The situation may not, however, be the same today. Egypt itself has, since the Oslo Accords, embarked on a whole new realm of government-led ventures with Israel, including the creation of a joint company to market agricultural exports.[16] It has been an avid participant in attempts to create regional frameworks that include Israel, including EU designs for a Mediterranean free trade area and a Middle East regional development bank.

In January 1995 Jordan signed a free trade agreement with Israel and the PA, creating in effect a customs union between the three. Palestinians have as much to fear from Jordan's superior economic strength as they do from Israel's, although inevitably they will prefer to be economically linked to Jordan rather than to Israel. There is always considerable concern among Palestinians, for example, that Jordanian banks are not reinvesting Palestinian deposits in Palestine, and there is evidence that this is true (see Chapter 7 in this volume). The Jordanians also have reservations about Israel's dominant economic status in the grouping, but they believe that Jordan's own viability will ultimately depend on regionally open borders and coordinated development. They have much to gain from cooperative ventures with Israel and the Palestinians in areas such as water, transport, phosphate production and marketing, and the free movement of labour. Israel sees Jordan as an essentially small market for its goods – in 1992 Jordan imported only 17.5 per cent of the value of Israeli imports[17] – but the principle of economic opening between Israel and the Arab states is worth pursuing in this instance for itself alone. Israeli products will also have to pass through Jordan if they are to reach the southern Gulf states or Iraq by land.

2. *Arab states moving towards de facto economic normalization.*
Examples in this category include Morocco and Tunisia. They are both engaged in the EU partnership plan of action which envisages an eventual Mediterranean free trade zone by the year 2010. Both openly admit that they no longer observe the Arab boycott, both have been fully engaged in regional economic summits, save the one at Doha, both have formal channels of communication open with the Israeli government (liaison and interests sections) and both are deeply committed to the processes of economic liberalization and regional economic engagement.

Although Turkey is a non-Arab state, it is worth remembering that this Middle Eastern country, which is both closer to Europe and rather more economically developed than many others in the region, has also recently agreed with Israel to scrap all tariff barriers between them by the year 2000 as a part of their mutual Mediterranean free trade zone commitments. Existing trade between the two countries is still small (less than $500 million), but is expected to expand to as much as $2 billion by the time the barriers are removed.[18]

3. *Arab states moving towards economic cooperation.*
The Gulf Cooperation Council (GCC) states provide excellent evidence of the tensions surrounding developing ties with Israel. In September 1994 they collectively announced that they would lift the secondary boycott against Israel. This was to some extent rather farcical – Israeli products have been reaching the Gulf for years via dummy companies in Malta, Italy, Cyprus and Greece[19] – but it did set the precedent for direct intergovernmental ties. The GCC countries sent public and private sector delegates to both Casablanca and Amman and began publicizing unilateral deals that had been made with Israel as early as April 1994, such as the Omani agreement on solar energy development and its offer to host a research centre on desalination under the auspices of the multilateral talks on water. Even Egypt and Jordan grew nervous of the apparent willingness of the GCC states to move ahead unilaterally; a mini-summit was convened in January 1995 at which they tried to convince Saudi Arabia to restrain its Gulf neighbours to prevent the Syrian–Israeli talks from falling too far behind events and weakening the Syrian position. Oman was unimpressed, and in October 1995 became the first GCC state to establish official relations with Israel. Qatar and Saudi Arabia have both made agreements with Israel on air links or airspace, and Oman and Qatar sent official representatives to Prime Minister Rabin's funeral at the end of 1995. Rabin himself, shortly before his death, had visited Oman in 1994 and met officials from Qatar in New York to agree on the details of the liquified natural gas deal which was cemented in 1999.

Economic ties with the GCC are likely to continue to proceed rather faster than diplomatic ties, a pattern which is not new to Israel. Indeed, Israel has often sought exactly this process in the past in order to create conditions which make it difficult for a process of rapprochement, however slow, to be reversed or held up. The establishment of economic ties with the Muslim Central Asian Republics is a case in point.[20] Israel views the GCC states as offering investment capital in the long term, as well as representing one of the largest consumer markets in the world, worth over $50 billion a year.[21] Israel can offer precisely the technology the GCC needs in water conservation and irrigation, agriculture, energy and potentially arms sales. Moreover, it sells high quality finished products and consumer goods which the GCC states can afford.

The GCC states are, however, extremely cautious in assessing the benefits to be gained from economic relations with Israel. At the close of the first GCC conference on Middle East peace and its economic impact in January 1996, they issued a statement asserting that the lifting of the primary boycott against Israel would have to wait. The lifting of the secondary boycott had brought new investment to Israel but little new interest in the GCC states. Instead, they found their role to be increasingly that of financiers to regional projects and a source of oil, a role they will increasingly be unable to play (see Chapter 2 in this volume). The GCC states, they declared, "must create a common market to fight the negative economic consequences of the peace process."[22] The GCC states have indeed been trying to establish such a common market for a while now, and many analysts have suggested that a regional common market should be established for the Arab world as a whole before economic relations with Israel are consolidated, in order to strengthen the bargaining position of the Arab states.

4. *Arab states currently rejecting economic links with Israel.*
Any Israeli peace with Syria will be bound, ultimately, to include political and economic normalization, that being a key demand of the Israelis. Syria's own economy, after a brief period of oil-fueled revival, is again suffering from stagnation and atrophy. Peace may or may not bring dividends of economic aid, a reduced military burden and new foreign investment, but President Assad remains sceptical that the economic bonus of peace can make up for the political and strategic concessions that it will require (see Chapter 6 with particular reference to military budget concessions). Other states in this category include Lebanon, Libya and Iraq.

JUST HOW STRONG IS ISRAEL'S ECONOMY?

What is clear from the above categorization is that all the Arab states remain nervous of Israel's potential to dominate any regional economy. The debate over the relative strength of Israel is not new, but certain characteristics of the Israeli economy are, and they deserve attention.

The Oslo agreement provided the basis for the international political rehabilitation of Israel and, it now appears, a new stage in its economic development. Within a year of the signing of the agreement, Israel had established diplomatic relations with over 20 new countries and more have followed suit. Although these have included states from around the world, including South America and Oceania, Israel has concentrated its efforts on Southeast Asia. Relations were established with China, India and Mongolia in 1992, followed by Vietnam, Cambodia and Laos in 1993. In 1994 Prime Minister Rabin embarked upon an East Asia tour, visiting China, Japan, Singapore, both

Koreas, Thailand, the Philippines and Malaysia. Countries which had previously observed the economic boycott now lined up to sign economic and trade agreements with Israel, which included opening their markets to Israeli exports, quoting Israeli stocks on their exchanges and establishing joint ventures in everything from agricultural equipment to arms production.

In the first nine months of 1994 alone, Israeli exports to Asian countries increased by a third, accounting for 12.4 per cent of total Israeli exports (compared to only 8.1 per cent in 1992).[23] In 1993 bilateral trade with South Korea increased by 50 per cent, and in 1995 China became a prime and welcoming target for Israeli defence exports, industrial technology and agricultural products. The irony of the peace process is that Israel's vision for itself is not so much as the dominant state of the Middle East but as a new "tiger" in the international economy. It is taking advantage of the political benefits of peace to launch a drive for its own international economic development.

One must ask how realistic are the claims of such Israelis as the current Prime Minister, Benjamin Netanyahu, to the effect that Israel can become a "tiger" by doubling its per capita income in the next 15 years.[24] Israel has certain economic characteristics that suggest it may be possible. It has a highly educated and technologically proficient workforce and a high-tech industrial base which is no longer dependent on technology transfer for its development and which is constantly invigorated by the highly developed military-industrial complex. Leading Israeli technology companies such as Indigo and ECI are establishing their own subsidiaries in Germany, the United States and elsewhere. Equally, since the lifting of the secondary boycott, multinational companies based in other countries have begun to move into Israel, establishing offices and starting joint ventures with Israeli companies. The US ambassador to Tel Aviv was quoted as having said that:

> U.S. companies are only just beginning to understand Israel's true economic potential and the opportunities it provides – not just in marketing, but also in terms of investment. There is a real sense of an awakening awareness in the United States that Israel can and will become the Asian tiger of the Middle East.[25]

The full range of multinationals are now showing interest in the post-boycott Israeli economy. Companies such as General Motors, Westinghouse, Salamon Brothers, Cable and Wireless, Daimler Benz and Siemans have all shown interest, and some have actually moved into Israel, thereby negating what until now had been the principal damaging effect of the Arab boycott.[26] Such firms do not see Israel as a source of finance, "sweat shop" labour, but as a partner for finance, investment and research and development. Israel itself is not targeted as a major market for products, but as a gateway to markets in the Far East (and to a *lesser* extent the Middle East) and a source of technological product input. One example is the establishment of a Nanonics lithography electro-optics factory in Jerusalem by a collaborative company including the Federman family, Daimler Benz and the Gemini Venture Capital Fund.

The Israeli labour force includes 138 scientists and technicians per 10 000 workers, as compared to figures of 80 in the United States, 78 in Japan and 45 in Taiwan (see Table 3.1). Israel's research and development (R&D) expenditure as a percentage of GDP rivals that of Germany and surpasses that of the United States and most of Europe (see Table 3.2). Its expenditure on education has, moreover, increased by 70 per cent over the last two years, with the deliberate intent that high-tech innovation should continue to fuel an economic renaissance for the country. There are currently 70 technology-led Israeli companies, including world leaders such as Scitex,[27] quoted on the

Table 3.1 Scientists and technicians per 10 000 workers

Israel	**138**
United States	80
Japan	78
Netherlands	62
Germany	60
Sweden	55
Canada	48
Australia	48
Taiwan	45
United Kingdom	40
South Korea	35
Singapore	28
Argentina	20
Egypt	18

Source: Israeli Ministry of Industry and Trade, *Guardian*, 10 February 1996.

Table 3.2 Civilian R&D expenditure as a percentage of GDP

Japan	3.0
Germany	2.7
Israel	**2.2**
United States	2.1
France	2.0
Denmark	1.7
United Kingdom	1.7
Italy	1.3
Canada	1.3

Source: OECD, Israeli Centre of Business Statistics, *Guardian*, 10 February 1996.

New York stockmarkets with a capitalization in excess of $8 billion. A further 55 such companies are quoted on the TASE with a combined market value exceeding $3 billion. Israeli companies lead the world in industries such as the multimedia industry (producing CD-Roms) although they often leave the international marketing to US partner companies.[28] A good example might be Nice Systems, based in one of Israel's self-styled "Silicon Valley" industrial parks and a world leader in computer telephone integration and the migration from analogue to digital recording. A spin-off from the military, Nice Systems was floated on the TASE in 1991 and recently completed a hugely successful share sell-off on the Nasdaq stock exchange.[29]

The liberalization of the Israeli economy, in progress since the mid-1980s, albeit often at a snail's pace and with the state still retaining an intrusive role in the economy, has prepared the Israeli economy well for this new situation. In 1994 the government took steps towards the removal of foreign exchange controls and the internationalization of financial markets. Competition has been introduced into the banking sector, and financial services have now become the target of foreign interests. In 1994 the so-called "big" accountancy firms,[30] which between them control 95 per cent of the world accountancy market, targeted Israel as a new and growing market for their services, the most significant factor in their calculations being the imminent demise of the Arab boycott. Mr. Danny Doron, president of the Institute of Certified Public Accountants in Israel, said of this development: "The firms are moving here on the belief that the peace process is a done deal."[31]

Meanwhile, some of the big names in American business are contenders for the Israeli banks scheduled for privatization. Larry Tics, Charles Bronfman and Ted Arison are contending for control of Bank Hapoalim, while others, including some of the European banks, are reported to be interested in buying the Mercantile Discount Bank.[32] European and Japanese banks are for the first time competing with the United States to underwrite privatizations, and senior international bankers recently described Israel as "the most exciting story around at present".[33] The American brokerage house, Morgan Stanley, has included the TASE in its table of emerging markets exchanges, increasing the interest of foreign investors. The Israeli stockmarket, now free of regulations hostile to foreign investors, has over 600 companies quoted on it, rivalling Indonesia and Argentina. Israeli companies are rapidly attracting foreign shareholders; noteworthy in this regard are the acquisition of a bloc of Bezeq shares by Cable and Wireless and the purchase of 22 per cent of Koor by America's Shamrock.[34] European and American fund managers have also been showing an interest in the TASE with evidence that they are starting to include Israeli companies in their investment portfolios.

This appeal to foreign investors is limited primarily to high-tech investors. Labour, because of its educational value, is not cheap in Israel; it is not the place to build factories aiming to exploit low wage costs. This has little to do with any lessening of the Arab boycott but reflects the high added value of Israeli labour and the relatively small labour force for entry into relatively privileged occupational positions. The exception is the interest which foreign capital has been showing towards investments in Israeli infrastructure projects, such as the Trans-Israel Highway and the Carmel Tunnel. The high level of government commitment to infrastructure investment, particularly in those areas designed to favour industry and production, such as transport, water and energy, attracts investors who see the country as a fast-growing, high-potential area offering rewards for low risks. Israeli firms are viewed as strategic partners for foreign capital in this process. In the eyes of the Israelis: "One thing is clear – after years of frustrating attempts to attract the 'big names' in world economics to Israel, the effort is beginning to bear fruit, and not just because of the peace process."[35]

If one looks at the structure of trade for Israel, and bearing in mind that trade accounts for up to 75 per cent of GNP, its principal imports are dominated by investment goods, although raw diamonds represent almost as much (see Table 3.3). Exports, however, which have been growing at an average of 10 per cent per year until 1995 and 8 per cent in that year, are vastly dominated by manufactured goods (over 88 per cent) and are highly diversified, including processed diamonds, metals, machinery and electronics, chemicals, textiles, clothing, rubber, plastics and processed food products (also see Chapter 8 in this volume). Principal trading partners are America and the European Union, but increasingly Japan, Hong Kong (accounting together for nearly 10 per cent of exports in 1993 and more than that in 1994) and other East Asian states. A recent reversal in the terms of trade has adversely affected Israeli exports, imports and the related and balance of trade, but this is unlikely to prove a prolonged problem for Israel.

Investment has picked up significantly in the last few years, with ratios moving in favour of plant and equipment and away from construction. Gross investment in industry grew by 20.4 per cent in 1991, 7.5 per cent in 1992 and 17.5 per cent in 1993, with most of it focused on advanced industries. One problem which has arisen is that the government incentive of a 38 per cent

Table 3.3 Principal Israeli imports (US$ million)

Investment goods	4 509
Diamonds	4 124
Fuel	1 658
Consumer non-durables	1 548
Consumer durables	1 497
Other production inputs	10 432

Source: Economist Intelligence Unit, *Country Report*, 1994/95.

contribution to investment costs of foreign companies investing in Israel has led to a much larger than expected burden on the government bill. Intel have netted over $600 million in subsidies to their investments in Israel, while Motorola, Vishay and Tower Semiconductors have between them netted over $52 million.

While successive Israeli governments may have been, since the economic stabilization plan of the mid-1980s and the subsequent moves towards economic liberalization, attempting to transform Israel's economy into a capitalist "baby tiger", it is still true to say that the political repercussions of the initial advances in the Arab–Israeli peace process have provided the conditions for these apparent early stages of "take-off". Economic performance in recent years has been impressive. Although privatization has apparently stalled, and inflation has remained a problem (at around 14 per cent), growth has averaged 7 per cent per annum since 1992 and per capita income has risen from $12 600 in 1992 to $15 600 in 1995.[36] This latter figure, currently on a par with Ireland or New Zealand, is expected to rise dramatically in the next few years – targeted at $20 000 by the year 2000.[37] GDP per person in Israel is now higher than in Taiwan, South Korea, Argentina, Chile, Malaysia, Mexico, Thailand, Brazil, Russia, Turkey, the Philippines or India.[38] The share of GDP emanating from the business sector grew by 39 per cent between 1990 and 1994. Israel has achieved solid sovereign currency debt ratings[39] and has seen a sharp drop in its "risk factor" in terms of credit ranking. Analysts in Israel have calculated that improved credit ratings will save Israel up to $7 billion in debt service costs over the next ten years.[40]

There are, of course, still problems for Israel's economy. Inflation remains a bug in the system, although targets of 8 per cent have been reached in the last year. Monetary instability remains a threat. Government-owned defence industries (Elbit, Rafael and IAI) are proving troubled by the costs of restructuring, as are the major firms like Scitex and Indigo which have faced recent reductions in demand for their products. They are, however, still investing in product development for the future and enacting structural reform programmes to gear them up for a more competitive future. On the macroeconomic scale, the size of absolute debt has increased in recent years largely as a result of government investment-oriented consumption and immigrant absorption. In relative terms, however, the debt-servicing ratio has been reduced from 25 per cent of export revenues in 1986, to 16 per cent in 1993. Total debt as a proportion of GNP fell from 80 per cent in 1985 to 37 per cent in 1989, 27 per cent in 1993 and just 22 per cent in 1995.[41]

A word must be said here about foreign aid. There is a mistaken tendency in Arab circles to believe that Israel's receipt of foreign aid (specifically US aid although not USAID) indicates that the Israeli economy is weak and dependent. Observers of the Malaysian and South Korean experiences know that aid which enables a government to invest in industry-oriented infrastructure actually strengthens a developing economy. Furthermore, over half of

US aid to Israel comes directly in the form of military equipment – much of which has represented a vast technology transfer during the past two decades – providing a critical input not just to military development but also to civilian research and technology. Israel does not depend on foreign aid because it is weak; rather, it uses the availability of a virtually "no strings attached" supplementary income to reinforce its existing economic strength.

This situation, does, of course, have a downside. In the past that income has been used to sustain an artificially high standard of living through state welfare distributions. This is much less true today, when most of the economic aid is used to service debt to the US or for investments in education and infrastructure. The gift of foreign aid in general is becoming a politically hot topic in the US and most Israelis acknowledge that it will only continue for a limited period of time. Many Israeli economists will welcome external aid's eventual demise, believing it has artificially distorted the Israeli economy for long enough and, with a lower debt-service ratio, it is not now needed as it was in the past.

In concluding this analysis of Israeli economic strength, one can say that Israeli economic development is being firmly steered towards and is responding well to a global strategy for marketing its goods and attracting investment.[42] Although Israel has outlined its commitment and desire for regional economic development, that is not the basis of its own development strategy. Israel seeks to utilize the results of its liberalization programme and its high-tech, skilled labour force economy to engage fully and advantageously in the present process of globalization. The achievement of peace in the region is the essential step towards opening global as opposed to simply regional markets. Equally, Israel's demand for the lifting of the Arab boycott was aimed not only at Arab–Israeli trade, but more with a view to attracting the large multinationals to Israel. As the former Israeli Minister of Industry and Commerce, Micha Harish, said: "Today these companies realise that we are the most important market in the region and that it pays for them to get a foothold here."[43] The essentially outward-oriented strategy envisages the European Union, the United States and increasingly East Asia as the markets for Israeli goods and the source of capital. The Israelis themselves said at Casablanca: "In the immediate period of the plan, the potential for foreign trade ties with the Middle Eastern countries is very limited, because of major differences between their economies and the trade structures of the countries."[44]

PROSPECTS FOR THE REGION

However, if all this is intended to demonstrate that Israel is increasingly, and directly as a result of the peace process, geared up to the global economy, it does not imply that Israel can do without its regional context.

There is already growing evidence that the region is experiencing a new (if as yet nascent) labour mobility between Arab states and Israel based on these developments in global capital. With its high labour costs, Israel must currently seek markets in the richer parts of the world such as Europe, Japan and the United States rather than in its own immediate neighbourhood. To counter this trend of Israeli labour pricing itself out of the low-skills market (in favour of high-tech production), some Israeli firms have been closing their factories in Israel and establishing new ones in lower wage countries such as Egypt and Jordan.[45] Delta, which produces textile items for large companies like Marks and Spencer in the United Kingdom or Gap in the United States, are all poised to open factories in Jordan, together with Jordanian investors, to take advantage of lower Arab wage rates. Similarly Macpell, which has closed 35 textile workshops in Israel, is planning to open a new branch in Amman. Israel and the PA have agreed to establish nine border industrial parks which will essentially provide the same service: cheap Palestinian labour for Israeli and international capital. Ironically, when Palestinian labourers from the West Bank and Gaza are being forced out of the Israeli labour market, there has been evidence of Arab workers from Jordan and Egypt taking their place. Driven from their own countries by economic recession, they are arriving in Israel on tourist visas and seeking illegal employment in the blue-collar sector. At present it is estimated that such workers number only a few thousand but they earn up to three times more in Israel than they would for the same work in their home countries.[46] Such labour migration adds a new dimension to a phenomenon which has characterized the region for 30 years.

While the Arab Gulf states are, to their annoyance, now being seen as little more than a source of capital to finance regional development. The fears: the resource-poor, labour-rich Arab states risk becoming labour pools for international capital, channelled via Israeli firms and joint venture partners. The facts: in general, the Arab world in recent years has proved itself unable to capitalize on the globalization process, at least in so far as the critical question of attracting foreign investment is concerned, despite trade and financial liberalization programmes. The GCC states, with their chronic overreliance on a narrow selection of oil-related exports, and protectionism, are particularly good examples of this. In some instances, the business environment simply remains too restrictive to attract foreign investment.

As Field and Wilson point out, obstacles include lack of unified customs structure or common investment policy, restrictions on cross-border movement of goods and people, unwritten rules that prevent foreigners from buying equity shares, cumbersome government bureaucracies and state-owned monopolies, the lack of corporate transparency, poor flow of business information and a complete absence of ministerial accountability. Foreigners are prevented from owning land or majority shares in joint ventures, and the family connections of Arab Gulf businesspersons count more than the financial solidity of potential foreign investors. The socio-political structures of the Gulf monarchies are highly resistant to the kinds of changes which inevitably mean a loss of government control over the resources and direction of the economy.[47]

The Middle East countries best placed to take advantage of globalization are those which have already advanced significantly along the path of economic liberalization, such as Tunisia and Turkey, and to a lesser extent Oman, Qatar and UAE, which have worked hard to diversify their exports and create a regulatory environment that is attractive to foreign investors. Where government restrictions on foreign investment are raised, Israeli capital – or joint-venture capital – can also make an entrance, for example the introduction of the Israeli Tahal water company into Morocco in late 1995. Tahal now owns a subsidiary company, Mideast Tahal, which utilizes World Bank and African Development Bank funds to participate in the Moroccan water planning sector as it undergoes privatization. The essence of globalization is that it is driven by private companies, not by governments. The GCC states themselves are aware of this and cast nervous eyes at even their poorest neighbours like Jordan, whose open trade policy with Israel has provided it with the potential to attract Israeli or Israeli-channelled investment.

Export diversification is essential if countries are to gain from globalization. Riordan *et al.*[48] have pointed out that oil represents nearly 90 per cent of the merchandize exports of the Middle East and North Africa (MENA) region (for more on MENA as a region, see Chapter 4 in this volume). By comparison, primary commodity exports in East Asia represented only 26 per cent of exports. The value of manufactured exports in Middle Eastern states is still very low, with Israel clearly leading the field (see Table 3.4).

Riordan *et al.* conclude that the MENA region has so far been largely excluded from globalization and that this situation is likely to become worse in the future. With the economic transition currently taking place in Eastern

Table 3.4 Value of manufactured exports, 1993 (US$ billion)

Israel	15.906
Turkey	6.771
Morocco	2.346
Tunisia	2.135
Saudi Arabia	1.749
Algeria	1.686
Egypt	0.793
Iran	0.676

Source: World Bank, *World Development Report, 1993*, cited in Rodney Wilson, *Economic Development in the Middle East* (London: Routledge, 1995).

Europe, China and elsewhere, the manufactured products of the MENA region (Israel excluded) are unlikely to be able to face the competition of other low-income manufactures exporters. Overreliance on oil and oil-derived exports makes income for the region highly volatile, and many governments have proven themselves unable to open their economies in sufficient time to be "ahead of the game". The GNP of Arab states amounted to approximately $483 billion in 1995, of which $102 billion derived from oil.[49] Intra-regional trade is unlikely to fill the income gap. Rodney Wilson concludes:

> There is little sign of any promising regional economic cohesion in the Middle East....Despite so-called open-door policies, such as Egypt's *infitah*, it is by no means clear that the economies of the region are really opening up, either internationally or even to their neighbours.[50]

Inter-Arab investment, likewise, falls short of its proper contribution to regional development. The vast majority of Arab businesspersons invest outside the region, usually because of the poor investment environment within. The president of the General Union of Arab Chambers of Commerce has given figures of 98 per cent of Arab investment going outside the region, amounting to $670 billion, while just 2 per cent is directed inward.[51]

CONCLUSION

If one examines the Middle East broadly, then, one can see not a developing regional economy but rather the consistent fragmentation of the region. On the one hand, those states which *have* opened up their economies, like Tunisia and Morocco, are able to take advantage of what Riordan *et al.* call "windows of opportunity", such as the European Union's Mediterranean Initiative, "which offers the potential for expanded free trade and foreign investment, increased official finance from the European Union and enhanced regional integration among the EU and MENA countries themselves."[52] They can take advantage of the peace process to reduce the risks associated with investment in their countries and coordinate regional economic activities with other similar states to their mutual advantage. The European Union's continued interest in creating a functioning Mediterranean free trade zone will provide states that have opened their economies with access to advantages they cannot get from those among their neighbours which have not opened up. Those which remain closed even within their own region may be forced to turn increasingly inward upon themselves, resorting again to import substitution and declining in relative terms compared to the rest.

Relations between Arab states and Israel will depend greatly upon the degree of openness to the international economy generally. Partnerships through intermediary organizations like the European Union will soften the impact of initial direct relations. Economic openness clears the path for private capital, whatever its country of origin, and while Israel will generally have the upper hand in terms of its national economy, the transaction is essentially one of private capital transfer and exchange, not of any national colouring. Fears of an Israel that economically dominates and subjugates the region become irrelevant when the Israeli state is seen simply as a conduit for international capital, multinationals and joint venture projects, and as one partner of many in an EU-type multinational collaborative free trade venture.

Jordan can see a potential "window" for itself as the new "laundry" for Israeli goods, replacing Cyprus. It can also be the site for "finishing" Israeli products, extracting rent and taking advantage of liberal export duty laws. Those Arab states which are not geographically contiguous to the Mediterranean or which remain closed economically will be marginalized from this process and thus the Middle East may be increasingly split, not on the basis of Arabs and Israelis, but on a Mediterranean–Orient axis.

The Arab states face a choice in how they proceed with the economics of the peace process. Israel is already taking advantage of the peace process to leap into the globalization pool and swim. It is not dependent for its economic health on willing and welcoming regional partners, although it would have much to gain from regional economic cooperation and integration. Likewise, most Arab states now realize that they cannot invest in their ambitions for healthy economic development in their own region alone. They too must learn to swim in the bigger global pond. Regional trade openness and cooperation would certainly increase their ability to float in the first place, and steps towards at least inter-Arab economic openness and integration would be a good starting point for building up their own economies to a position where they can cooperate with, and perhaps even take advantage of, Israeli regional strength. To this end, a number of Arab states have been engaged in developing long-term strategic visions, many of which aim to determine what their post-liberalization policies should be. The three principal challenges will be the still-excessive rate of population growth, the relative decline in oil-derived income and the need to increase and diversify exports.[53]

There will still be winners and losers. The Palestinians are still being excluded from the economic development process, and international aid has not led to peace-building on a scale relevant to its size (see Chapter 11). And, while infrastructure building, if it takes place, might repair some of the damage being done by Israel in its nearly 30 years of occupation, aid that goes solely to infrastructure does not equate with sustainable development, and in any case the current terms of the Israeli–PA agreements still allow Israel to impose restrictions on or even prevent such development.[54] For its own reasons, Israel continues to marginalize Palestinian labour, trade and production. Those Arab states with poor resource bases and low skills may become sweatshop labour for the capital of the others, or they may simply be excluded from a regional economy. The wealthy GCC states will be protected by their oil incomes from the worst effects of their failure to take the plunge; wealthy Gulf businesspersons may make money from essentially speculative deals with Israel, and their governments may benefit from co-operation in water, tourism and environmental protection. But these states will not benefit from the real possibilities of marrying Gulf money with Israeli skill.

If all this sounds like an advocation for complete reconciliation with Israel, it is not. The stakes are too high for absolute acquiescence. There are two critical questions to be asked about the desirability of divisions from the economics of peace in a global rather than regional context. First, the Arab states need to consolidate their own position by developing linkages and ties among themselves before opening up to Israel. An Arab economic region could capitalize on its common resources rather than being characterized by the weaknesses of individual states, and it could encourage governments to deal with long-term economic needs rather than short-term and superficially advantageous goals. This development in inter-Arab trade, investment and liberalization should be considered as a part of a wider process of preparing itself for regional legal harmonization as well as for economic globalization – and *in that context* for integration and normalization with Israel. As long as such opening is not part of a considered policy of general opening to the world and thoughtful economic restructuring (with the proviso of appropriate welfare provision), then economic relations with Israel will end up being the domain of speculative businesspersons who make a fast buck out of exploiting the weaknesses of their own economies.

Second, the Arab states can remember that economic links are a two-way business. With Israeli economic interests vested in good relations with Arab states or a common EU partner, the Arabs too gained bargaining position they have not exploited. After all, if the current development of Israel's international position has been the result of the peace process, then a reversal in the process could potentially threaten Israel's relations elsewhere.

The aim must surely be to find a way to deal with Israel that does not diminish the potential for the Arab states and the Palestinians. There is little to be gained by refusing to deal with Israel, particularly if the Zionist state can still use the peace process to launch its bid for enhanced alliances with firms in developed nations. There is no doubt, however, that a supportive regional environment would benefit both Israeli and Arab ambitions and that fact, coupled with realistic economic policies of their own, can provide the

Arab world with a strategy for facing the challenge of regional development in the next century. This may not be an ideal scenario, but the time for aspiring to deals in the Middle East has passed, and present realities demand a focused and dynamic approach to the region's political economy and to global market participation.

Notes

1. Stephen Graubard, *Mr Bush's War* (London: Tauris, 1992), p. 165.
2. For a relatively user-friendly introduction to globalization, see Malcolm Waters, *Globalization* (London: Routledge, 1995).
3. This has been discussed by the author in "Israel and the Palestinians: The Economic Rewards of Peace?" CMEIS Occasional Paper no. 47, March 1995. The same conclusion has been drawn by international agencies such as UNCTAD and the ILO; see International Labour Organization, Report of the Director General, 80th Session, Appendix II and Prospects for Sustainable Development of the Palestinian Economy in the West Bank and Gaza Strip, UNCTAD/DSD/SEU/2, 27 September 1993, Geneva.
4. See Harry Magdoff, "Globalization – To What End?" in Ralph Miliband and Leo Panitch, *New World Order? Socialist Register 1992* (London: Merlin, 1992), pp. 45–75.
5. Samir Amin, "Fifty Years is Enough", *Monthly Review* (April 1995), pp. 8–50. On a more global note, see Kenechi Ohmae, *The Decline of the Nation-State and the Rise of Regional Economies* (New York: The Free Press, 1996).
6. *Economist*, 3–9 February 1996, p. 44.
7. Represented through the Israeli–Palestinian Economic Cooperation Committee.
8. Full discussion of this issue can be found in "News from Within: The Mirage of Independence", Alternative Information Centre, Jerusalem, vol. 12, no. 1 (January 1996), and Murphy, "Economic Rewards of Peace", *op. cit.*
9. *Economist*, 10 February 1996, p. 68. For a more comprehensive discussion of the economic implications of Israeli border closures, see Fatima Ajiai's chapter in J.W. Wright, Jr. (ed.), *The Political Economy of Middle East Peace, the Impact of Competing Trade Agendas* (London: Routledge, 1999).
10. In December 1994 these foreign workers numbered around 54 000.
11. In 1994 the PA declared that it received less than a third of the moneys promised for its first year. Most of these were designated towards current expenditure costs, especially maintaining the Palestinian police force. See Eliyahu Kanovsky, "Middle East Economies and Arab–Israeli Peace Agreements", *Israel Affairs* 1(4) (September 1995), p. 33.
12. For example, the Northern Ireland company, Mivan, is contracted to build the £12.8 million UN hospital in the Gaza Strip.
13. Government of Israel, *Development Options for Regional Cooperation*, October 1993.
14. In an interview in *Ha'aretz*, 20 July 1995, Professor Eliyahu Kanovsky put it thus: "What do we have to buy from them (the Jordanians)? A very low level of compatibility exists between us and the Arab nations, and even more so with Jordan. We can sell Jordan quite a lot of things, however they want reciprocity, and the problem is that they have nothing to sell to us. The Jordanians produce phosphates, vegetables, fruits, potash and fertilizers. There is no demand for their products in Israel."

15. Samir Abdullah, “The Middle East Peace Dilemma: Bilateral Political Negotiations for Multilateral Economic Cooperation”, Economic Research Forum Working Paper Series, no. 9526 (Cairo, 1996), p. 8.
16. The company includes the Israeli marketing agency, Agrexco, which is half owned by the Israeli government, as well as a consortium of Egyptian exporters and Egypt Air. The company plans to build a new terminal at Cairo airport specifically to export Egyptian and Israeli agricultural produce to Europe and the Persian Gulf, with Israeli banks providing most of the investment capital.
17. Nadav Halevi and Ephraim Kleiman, Hebrew and Tel Aviv Universities, “Trade Relations between Israel and Jordan: Risks and Considerations”, quoted on Israeli Information Service Gopher israel-info.gov.il, 20 July 1994.
18. *Financial Times*, 12 March 1996.
19. Israel had some covert agricultural ties with Qatar and Oman, and all the GCC countries were recipients of Israeli pharmaceuticals, irrigation equipment, electronics, seeds and chemicals. According to Israeli sources, secret Arab–Israeli trading totalled at least $200 million per year. *Middle East International*, no. 512 (3 November 1995), pp. 16–17.
20. See Anoushiravan Ehteshami and Emma C. Murphy, “The non-Arab Middle East States and the Caucasian/Central Asian Republics: Iran and Israel”, *International Relations* 12(1) (April 1994).
21. *Arab Press Service Report*, 27 November–4 December 1995.
22. *Arab Press Service Diplomat*, 13–20 January 1996, SP42, pp. 6–7.
23. *Financial Times*, 7 December 1994.
24. *Financial Times*, 30 January 1996.
25. In Yaroslav Trofimov, “Looking for a Piece of a Peace Dividend”, *World Trade* (January 1996), pp. 34–5.
26. The journalist Avi Temkin said of the Arab boycott against Israel: “Since its inception [it] has been a relatively effective weapon. Official estimates put the damage caused by the boycott [to Israel], mainly in its secondary and tertiary aspects, at some $40 billion. Even if this figure is inflated, the boycott was clearly effective in blocking the formation of working relations between Israel and multi-nationals, from Europe and Asia in particular.” Avi Temkin, “The Arab Boycott: Prospects for Dismantlement and its Implications for the Israeli Business Environment”, *Economic Dimensions of the Middle East Peace Process*, Economist Intelligence Unit, 1994.
27. Which revolutionized pre-press printing a few years ago.
28. See, for example, “Developing a CD-ROM? Israel’s Got the Talent, Location, Lower Costs”, *Christian Science Monitor*, 30 June–6 July 1995.
29. *Financial Times*, 13 March 1996.
30. Arthur Andersen, Price Waterhouse, Ernst and Young, KPMG, Coopers and Lybrand and Deloitte and Touche.
31. *Jerusalem Post*, 15 April 1994. The political intentions of these firms are explored in Shimon Bich’or’s chapter in J.W. Wright, Jr. (ed.), *Structural Flaws in the Middle East Peace Process* (London: Macmillan, 1999).
32. *Business Magazine – Ma’ariv*, 9 May 1995.
33. *The Middle East*, no. 242 (February 1995), p. 30.
34. Another development in telecommunications was the bid by MCI Communications, the second largest US long-distance telecoms operator, as part of a British Telecommunications-led consortium for one of two international telecoms services in Israel. Competition for the license came from Singapore, Korea, Germany, France and the United States, from major multinational communications companies. *Financial Times*, 22 February 1996.

35. *Business Magazine – Ma'ariv*, 9 May 1995, pp. 4–5.
36. *Financial Times*, 9 February 1996.
37. David Brodet, Israeli Treasury Budget Director, provided this prediction in *Jerusalem Post International*, 10 September 1994.
38. *Economist*, 9–15 March 1996, p. 146.
39. Standard and Poor, for example, rated it at BBB+ in 1993.
40. Dr. Nadine Baudot-Trajtenberg, Fourth International Conference of Jewish Media in Jerusalem, 1995.
41. Recent economic data is taken from Economist Intelligence Unit *Country Reports and Profiles, 1994–1995*.
42. For a detailed analysis of recent Israeli economic performance see International Monetary Fund, "Israel – Recent Economic Developments", Staff Country Report no. 95/105, Washington DC, October 1995.
43. Roni Ben Efrat, "Israel's Economy Marches Out to Conquer the World", *Challenge*, no. 33 (September–October 1995).
44. Samir Abdullah, "Middle East Peace Dilemma", *op. cit.*
45. Alternative Information Centre, "News from Within", *op. cit.*, p. 11.
46. Kamal Ja'afari, "Foreign Arab Workers in Israel", *Challenge*, no. 35 (January–February 1996), pp. 14–15.
47. Robin Allen, "A Thirst in the Desert States", *Financial Times*, 30 January 1996.
48. E. Riordan, U. Dadush, J. Jalali, S. Streifel, M. Brahmbhatt and K. Takagaki, "The World Economy and Implications for the MENA Region, 1995–2010", Economic Research Forum Working Paper no. 9519, Cairo, 1995.
49. *Arab Press Service Diplomat*, 27 May–3 June 1995.
50. Wilson, *Economic Development in the Middle East*, *op. cit*., p. 175.
51. *Arab Press Service Diplomat*, 27 May–3 June 1995.
52. Riordan *et al.*, "The World Economy" *op. cit.*, p. 1.
53. See Economic Research Forum, no. 3, Cairo, October 1995.
54. For evidence of the continuing underdevelopment or "de-development" in the occupied territories, see Sara Roy, *The Gaza Strip: The Political Economy of De-Development* (Washington DC: Institute for Palestine Studies, 1995); and International Monetary Fund, "West Bank and Gaza Strip – Recent Economic Developments and Prospects and Progress in Institution Building", Background Paper Issued in Connection with the 1995 Article IV Consultation with Israel, Washington DC, October 1995. Also see *Tanmiya*, no. 41 (December 1995), The Welfare Association, Geneva.

4 Is MENA a Region? The Scope for Regional Integration

Mohamed A. El-Erian and Stanley Fischer[1]

INTRODUCTION

Despite many attempts since World War II to promote trade and policy cooperation in the Middle East and North Africa (MENA), economic interactions within the region have remained limited. There is no unique way to define the MENA region. The most comprehensive definition covers 24 countries: the 21 members of the Arab League (Algeria, Bahrain, Djibouti, Egypt, Iraq, Jordan, Kuwait, Lebanon, Libya, Mauritania, Morocco, Oman, Palestine, Qatar, Saudi Arabia, Somalia, Sudan, Syria, Tunisia, the United Arab Emirates and Yemen), as well as Iran, Israel and Turkey. More limited definitions have been used, the most restrictive being that encompassing Egypt, Israel, Jordan, Lebanon, Syria and the West Bank and Gaza. For the purposes of this chapter, MENA is defined to cover four Maghreb countries (Algeria, Libya, Morocco and Tunisia), the seven countries situated at the geographical centre of the region (Egypt, Iraq,[2] Israel, Jordan, Lebanon, Syria and the West Bank and Gaza) and the six member countries of the Council of the Arab States of the Gulf, or GCC (Bahrain, Kuwait, Oman, Qatar, Saudi Arabia and the United Arab Emirates). Recent progress in the Arab–Israeli peace process and steps by several countries towards external economic liberalization have focused increasing attention on the economic potential of MENA *as a region.* This attention comes at a time of renewed global interest in regional arrangements, be they among industrial countries (such as the European Union), industrial and developing countries (NAFTA and APEC) or developing countries (Mercosur).[3]

There is a need in any region for a framework in which intra-regional issues – political, security and economic – can be addressed on a regular basis, and most regions have many, overlapping, regional organizations. A recent OECD survey identifies three reasons countries seek greater regional integration: (1) economic welfare gains; (2) increasing the region's collective political bargaining power in extra-regional issues; and (3) achieving other non-economic national goals, such as meeting security concerns and preventing future conflict.[4]

A region is defined by several characteristics, the most basic of which are geography and culture. However these two aspects say little about the extent of, or the potential for, welfare-enhancing regional economic interaction, which are also determined by economic and political factors. The more similar the economic and political systems, and the more similar the political objectives of a region's composite states, the easier it is to promote effective regional economic integration. The returns to economic integration will also reflect the relative resource endowments, including human capital, of the participating countries, albeit not in a unique and unambiguous manner.[5]

It is these factors – the degree of actual and potential economic and political coherence among countries, and the potential returns to integration – that provide the basis for our exploration of the extent to which MENA is a region, and the extent to which it might gain from becoming more economically integrated. In the next section we discuss the defining characteristics of a region in more detail. In the subsequent section we assess the extent to which MENA meets these criteria, both in absolute terms and relative to other regions in the world economy. After that we discuss the scope and requirements for enhanced regional integration in MENA, followed by our concluding remarks.

WHAT IS A REGION?

At the most basic level, regions are defined in terms of *geography*: they are usually contiguous land masses or share a common littoral. Geography is a significant determinant of the proximity of agents to markets within the region – an aspect that assumes greater importance the higher the costs of transportation and communication, as demonstrated, for example, by the work on gravity models.[6] It also plays an important role in facilitating contacts among residents of the region, be they government officials, businesspersons or journalists. Of course, geographical proximity is also an almost necessary condition for active enmity, with the exception of great-power states; even so, proximity may contribute to creating a general sense of belonging, if only to the extent that problems are shared or need to be dealt with jointly if they are to be solved.

There are two important qualifications to the influence of geography. First, proximity *per se* is not normally sufficient to create contacts within a region that affect the daily lives of its residents in a meaningful way. For this, higher degrees of coherence are needed. Second, technological changes (particularly in information and communications) have sharply reduced the effective distances between countries, as have changes in economic strategy away from inward-based policies toward those promoting cross-border activities. The influence of technological change on regional integration is ambiguous. At the same time that technology has made the globe smaller and encouraged globalism, it has facilitated intra-regional travel and communications to the point where it is often quicker for a businessperson or policy-maker to visit a neighbouring capital than a provincial centre, thus encouraging regionalism.

Commonality of *culture* provides a strong bonding element in any region. Dominant history, language and religion facilitate personal interactions, with a favourable impact on trading relations, tourism, labour and investment flows. They are also likely to enhance perceptions of a mutuality of interests in multilateral deliberations as well as in bilateral negotiations with other states or regions, and now with agencies like the World Trade Organization.

An illustration of the operation of these factors is provided by a recent analysis of the experience of the European Union. European economic integration has of course been characterized by geographical contiguity and a shared if ambiguous history, which after two world wars pushed in the direction of integration as the alternative to future conflict. Looking at the initial stages of the European integration, the effective postwar shrinkage of Western Europe to a core of six largely Catholic countries, which formed the original European Coal and Steel Community, ensured a strong common cultural tradition which, in turn, facilitated economic and political integration.

There may well be a close relationship between cultural and political factors; in particular, cultural factors may influence the political configuration of a country, as summarized in the form of government and stability of political institutions and traditions.[7] Two specific political aspects affect the likely coherence of a region: first, the cross-national consistency of political regime-type; and second, the political commitment of the various states to the region at large.

The more stable and similar the political institutions and systems of governance within a region, the easier and more effective the process of integration,[8] particularly for countries sharing a democratic approach. And, in committing themselves to regional objectives *per se*, in both economics and governance, political leaders throughout the region must be both willing and able to override national goals that would otherwise tend to undermine regional integration. Political commitment to regional integration may be driven in part by official perceptions regarding the likely economic benefits, but it is also powerfully affected by political and security-related considerations. This was certainly the case in Europe, and it is again evident in EU consideration of eastward expansion.

When regional affiliations begin to take institutional form, they may initially be expressed within a political but not an economic framework; such was the case in the Americas, where the Organization of American States was set up prior to regional economic arrangements. However, security concerns aside, it is not obvious what states would discuss within a political framework that did not address economic issues. Further, the success of the European enterprise in achieving political objectives through economic integration has cast a new light on the potential benefits of intra-regional economic cooperation. At the same time, economic cooperation is not possible within a given region without a basic political commitment to closer interstate relations within that region. The level of political commitment may in turn depend on an evaluation of the economic benefits of integration to the individual states, and on the success or failure of any initial steps that might have already been taken the direction of regional economic integration.

Both economic and political factors suggest that economic integration is more likely to be beneficial the more similar the participating countries. Integration among similar countries reduces the scope for trade diversion since these states are already likely to be producing and importing similar goods. Such integration is likely to enhance intra-industry trade and widen the product variety available to consumers; it can also serve to lessen the monopoly power of local producers, with imports of close substitutes providing increased market discipline. Similarly, integration is less likely to trigger strong opposition from interest groups if countries are highly similar. For example, the more similar the countries, the smaller the differences in wages and work conditions. The opposition of American labour to the Mexican accession to NAFTA, which was far stronger than opposition to free trade with Canada, illustrates this tendency.

These points serve to highlight the potential challenges facing the integration process in the MENA region, with its pronounced differences in political and economic structures. In considering regional economic integration, the choice is often posed as one between regionalism and multilateralism as mutually exclusive options. If regional liberalization were incompatible with multilateral liberalization, the choice would be clear, particularly in MENA: pursue multilateralism. But the two processes may take place at the same time, and we assume henceforth that closer regional ties in MENA will not come at the expense of multilateral liberalization.

Regional economic arrangements may be characterized as taking one of several possible forms:

(1) preferential trading arrangements, in which regional trading partners enjoy more favourable trading conditions, including lower tariffs, than other countries;
(2) a free trade area, in which trade within the area is not subject to taxation, but where external tariffs on third parties may differ among member countries;

(3) a customs union, in which a common external tariff is applied, and more generally in which all members of the region treat all conditions of trade with extra-regional economic partners in a similar fashion;

(4) a common market, in which trade in goods and capital flows within the region are free, where market conditions (including standards) have been made uniform so that producers in one country do not have to face non-market restrictions while selling their products in other countries in the common market, and where restrictions on labour flows are more limited; and

(5) an economic union, where members eventually share a single currency, and the concept of national residency is eliminated in all economic relations through two key principles: mutual recognition and minimum harmonization.[9]

These forms are listed in ascending levels of intensity of economic integration. They should be thought of as points on a continuum rather than an exhaustive listing of alternative institutional arrangements. The higher the level of integration among member countries, the greater the loss of discretionary national policy-making capability in areas covered by the regional arrangements. As the integration process strengthens, efficiency dictates that region-wide institutions assume growing power for proposing, regulating and supervising the rules that are needed for the operation of a single market.[10] While economists might view such changes as superior methods of coordinating and/or pre-committing on relevant economic policies, politicians tend to view them as a loss of sovereignty or state authority. As such, enhanced integration has often proved controversial among members of the European Union,[11] with monetary union the most contentious example.

REGIONAL CHARACTERISTICS OF MENA

To what extent, then, does MENA constitute a region? While geography and culture favour regional integration, the absence of political and economic prerequisites has so far limited the scale of market and institutional integration.[12] The MENA region covers a contiguous geographical land mass extending from the Atlantic Ocean in the west to the Arabian Sea in the east. Its land mass of 15 million square kilometres is almost equal to that of the European Union and three-quarters that of Latin America. While tending to be characterized by harsh climates and limited ground water and rainfall, the region is rich and diverse in its natural resources: important crude oil and gas reserves, numerous non-fuel mineral and non-mineral resources, and some very productive agricultural pockets.[13]

In some respects MENA is unusually culturally homogenous. Arabic is the primary language in all countries of the region except Israel, and is an official language in all countries; Arabic and Hebrew are closely related. Monotheistic religions, with historical relations among them, dominate the region. In every country but Israel the population is predominantly and in most cases overwhelmingly Muslim. The Arab countries in the region share a rich heritage, part of which is also shared with Israelis, but relations have had a checkered history and in recent years the region has been dominated by the human suffering, hostilities and mutual distrust associated with armed conflicts, particularly but not exclusively the protracted Arab–Israeli conflict. Reflecting religious and historical influences, the culture in several MENA countries endorses commercial activities. Nationals of the region have a well-established entrepreneurial reputation, a fact which is illustrated by the success of individuals of Lebanese and Palestinian origin around the world, especially in Latin America, West Africa and North America.

This extent of language and religious coherence compares favourably with other regions. The similarities of language are considerably greater than in they are in the European Union, for example. Latin America has similar coherence with respect to language but less diversity with respect to religion.[14] APEC, the emerging regional bloc seeking to establish a free trade area in the Asia-Pacific region by 2020, is considerably less homogeneous in terms of language, religion and historical heritage than is MENA.

The populations of MENA countries (see Figure 4.1) range from more than 60 million in Egypt to around one-half million in the smaller GCC countries (Bahrain and Qatar). Many countries in the region have experienced high population growth rates and rapid labour force growth, and have a large share of young people in their populations.[15] Urban population accounts for around 70 per cent of the total, well above the average for developing countries (44 per cent), below that of the EU (74 per cent), and similar to that of APEC and Latin American countries.[16] Israel has the highest urbanization rate (90 per cent) and Egypt the lowest (44 per cent).

The basis of international relations within the region has been dominated since World War II by Arab nationalism, the Arab–Israeli conflict, and since 1973 by the political-economy of oil. The political peak of Arab nationalism was attained in the 1960s. However, the political unity of the Arab bloc, as exemplified in the activities of the Arab League and other Arab regional organizations, was adversely affected by two events in the last 20 years: the Egyptian–Israeli peace treaty in 1979; and the 1990–91 regional crisis triggered by Iraq's invasion of Kuwait and the subsequent war against Iraq. The erosion in Arab political unity has been accompanied, first, by fluctuating tensions among certain Arab countries, and, second, by the emergence of security and economic arrangements among subregions, most notably the Gulf Cooperation Council (GCC).

Figure 4.1 MENA population, 1994 (million)

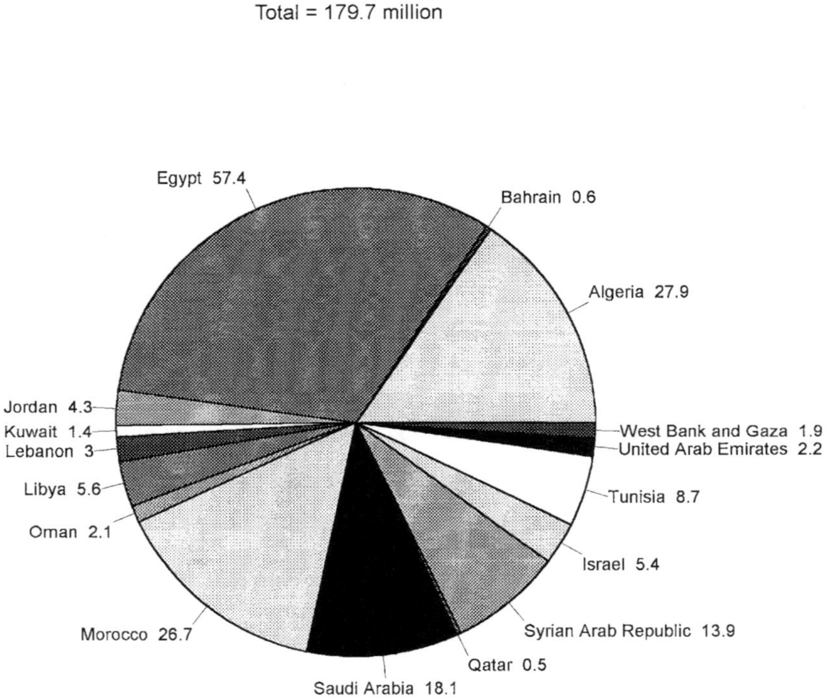

Source: World Bank, *Social Indicators of Development.*

More recently, progress in the Arab–Israeli peace process since the end of the Cold War has forged new economic and political linkages in the region, the most important being the developing Israeli–Jordanian–Palestinian nexus. Despite this, powerful divisions of opinion both among and within countries on the desirability, pace and nature of this peace have cast a shadow over the possibilities for a regional integration that includes Israel. While the history of regional integration efforts in Europe and now in Asia suggests that enhanced regional integration can help cement peace, forward motion in the latter regard requires the development of strong constituencies within each country supporting the terms of the peace.

The region remains diverse in regard to political systems and governance. Democratization has not proceeded very far in several countries, and there has been little political commitment to regional goals. Very few of the numerous regional political initiatives have been translated into sustained and effective institutional foundations. Time and again, national considerations have undermined regional efforts.[17]

On the economic front MENA is remarkably unintegrated, in terms of both the extent of economic interactions within the region, and the absence of an effective framework or institutions responsible for formulating and implementing rules and policies to influence, regulate and supervise economic relations. First, the scale of intra-regional merchandize trade is limited, amounting to only some 7 or 8 per cent of total exports and imports; this compares to over 60 per cent in the European Union, over 30 per cent in Asia and around 20 per cent in the Western hemisphere (see Table 4.1). For no country in the region does trade with other MENA countries amount to more than 25 per cent of total trade, and the (unweighted) average share of intra-MENA trade for the 15 countries in Table 4.2 is under 10 percent.

With the exception of mineral fuels, there is no category of commodities for which intra-MENA trade is very important.[18] As a result of the Arab–Israeli conflict there has been virtually no trade between Israel and the Arab cordon states; even after 1979 there was very little trade between Egypt and Israel.[19] Capital transactions have also been relatively limited, with the exception of large official flows from the oil-exporting economies to other Arab countries, particularly following the 1973–74 and 1979–80 oil price increases.[20] Tourism and other non-factor service flow patterns have also been quite segmented. Some countries, primarily Egypt, Jordan, Lebanon, Morocco and Tunisia, have received substantial tourist flows from within MENA. For other countries, particularly Israel, regional tourism has been inhibited by political and security considerations.

Labour movements have been more important, taking the form of flows from the non-oil economies to the GCC economies,[21] as well as Palestinian labour working in Israel. In the 1990s these flows were subjected to major restrictions and there was recent substitution of Asian labour for Arab labour in both cases, causing unemployment in the North. MENA does not enjoy the type of labour mobility found for example in the European Union,

Table 4.1 Intra-regional exports, 1990–2 (percent of total exports)

	1990	*1991*	*1992*
Industrialized countries	76.3	74.9	74.0
of which:			
European Union	66.0	66.8	66.8
Developing countries	35.8	37.7	39.5
of which:			
Africa	7.2	7.4	7.7
Asia	33.3	36.0	37.8
MENA	8.7	7.7	7.4
Western hemisphere	18.1	20.0	22.7

Source: International Monetary Fund, *Direction of Trade Statistics*.

Table 4.2 MENA countries: trade patterns, 1989–94 (percent of total trade, except as indicated)

	Industrialized Countries	*EU*	*USA*
Algeria	88.6	67.3	14.4
Bahrain	20.2	8.1	4.9
Egypt	67.9	41.0	15.1
Israel	78.8	41.9	22.1
Jordan	41.5	24.3	8.9
Kuwait	62.0	29.4	15.3
Lebanon	56.0	39.0	6.0
Libya	82.3	76.7	0.2
Morocco	68.8	55.6	4.9
Oman	47.6	14.9	5.5
Qatar	67.7	15.6	4.8
Saudi Arabia	66.8	25.3	19.6
Syria	55.8	43.3	4.0
Tunisia	80.3	69.9	3.4
UAE	55.1	17.0	5.4

Source: International Monetary Fund, *Direction of Trade Statistics.*

where citizens of one country have the right to work in other countries. Finally, there has been little regional economic policy coordination, with the exception of the GCC, and through the mechanism of OPEC.

Nonetheless there is potential for far greater intra-MENA economic interaction policy harmonization. The region has a diverse natural, human and financial endowment base that is spread among many of its member countries. Its high initial trade barriers suggest a scope for trade-creating gains from regional integration. With an average per capita income well above that of developing countries as a whole, and with almost 5 per cent of the world's population, it offers a large market with considerable purchasing power. It has well-established trade links and relatively accessible intra-regional trading routes. Finally, the commonalities of language and cultural affinity should facilitate labour and tourist flows within a substantial part of the region.

Despite these potential advantages, it is often argued, correctly, that the similarity of resource endowments among many countries in the region and the greater proximity of the Maghreb countries to Europe than to the Mashreq (Arab East), will keep intra-regional trade limited.[22] Nonetheless, while regional states will continue to trade mostly with extra-regional partners, the current levels of trade within the area are below the levels that could be attained if economic relations among the countries of the region were freer.[23] In addition, most types of economic interaction within MENA, with the important exception of labour flows, remain remarkably limited.

THE SCOPE FOR REGIONAL INTEGRATION

MENA's overall economic performance in recent years has fallen short of potential.[24] The regional per capita income has stagnated, investment and domestic saving rates are low (Figure 4.2), and the productivity of investment has been disappointing. An insufficiently diversified economic base makes the region extremely vulnerable to unfavourable external shocks.[25] The resulting economic and financial challenges are compounded by high unemployment, a growing number of entrants into the labour force and poor social indicators.

What, then, is the rationale for greater regional interaction, and what means might be used in order to realize its potential gains? The region requires economic policy changes, most of which are also needed to benefit from the globalization and integration of the international economic system (see Chapter 3 in this volume), and in order to fully participate in groups like the World Trade Organization. Indeed, MENA will attain a higher level of regional economic interaction simply by implementing the policies that would be needed to benefit from the changes in the world economy.[26] Moreover, the pursuit of MENA integration within the overall context of multilateral externally-oriented policies would further growth in the region. Political factors are likely to constrain the pace of integration over the next few years, but as the European experience suggests, even the most ambitious plans need time to develop.

The Case for Regional Integration

Although most countries in MENA will continue to trade mostly outside the region, primarily with Europe, the United States and Asia, both the volume and the share of regional trade have the potential to rise significantly. This is the main reason for believing that substantial economic gains could be obtained through greater regional integration.[27]

There is a wide diversity of factor endowments within MENA, most strikingly in labour and natural resources, as well as differences in the extent of economic diversification.[28] Much of the trade within the region is based on this diversity, with oil the main traded commodity and labour the main traded factor. Closer regional integration is unlikely to lead to much trade diversion in these commodities but should promote greater merchandize trade in other commodities. Beyond its effects on merchandize trade, regional integration would boost service flows and intra-regional investments. MENA residents hold a very large share of their portfolios outside the region, with estimates ranging from $350–600 billion. Given the right economic policies in recipient countries, even a small re-allocation of portfolios in favour of regional activities would make a large difference in the

Figure 4.2 Developing countries and the MENA region: growth, investment and savings, 1989–94

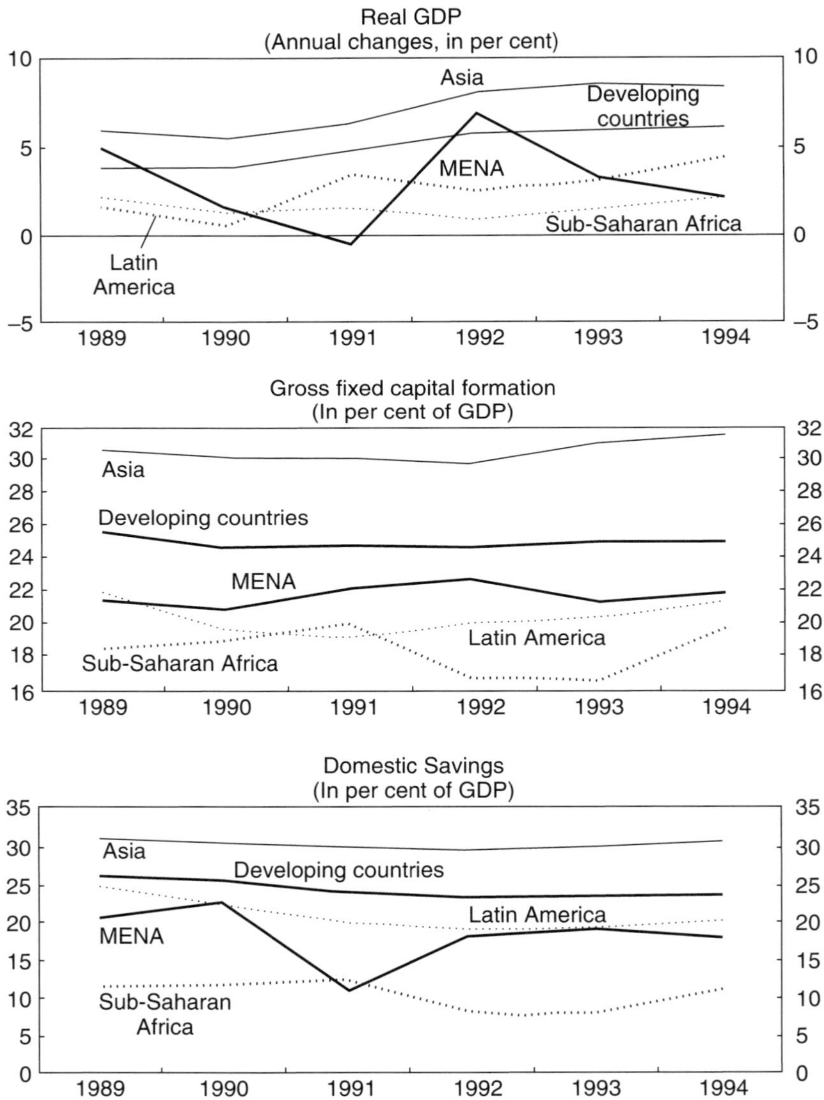

Source: IMF, *World Economic Outlook.*

region's investible resource base (see Wilson below). The right policies would be encouraged if regional integration efforts included an attempt to develop an investment code conforming to the highest international standards and practices.

There would also be gains from policy harmonization, particularly in reducing the cost of competitive tax exemptions and concessions – aspects that undermine the tax base and are tending to proliferate in the region. Thus, progress towards Arab–Israeli peace provides both an opportunity for moving towards greater political coherence within the region, as well as providing some direct economic benefits.[29] A comprehensive regional peace, if it occurs, will permit reductions over time in MENA military spending, which is the highest in the world as a share of GDP.[30] It should also increase the returns to investment by reducing country risk and opening up opportunities for regional projects in such areas as power generation, tourism and water management. And, of course, peace would make states more inclined to seek out agreements on measures to promote or facilitate intra-regional private sector economic activities.

There are also a few qualifications and some critical questions to consider. First, overcoming the legacy of recent history will take time; the length of time will depend on the perceived nature and dividend of the peace arrangements and their institutional support. Second, the Arab–Israeli conflict is only one, albeit the most important, of the conflicts and uncertainties facing MENA countries. Third, the scope for regional integration may be undermined by real or imagined perceptions of unequal allocations of the gains and losses associated with regional integration. Already there is concern in the Arab countries that Israel will become economically dominant and contribute to the de-industrialization of other countries. Will Israeli integration retard Arab industrialization processes? More likely, the relative size of Israel in the regional economy can be expected to decline over time as other countries, further from the technology frontier, grow more rapidly.

Policy Implications

Given the current outlook for the region, the policy implication of this analysis is not that countries in the region should set as their first economic policy priority the goal of embarking on the complex processes leading to the creation of an EU- or NAFTA-type arrangement. Rather, each country should focus first on domestic economic policy reform, second on the associated process of integrating into regional economies, and third into global markets through multilateral trade and payments liberalization. Successful liberalization will promote regional interaction.

It is critical to continue structural reforms aimed at de-regulating and decentralizing MENA economies. As noted earlier, some MENA economies are among the most protected in the world. In addition to denying consumers access to world-quality goods, high tariff and non-tariff barriers have reduced the efficiency and responsiveness of the production sectors in several MENA economies. To be sustainable and effective, the liberalization of the external trade and payments regimes will have to be accompanied by appropriately tight macroeconomic policies, by strict implementation processes, and by concurrent progress on domestic structural reforms, particularly those affecting investment labour, and financial markets.

Progress at the national level holds the key to increased integration within the MENA region. The experience of other regions, particularly the Asia-Pacific area, illustrates the advantages of open regionalism in emerging market development. One possibility may be for regional economic integration in MENA to evolve from an initial subset of core countries, starting perhaps from the Israeli, Jordanian and Palestinian economies and broadening to include the other states in the heartland of MENA, first Egypt, then as the peace process unfolds, Syria and Lebanon, and perhaps eventually Iraq. Similar processes can be envisaged within both the GCC and the Maghreb. Over time, and as more countries in the MENA region progress in deregulating and liberalizing their economies, cross-linkages among these groupings would strengthen MENA-wide economic ties.

The process of economic integration among these states will be strengthened by their development of strong trading ties with major partners outside the region (through free trade arrangements with the United States and the European Union, for example). The European Union's Mediterranean Basin Initiative contains incentives not only for closer economic ties between European Union countries and those in the southern and eastern Mediterranean, but also for closer ties among the latter group of countries themselves. Israel, Morocco and Tunisia have already reached association agreements with the European Union, while Algeria, Egypt, Jordan and Lebanon are in the midst of negotiations to reach similar accords with the Europeans. While the liberalization schedule under these agreements is spread over 12 years, and while full liberalization does not apply to agriculture, their encouragement of regional integration could be very important.[31]

Even though domestic reforms and multilateral liberalization could serve as the main engines of greater economic integration in MENA, there is also a clear need for measures aimed directly at regional interaction: these include reducing divergences in regulatory frameworks (including customs nomenclatures), improving road and rail transportation and abilities to move goods between countries, enhancing communications, and developing facilities for regional export financing. To the extent possible, these measures should be harmonized with best international standards and practices. In addition, several studies point to significant opportunities for regional projects with high payoffs. These include electricity generation (particularly better linkages of power grids), water management and tourism.

Such direct regional cooperation efforts would be enhanced by the creation of an appropriate institutional framework. There is a need for a forum in which countries from within the region can meet to discuss regional economic problems and do the work needed to develop solutions. This organization would be similar to the OECD in emphasizing policy coordination and discussion but would go beyond the OECD in having an action-oriented policy research staff dedicated to finding solutions to the problems and plans that emerge from discussions among policy-makers. In addition, there is a need for a regional financing organization, the primary objectives of which would be to finance interstate public projects within the region and to provide financial and informational assistance for the development of the private sector in all the member countries. [Note: Saudi vetoes this and it is no longer on the table.]

CONCLUSION

Increased regional interaction, particularly in the context of outwardly oriented development strategies, can enhance economic welfare through specialization and rationalization of consumption and production activities, increase the region's collective political bargaining power in extra-regional fora and improve security considerations. These considerations go a long way in explaining the renewed worldwide interest in regional arrangements, including in the Americas, Asia and Europe.

As Queen Noor points out above, countries in the MENA region face important political, social and economic challenges. Success toward peace will not happen without integrated approaches. Still, meeting these challenges is easier in the context of economic growth than within the context of the economic stagnation that continues in most countries of the region. Indeed, sustained high economic growth is required if MENA is to address its unemployment problem, find jobs for the large numbers of young people about to enter the labour market and improve its social indicators. The main key to economic progress for each country is the reform of the national economies in such a way as to enable them to take advantage of the process of globalization and integrate with the world economy.

There are many indicators – geographical, cultural, social, political, and economic – that point to a scope of considerable gains from greater economic interactions within the MENA region. However, the Arab–Israeli conflict and the lack of inter-Arab coordination, as well as inappropriate economic policies, have kept intra-regional economic interactions at an abnormally low level during recent decades. Merely restoring these interactions to their natural levels would give an important impetus to economic growth within the region. The continuing peace process, if it succeeds, will offer an important opportunity for enhanced economic cooperation within MENA. And, as the post-World War II Western European experience demonstrates, such cooperation would strengthen not only the economic well-being of countries in the region, but would also feed back to reinforce the peace. What is required are steadfast national commitments to structural reforms on the part of all MENA countries, including continued multilateral liberalization, the removal of impediments to regional economic interaction and the strengthening of the institutional framework.

Notes

1. International Monetary Fund; Fischer is on leave from MIT. An earlier version of this Chapter was presented at the meetings of the International Economic Association in Tunis in December 1995. We are grateful to our discussant in Tunis, Ephraim Kleiman, for his comments and suggestions, and to Nigel Chalk and Peter Kunzel of the IMF for their assistance. The views expressed are those of the authors and not necessarily those of the International Monetary Fund.
2. Iraq is included in our definition of the MENA region, but due to the unavailability of statistical data it is omitted for the purposes of statistical analysis.
3. For reviews of regional trade arrangements see M. Leanne Brown, *Developing Countries and Regional Economic Cooperation* (Westport, Conn.: Praeger, 1994); Augusto de la Torre and Margaret Kelly, *Regional Trading Arrangements*, IMF Occasional Paper no. 93, International Monetary Fund, Washington DC, 1992; and Jaime De Melo and Arvind Panagariya (eds), *New Dimensions in Regional Integration* (Cambridge: Cambridge University Press, 1993).
4. Organization for Economic Cooperation and Development, *Regional Integration and the Developing Countries* (Paris: OECD, 1993).
5. Traditional trade theory suggests that the potential payoffs from the opening of trade among countries that formerly did not trade with one another or the rest of the world are higher the more complementary are the structures of their economies. However, the creation of a customs union among countries that could trade before is more likely to be welfare-enhancing for its members the more similar the range of goods they produce, for trade creation is more likely to dominate trade diversion under those circumstances. See for instance Nadav Halevy and Ephraim Kleiman, "Regional versus Non-Regional Integration: The Case of the Middle East", mimeo, Hebrew University, Jerusalem, 1995. This result may be strengthened by taking into account intra-industry trade based on increasing returns.
6. See Carlos M. Asilis and Luis A. Rivera-Batiz, "Geography, Trade Patterns, and Economic Policy", Working Paper, WP/94/16, International Monetary Fund, Washington DC, 1994; Jeffrey Frankel, Ernesto Stein and Shang-jin Wei, "Continental Trading Blocs: Are they Natural, or Super-Natural", NBER Working Paper no. 4588, National Bureau of Economic Research, Cambridge, Mass., 1993; and Paul Krugman, *Geography and Trade* (Cambridge, Mass.: MIT Press, 1991).

7. Benjamin H. Higgins and Donald J. Savoie, *Regional Development Theories and their Application* (London: Transaction Publishers, 1995).
8. See, for example, OECD, *Regional Integration and the Developing Countries, op. cit.*
9. Under the principle of mutual recognition, laws and regulations enforced in one country are recognized by all other members of the Union. The minimum harmonization principle requires members to harmonize regulations at the minimum level among countries in the Union; the principle prevents competition between rule books from leading to disruptive deregulation. See the discussion in Tommaso Padoa-Schioppa, *Tripolarism: Regional and Global Economic Cooperation* (Washington DC: Group of Thirty, 1993).
10. In the European Union, central institutions may also have the power to approve these rules.
11. See, for example, Frank J. Strain, *Integration, Federalism and Cohesion in the European Community: Lessons from Canada* (Dublin: Economic and Social Research Institute, 1993).
12. As the names imply, market integration relates to the economic relationships among goods and factors within the region, while institutional integration refers to the extent of legal and institutional relationships. See Richard Cooper, "Worldwide Regional Integration: Is There an Optimal Size of the Integrated Area?", Yale Economic Growth Center Discussion Paper no. 220, November 1974.
13. The share of agricultural land varies from 3 per cent in Egypt and the United Arab Emirates, to 75 per cent in Tunisia.
14. This comparison abstracts from differences among sects within the major religions.
15. According to World Bank data, the average annual rate of population growth has been 3 per cent. Over half the region's population is below the age of 17. The total labour force has been increasing at an annual rate of 3.5 per cent (4.9 per cent for female labour participation), well above the developing country average of 2.2 per cent.
16. Data derived from World Bank, *Social Indicators of Development* (Washington DC: World Bank, 1995).
17. See E. Ghantus, *Arab Industrial Integration: A Strategy for Development* (London: Croom Helm, 1982).
18. Additional information may be found in Stanley Fischer, "Prospects for Regional Integration in the Middle East", in De Melo and Panagariya, *op. cit.*
19. See Heba Handoussa and Nemat Shafik, "The Economics of Peace: The Egyptian Case", in Stanley Fischer, Dani Rodrik and Elias Tuma, *The Economics of Middle East Peace* (Cambridge, Mass.: MIT Press, 1995).
20. This is detailed in Pierre van den Boogaerde, *Financial Assistance from Arab Countries and Arab Regional Institutions*, Occasional Paper no. 87, International Monetary Fund, Washington DC, 1991.
21. Ruth Klinov estimates that about two-thirds of the eight million migrant workers in the GCC in 1985 were Arabs. See Ruth Klinov, "Recent Trends in Migration-for-Work from Middle Eastern Countries", paper presented at the conference entitled "The Economics of Labor Mobility in the Middle East", Kennedy School of Government, Harvard University, Cambridge, Mass., 1991. Nemat Shafik argues that trade in labour services has been the most successful element of regional integration, because the obstacles to trade in goods have been greater than those to labour movements. Nemat Shafik, "Has Labor Migration Promoted Economic Integration in the Middle East?", MENA Discussion Paper no. 1, World Bank, Washington DC, 1992.

22. See for instance the argument developed in Halevy and Kleiman, *op. cit.*; A similar view is expressed in Fischer, *op. cit.*
23. See, for example, Karolina Ekholm, Johan Torstensson and Rasha Torstensson, "Prospects for Trade in the Middle East and North Africa: An Econometric Analysis", paper presented at the ERF Conference on Liberalization of Trade and Foreign Investment, Istanbul, 16–18 September 1995.
24. For details see Mohamed A. El-Erian, Sena Eken, Susan Fennell and Jean-Pierre Chauffour, *Macroeconomy of the Middle East and North Africa: Exploiting Potential for Growth and Financial Stability* (Washington DC: International Monetary Fund, 1995); and Nemat Shafik, *Claiming the Future* (Washington DC: World Bank, 1995).
25. For example, the variance in terms of trade for the MENA countries in 1989–94 was 15 times higher than that for developing countries as a whole and over 30 times that of industrial countries. Fluctuation in oil prices was not the only factor. Thus, the non-oil MENA countries recorded variances that were 31/2 and 7 times higher than those for developing and industrial countries, respectively.
26. The example of the dynamic Asian-Pacific economies is particularly relevant: outwardly-oriented development strategies have been associated with intensified regional economic interactions without official trade discrimination or significant formal institutional support. See Ross Garnaut and Peter Drysdale (eds), *Asia Pacific Regionalism* (Australia: Harper Educational, 1994).
27. The region contains some of the most open (e.g., the GCC) and most closed (e.g., Egypt) economies in terms of traditional indicators of international trade activity.
28. In some countries, a single sector accounts for over half of GDP (e.g., oil in the GCC economies and hydrocarbons in Algeria). Others, such as Israel, Morocco and Tunisia, are more diversified with an important manufacturing component, albeit varying in terms of the preponderance of high-tech industries.
29. For details, see Fischer, Rodrik and Tuma, *op. cit.*
30. See Daniel Hewitt, "Military Expenditure Worldwide: Determinants and Trends", *Journal of Public Policy*, 12 (1995); and Malcolm Knight, Norman Loayza and Delano Villanueva, "The Peace Dividend: Military Spending Cuts and Economic Growth", IMF Working Paper, WP/95/53, International Monetary Fund, Washington DC, 1995. Military spending is unlikely to be reduced significantly in the early stages of the peace process; indeed, redeployments may require increased spending. However, military spending should decline as confidence in the durability of the peace increases.
31. For a more sceptical view of the Mediterranean Basin Initiative, see Bernard Hoekman and Simeon Djankov, "Catching Up with Eastern Europe? The European Union's Mediterranean Free Trade Initiative", Discussion Paper no. 1300, Centre for Economic Policy Research, London, November 1995.

5 Will an Arab–Israeli Peace Bring a Trade Dividend?

Elias H. Tuma

INTRODUCTION

In this chapter I shall briefly survey the obstacles to trade and development in the core Arab–Israeli region, with emphasis on the obstacles that are not related to war and peace. Next I discuss the extent to which a regional peace would help to alter the negative conditions and enhance development, growth, and consequently trade. Then I explore the extent to which the direction of trade and economic cooperation among former enemies might be enhanced without infringing on the independence, sovereignty and economic welfare of the individual countries involved in the peace process; this is followed by a set of general conclusions.

Probably the most simple and misleading answer to the title question is that peace will bring a trade dividend. It is simple because in theory and in a perfect and larger market trade should increase. It is misleading because theory and practice do not always coincide. Because the Middle East can hardly claim to have a perfect market, it is difficult to calculate a precise dividend. Besides, a peace trade dividend implies that the volume of trade will increase and its direction will change to favour the parties concluding a peace agreement. The size and composition of the trade basket are a function of the income level or the purchasing power that can be allocated to foreign trade. The direction of trade, however, is a function of the terms of trade, economic complementarity, and the costs and benefits of trading with one party or another. The costs and benefits in this case include social, psychological and political dimensions of trade relations. Therefore, to answer the question we have to assess the impact of peace on the levels of income and purchasing power, the terms of trade, and the relative costs and benefits of trading among former enemies. It is necessary also to examine the degree of complementarity between the relevant economies.

The focus of the current peace process in the Middle East is between Israel and its immediate Arab neighbours, especially the Palestinian Authority, Jordan and Egypt. All other Arab countries are either holding off from a peace agreement, as Lebanon and Syria are doing, or they are proceeding to promote economic relations with Israel without formalizing a peace agreement, as some of the Gulf states, namely Qatar, have begun to do. The focus of this chapter is the likely impact of peace on trade between Israel and its immediate Arab neighbours which have already concluded peace agreements with it, namely the Palestinian Authority, Jordan and Egypt.

Since the process began, related literature has been replete with predictions that an Arab–Israeli peace would lead to trade expansion, economic cooperation, and possibly to economic blocs and eventual prosperity. These studies may be classified into three categories: normative, idealistic and prescriptive. The normative studies tend to assume that in the absence of war, trade flourishes, and since war has been a major obstacle to trade between Israel and the Arab states, once peace prevails, trade will flourish. However, neither assumption is valid: war is not the only obstacle, and trade among countries at peace does not always flourish.[1]

The idealistic studies presume that once peace prevails the Middle East countries will restructure their economies, harmonize their trade regulations, cooperate closely with each other to reap large scale benefits, and enhance the level of complementarity between them. These studies are in a sense tautological: by stipulating that certain forms of restructuring and cooperation lead to economic benefits, they conclude that if the Middle East countries behave accordingly, they will reap those benefits. But will they? Why have countries that are not at war with each other done so?[2]

The prescriptive studies are in many ways politically-oriented and aim at convincing the relevant parties that peace will reward them with major trade benefits because certain developments will follow to make the benefits possible. Such studies, however, proceed to outline steps to be taken in the aftermath of peace agreements in order to achieve the prescribed results.[3]

What these studies have in common, in addition to an optimistic viewpoint, is a failure to analyse other factors that influence economic relations besides war and peace, namely the institutional, social and psychological forces that determine the volume and direction of trade. A deeper study of the Middle East *political economy* would cast doubt on the assumptions and conclusions therein. In contrast, I propose the following hypotheses:

1. Peace between Israel and the Arab states is a necessary but not a sufficient condition for trade expansion between them. Peace alone is not sufficient to raise incomes or the purchasing power allocated to trade, nor is it a sufficient condition to redirect trade in favour of trade with previous enemies. For these parties to expand trade between them there has to be a certain degree of complementarity between their economies. They also have to overcome historically-ingrained feelings of voluntary separation and enmity before they will trade freely and apply economic rationality to their trade relations. The level of complementarity between the economies of Israel and the Arab states is low and the social-psychological hurdles are deeply ingrained. Therefore it is unlikely that peace agreements between them will greatly enhance mutual trade or invest-

ment. The low complementarity becomes especially evident once labour mobility, which is politically determined, has been neutralized.
2. The levels of income and trade-intended purchasing power depend on investment, job-creation and the distribution of income. None of these factors can be expected to respond positively to the end of war and the proclamation of peace unless the institutional obstacles to growth are removed. That, however, requires more than the signing of a peace agreement to realize; it requires policy implementation and planning.
3. Peace may still have a positive impact on trade if the parties proceed slowly and cautiously in order to allow the peoples of the region to adapt to the peace framework, assess the costs and benefits of new trade relationships and become confident that no new trade partner will dominate the others through trade between them.

OBSTACLES TO DEVELOPMENT AND TRADE

Jordan, Egypt and the occupied Palestinian territories suffer from relatively low per capita incomes, low levels of saving (though the saving rate may be high) and low productive investment. Hence income levels continue to be low and therefore trade remains limited because of the underlying negative factors that restrict development and expansion. In recent years the per capita income has declined in Egypt, Jordan and among the Palestinians, while the rate of increase in Israel has also declined. Improvement in Syria has been slight; only Lebanon has been enjoying an economic revival after a major economic collapse.[4] Rapid population growth, underdeveloped institutional structures, lopsided education that favours book learning over analytical and entrepreneurial activities, and a government structure that tends to depend on rent and foreign aid at the expense of hard decisions to promote development are major hindrances. These forces are buttressed by forces of traditionalism and religion that undermine individual free thinking in favour of depending on or acquiescing to a higher authority.[5]

Defence expenditure, often at the expense of productive and development expenditure, is another obstacle to development and trade. Although the war psychology may increase the rate of saving and investment, the form investment takes can hardly be productive, especially when much of the military equipment and arms are imported. In that sense, defence expenditure tends to increase trade in military goods at the expense of trade in other commodities.[6] This trade dynamic has had variant influence on the region's national economies (as Looney points out in Chapter 6). The poor countries by and large do not profit from arms trade, though rich countries often do.

Trade is also restricted because of the relatively low level of technology in Egypt, Jordan and Palestine, which reduces their competitiveness on the international market and limits their exports to less capital- and technology-intensive products, such as raw materials, agricultural products and crafts. This in turn limits the foreign exchange earnings and consequently the value of imports that can be financed domestically. It is not surprising in these circumstances to observe a close relationship between trade and the inflow of foreign exchange in the form of aid or loans. This dynamic also makes it difficult for these countries to participate in the economics of globalization that currently define trade relations in the industrialized West and in newly industrialized Asia (see Chapter 3 in this volume for more on this problem).

Finally, Egypt and the Levantine countries suffer from the poverty of resources relative to their populations, both in volume and composition. The resource–population ratio is one of the most strategic factors in development. Nevertheless, the ratio continues to decline because Arab governments fail to aggressively promote population control. The result is a vicious cycle: low income means poverty, and poverty sustains low income. The resource–population relationship is also affected by the highly skewed income distribution which favours the wealthy at the expense of a small middle-income group and a very large low-income group. Consequently, trade tends to be concentrated on luxuries and basic commodities (and/or military supplies) that are financed or subsidized by the government. Peace is unlikely to change the pattern of income distribution or the composition of the consumer trade basket. Trade is therefore limited by the absence of a mass consumption market in any of these countries.

Israel is an exception to most of the above conditions; it does share the burden of high military expenditure and poverty of resources (offset by a generous inflow of capital from the outside). Israel differs in one additional factor: it has turned its war expenditure into a military industry that is a major exporter of arms and earner of foreign exchange. While Egypt has attempted a similar approach, its tradable products are minor by comparison. Military expenditure in Israel has also been used in part to promote technological advance and economic growth by supporting domestic industry and productive employment.[7]

The discussion thus far has concentrated on the obstacles to trade and development as reflected by the volume of trade. The direction of trade is equally important in assessing the impact of peace on trade. Intra-regional trade is relatively small in the Middle East in general, and among the four countries in particular. Though Jordan records high levels of intra-regional trade, most of this trade is transit trade due to the political uncertainties in Lebanon and the economic embargo against Iraq.[8] The only major instance of high trade volume is between Israel and the occupied territories, which is forced on the Palestinians by Israeli military and political regulations. This high volume trade is certainly a function of Israel's continued occupation of the Palestinian territories.

Intra-regional trade in the Middle East is limited by a number of factors (see also Chapter 4). War and political conflict are only two such factors. A more important factor is the low level of complementarity between these economies in tradable commodities. While some countries have surplus land and others surplus labour, land is not mobile, and labour mobility is politically determined. Since most countries of the Middle East, with the exception of Israel, produce competitive trade commodities, they must look for trade partners elsewhere.[9]

Intra-regional trade, even in the absence of war, has also been limited by the low propensity among the countries of the region to cooperate with one another. Influenced by tribal and other traditional forms of social organization, most countries are still searching for national identity and internal political stability. The region's rulers struggle for a position of leadership, and they tend to emphasise nationalism rather than regionalism, and less rather than more cooperation (see Chapters 2, 3 and 4 in this volume for more comments on these points).[10] Bahrain and Jordan's new rulers seem to be following the paths laid for them by their predecessors. The exception to this pattern again is Israel which produces advanced technology and highly capital- and technology-intensive commodities in demand in other Middle Eastern countries. The ongoing Arab–Israeli hostilities, however, have precluded trade in these commodities, at least directly or openly. Trade with Israel through third parties has been known to exist, though not at a high volume and not with all Arab countries.

PEACE AND THE FACILITATION OF TRADE AND DEVELOPMENT

The obstacles to trade development which characterize Egypt, Jordan and Palestine are common to most countries of the Middle East, including those that have not been involved directly or indirectly in war with Israel or with others, such as Tunisia and Morocco. On the other hand, Egypt has had a peace agreement with Israel since 1978 and Jordan has had a virtual understanding of no war since at least 1970 when it received help from Israel against the Palestinians. A major question, therefore, is to what extent formal peace with Israel will remove the obstacles to trade. The answer can hardly be encouraging since the causes of low income and slow development are other than war. Therefore, peace can hardly eliminate those causes.

Probably the most significant impact of peace will be to reduce war capital destruction, military expenditure and waste of human capital. The impact therefore may be a redirection of expenditure to more productive investment and capital accumulation instead of capital replacement. In this sense more resources will be available for economic development, though not necessarily for growth. This impact, however, can be easily exaggerated. Egypt and Israel have been at peace for almost two decades and therefore one can hardly expect additional reductions in their military expenditures to result from their treaty at this late date. Israel and Jordan have had a virtual understanding of non-belligerency so that no military buildup by Jordan has resulted from the formal war situation. Israel and the Palestinians have room to reduce military activities against each other and redirect resources to a peace economy. Even so, Israel is not about to reduce its internal security operations *vis-à-vis* the Palestinians for some time to come, especially since a comprehensive and final peace arrangement has not been concluded.

The Palestinians, on the other hand, might be able to cut down on their military activities, since they have little room to maneuver militarily without instigating Israeli retaliation. In a sense the Palestinians have already been contained enough to prevent any new military buildups. Therefore some resources may be directed to economic development and growth, though it is unlikely to be permitted as long as the Israelis hold ultimate control. The poverty of the Palestinians under occupation, the large number of stateless refugees still in Lebanon and Syria, and the underdevelopment of economic and administrative institutions in Palestine cannot inspire great hopes for major increases in Palestinian income in the near future, unless massive aid from the outside materializes.

By contrast, reduction in Israel's military expenditure cannot be expected until there is a peace agreement with Syria and Lebanon. Even then, Israel may profit from military expenditure. Therefore, little change may be expected in the growth pattern of the Israeli economy and relatively small increases in the economies of Egypt and Jordan as a result of peace between them and Israel. Accordingly, the volume of trade may be expected to change proportionally, and composition of the trade basket should be expected to change only slightly in favour of non-military consumer and capital goods.

Another important impact of peace will be to reduce investment risk in the region and encourage the inflow of investment capital from the outside. As illustrated by Rodney Wilson (see Chapter 8), however, investment decisions are influenced by the expected profitability of the investment in addition to its security. The institutional and market structures in Egypt, Jordan and the occupied territories cannot be expected to change because of the peace agreements, since none of their economic environments are conducive to foreign investment. Even indigenous capital seems to flee these countries in search of more security and higher returns. And, as J.W. Wright points out (see Chapter 7), the lack of adequate banking facilities in the West Bank and Gaza Strip make financial relationships difficult to maintain.

Looking at the effects from a different standpoint, it is possible that peace would cause a reduction in the inflow of capital from the outside. Much of the aid has been generated by sympathy with one country or another facing hardship and the dangers of war. Is it not possible that as the threat of war subsides the related aid will also decline? Will Israel and Egypt continue to receive the billions of dollars they have been granted since Camp David after a comprehensive peace prevails in the entire region? Even if they do not face a reduction in the aid they receive, it is unlikely that can expect an increase; therefore the impact of peace in that case will be neutral.

The Wye Accords show that the Palestinians will receive continued aid to make sure their agreements with Israel are solidly cemented. This, however, can be expected to prevail only for a short period of time because neither Jordan nor Palestine will represent great danger to Israel. We have only to look at the aid promised to the Palestinians after they signed the Declaration of Principles in September 1993. Most of what has materialized has been used to finance administrative operations and internal security rather than economic development and growth (see Chapters 10 and 11 in this volume for further discussion of the problems of international economic aid to the Palestinians in the West Bank and Gaza). International donors have been made even more cautious with the Netanyahu government and the changes that have accompanied it.

The overall picture is as follows: peace can be expected to enhance economic development and growth only to the extent that some resources may be redirected from military expenditure to investment in a peace economy. However, no major increase in the available resources, domestic or foreign, may be expected until the institutional and administrative structures in the Arab countries have become more favourable to investment and growth.

Another serious obstacle to development which a regional peace agreement will not overcome is the sustained rapid increase in population in all Arab countries, and Israel will probably face significantly increasing problems of unemployment given the continued inflow of migrants and as the probable demobilization at peace prevails. Unless large sums of capital are invested and markets are guaranteed, Israel will face a major economic problem as a result of peace. Egypt and Jordan probably will not have to face demobilization since their militaries are not mobilized on a war footing. However, the sustained rapid increase of population continues to threaten those economies, and the peace process will do little to alleviate its effects.

Palestine will face a unique challenge in the event of peace, similar to one that Israel has itself faced: the absorption of returning refugees, should return become a real option. If it does, the number of returnees, although uncertain, could increase the population of the West Bank and Gaza by about 25–30 per cent due to refugee absorption. Added to the natural growth of the population, this increase is bound to create an economic havoc unless absorption capital is made available at the same rate of refugee integration in the Palestinian economy.

THE PROBABLE EFFECTS OF PEACE ON THE DIRECTION OF TRADE

The direction of trade responds to freedom of the market, economic complementarity and the terms of trade. Freedom of the market in this case includes freedom from both economic and political restrictions such as tariffs, quotas, prohibitions and binding treaties. In the absence of these restrictions trade will follow the self-interests of the buyers and sellers. A peace agreement does not automatically result in a free market. However, freedom of trade or the framework of a free market may be made an integral part of a regional peace. What cannot be made a condition is the social, psychological or attitudinal freedom of the market. Agreements between leaders cannot remove the internalized separation and mutual distrust of peoples that results from the long-term state of war: the protracted situation of cold peace between Israel and Egypt, even with their peace treaty in hand, should provide the necessary example. Therefore it is unlikely that trade between Israel and its other immediate neighbours will flow freely and abundantly in the aftermath of peace agreements between them, regardless of the assumptions made by the leaders and experts. The only way to guarantee increasing trade between these parties is to encourage trade through additional funds that may be made available to finance it. Even then, such funds must be relatively large in order to overcome resistance emanating from the ingrained antagonism accumulated during years of war and separation.

Assuming freedom of trade is assured in all respects – a broad assumption to say the least – trade among the signatories to the peace agreements must be based on economic complementarity between them. This factor is bound to be an obstacle. The only evident complementarity between Egypt, Israel, Jordan and Palestine relates to the supply of energy, labour and technology. Egypt has surplus oil and Israel already buys that oil. Labour supply, which is abundant in Egypt, Jordan and Palestine tends to be short in Israel, but labour mobility is governed by military and political factors rather than economic factors. Peace may ease mobility, but so far it has not. Israel has imported labour from Europe and Southeast Asia but not from Egypt. Jordan lost the Gulf market for its skilled workers but so far Israel has not opened its job market to large numbers of Jordanians.

Israel has employed Palestinian labour in varying magnitudes, determined largely by the whims of the leaders who use security as an excuse to open or close the gates. It has done so in order to take advantage of the relatively low wages and to reduce unemployment in the occupied territories with the aim of preserving a semblance of stability, since Palestinian labour under occupation still has no access to other markets. However, despite this, Palestinian labour in the occupied territories, which used to flow rather freely into Israel, has now been severely curtailed. And, of course, the Palestinian economy remains dependent on employment in Israel; a certain degree of similarity with the Bantustan system that used to prevail in South Africa is evident.

In the case of peace, Israel will have no political or military reason to employ Palestinian labour or, for that matter, to shut it out. Israelis, however, will still have the economic incentive of relatively low wages, but will Palestinian labour want to work for those low wages if Palestine becomes an independent economy with access to markets other than Israel's? In the short run, Palestinian labour may have no other option and might continue to work in Israel, thus sustaining trade between the two countries as a matter of mutual benefit and convenience. However, in the medium and long run, or when investment in the Palestinian economy begins to provide jobs, it is unlikely that Palestinian labour would want to continue to commute, accept relatively low wages, and to suffer humiliation, long hours of travel and little security of employment. Furthermore, the types of jobs Palestinians have held in Israel would become unacceptable to a Palestinian labour force that enjoys a relatively high level of education. In a condition of independence, Palestinian labour will become a competitor to Israeli labour rather than a complementary labour force to do the menial and unwanted jobs as they have done in the past. Thus, one of the major factors supporting trade between Israel and Palestine will be removed by a comprehensive peace agreement and an independently developing economy in Palestine.

The issue of complementarity is even more serious among the three Arab economies in Jordan, Egypt and the PA territories: all have surplus labour, depend on agriculture and services, import manufactured goods and technology and are short of capital. Theirs are competing rather than complementary economies. Any peace with Israel will not change this situation, and therefore, trade among them can hardly be expected to increase unless new conditional investments and finances are made available to enhance it.

There is still the question of whether Israel will be able to increase trade with the Arab states around it, given its advanced technology, highly-trained experts and potential to dominate the Arab economies. While the import of technology and human capital from Israel may be attractive to the Arab countries, one should ask why the Arab countries would rush to trade with their former enemy and risk economic domination by Israel. Leaving aside the social, psychological and political obstacles, trade between them must still be influenced by the terms of trade. Will Israel be able to offer better terms of trade for the Arab countries than what they enjoy with their other trade partners, with whom they have no political, military or historical conflict? In the short run Israel may be willing to offer extra-favourable terms in order to overcome those obstacles, but Israel cannot afford to offer better terms of trade than those prevailing on the international market for any length of time, unless, of course, the cost to it is offset by third parties in order to enhance cooperation in the region. That, however, is unlikely since the Cold War has ended and such cooperation has no strategic significance to any major power able to afford the cost. Thus we reach the same conclusion: peace would not alter the terms of trade and therefore could hardly affect the direction of trade between Israel and its immediate neighbours.

CONCLUSION

Yet, there may be a silver lining. Middle Eastern countries may still find ways to benefit from the economic cooperation that will become politically feasible if peace prevails. They may explore cooperation on specific projects, industries or policies towards other regions. They may explore ways to counter-balance the economic blocs forming in other parts of the world, or try to realize economies of scale in marketing, negotiating deals and concluding agreements with other countries and regions.[11] Thus, on the one hand, though the past history of economic cooperation in the Middle East is quite dismal, the possibility that a new peace environment may enhance cooperation cannot be entirely ruled out.

On the other hand, peace may induce the leaders of the four countries to turn their attention inward and concentrate on domestic economic issues, that is, to try to develop their own national economies and thus become able to cooperate with others on an equal footing. This means that they may opt to achieve certain levels of economic development and capital formation and to solve the social problems facing them before they consider formal cooperation agreements with other states.

It may also happen that the leaders of the Middle East countries will succeed in putting aside past conflicts and emphasise economic factors in making economic policy. In that case they may find mutual advantages in promoting trade and cooperation with each other. Doing so may lead to progress in coping with issues of demography, education, and institutional and administrative reform which would foster growth and development. Even modest achievements in these areas may create confidence and lead to formal economic cooperation among these countries.

Notes

1. Most of the normative studies tend to be free market-oriented and sponsored by the World Bank or the United States Agency for International Development (USAID). See, for example, Said El-Naggar and Mohamed El-Erian, "The Economic Implications of a Comprehensive Peace in the Middle East", in Stanley Fischer, Dani Rodrik and Elias Tuma (eds), *The Economics of Middle East Peace* (Cambridge, Mass., and London: MIT Press, 1993), pp. 205–24.
2. The best illustration is Riad Ajami's "A Middle Eastern Free Trade Agreement (MEFTA): Prospects and Possibilities" in Steven L. Spiegel and David J. Pervin (eds), *Practical Peacemaking in the Middle East*, Vol. 2 (New York and London: Garland Publishing, 1995), pp. 371–84.
3. A good illustration is Robert Z. Lawrence, *Towards Free Trade in the Middle East: The Triad and Beyond* (Cambridge, Mass.: Harvard University, 1995).
4. United Nations, "National Accounts Studies of the ESCWA Region", Bulletin no. 14 (1994), P. 4; World Bank, *Human Development Report*, 1995, 212.
5. See my "Institutional Obstacles to Economic Development: The Case of Egypt", *World Development* 16(10) (1988), pp. 1185–98.
6. World Bank, *Human Development Report*, 1995, pp. 182, 206.
7. For trade patterns see my *Economic and Political Change in the Middle East* (Palo Alto, Calif.: Pacific Books, 1987), especially table 8.1; United Nations, "National Accounts Studies of the ESCWA Region", 20–1; and World Bank, *Human Development Report*, 1995, pp. 212–3.
8. United Nations, "External Trade Bulletin of the ESCWA Region", 7th issue (1994), pp. 49–52.
9. World Bank, *Choosing Prosperity for the Middle East and North Africa* (1995), table 4.2, p. 67.
10. For past attempts to cooperate see my "Economic Cooperation and Middle East Regional Stability", in Spiegel and Pervin, *op. cit.*, pp. 287–301.
11. Riad Ajami, *op. cit.*, suggests regional water and agricultural projects as possibilities.
12. I have explored various possible economic combinations in the region as in Table 5.1, in *Beirut Review*, *op. cit*, p. 20. Israel, Jordan and Palestine (group #9) may be one such combination. Another would include Egypt (group #3). Though none of these combinations at present seems probable, all of them may at one time or another be possible.

Table 5.1 Conceivable economic cooperation sub-groups

Country	*1*	*2*	*3*	*4*	*5*	*6*	*7*	*8*	*9*
Algeria	X								
Bahrain				X					
Dijbouti									
Egypt	X	X	X				X		
Kuwait				X					
Iran					X			X	
Iraq					X	X		X	
Israel		X	X			X			X
Jordan		X	X			X			X
Lebanon		X				X			
Libya	X						X		
Mauritania	X								
Morocco	X								
Oman				X					
Palestine*		X	X			X			X
Qatar				X					
Saudi Arabia				X	X				
Somalia	X								
Sudan	X						X		
Syria		X				X		X	
Tunisia	X								
Turkey								X	
UAE				X					
Yemen				X					
Number of participants	8	6	4	7 GCC + Yemen	3	6	3	4	3

*Assuming a future Palestinian state.

6 The Budgetary Consequences of Middle East Peace: What are the Economic Impacts and Causal Linkages?

Robert E. Looney

INTRODUCTION

Gone is the superpower rivalry of the Cold War era and the strategic significance it lent to the Middle East. The end of Soviet support has caused several Arab governments to realign their foreign policies; Israel is no longer necessarily perceived as an enemy but in some circles is seen as a potential economic and political partner.[1] Clearly a major motivation for expanding defence expenditures has therefore been eliminated. Even so, there are still gaps in the defence systems of most states in the region, and most countries wish to modernize their armed forces. Even the peace process will not stand in the way of modernization, and actual defence spending is not expected to fall significantly for some time.[2]

It is commonly believed that the major constraint on new defence spending is the poor performance of regional economies and the strain on government budgets of maintaining a system of subsidies and social welfare. It follows that the pace of arms transfers may slow down as a result of the need to conserve resources, but the region is certain to continue spending heavily on security, even if the future enemy is more likely to be an Islamist than an Israeli.[3]

While not disputing that view, this chapter takes another approach. Specifically it examines whether and to what extent the eastern Mediterranean states and Saudi Arabia have become so accustomed to defence expenditures that a reduction in their levels or rates of growth might actually result in economic disruption. Clearly if large segments of the economy are adversely affected by reduced allocations to the military, there will be some limits to the extent to which military cutbacks occur. Whether or not the reluctance to make further cuts in defence expenditures will derail the peace process is problematic, but there is no doubt that this phenomenon may hamper both economic and political progress.

LITERATURE SURVEY: THE IMPACT OF DEFENCE EXPENDITURES

A body of conventional wisdom has amassed over the years concerning the causes and consequences of Third World militarization. More often than not in the academic literature this wisdom has been anecdotal and biased towards the standard "guns or butter" metaphor. Since the modern defence establishment is a heavy consumer of technical and managerial manpower and foreign exchange, resources that are especially scarce in the Third World, the conventional argument is that increased defence burdens should reduce the overall rate of growth.[4]

To test this theory, a rapidly growing body of empirical research has attempted to identify the impact of defence spending on various aspects of economic development and growth. Numerous studies have grown out of the debate but, unfortunately, no consensus has emerged. In the original study, Benoit[5] found strong evidence to suggest that defence spending encouraged the growth of civilian output per capita in less-developed countries.

This research has gone through various stages and levels of sophistication, with the initial studies largely based on ordinary least-squares regression techniques using Benoit's data-set for the 1950–65 period. The original research analysing Benoit's data-set[6] grouped countries on the basis of discriminant analysis with savings and investment used as variables. It was found that countries with relatively high levels of savings and investment experienced positive impacts on growth, while the impact was statistically insignificant for countries experiencing low levels of savings and investment.

On the other hand, Rothschild[7] concluded that increased military expenditures lowered economic growth by reducing exports in 14 OECD countries during the period 1956–69. In his examination of 54 developing countries for the sample period 1965–73, Lim[8] found defence spending to be detrimental to economic growth. Deger and Sen,[9] Leontief and Duchin,[10] Faini, Annez and Taylor,[11] Biswas and Ram,[12] and Grobar and Porter[13] also found evidence refuting the claim that defence spending stimulates economic growth.

In contrast, Wolf's[14] research examining the economic impact of Third World military expenditures utilising various sub-groupings of countries tended to contradict these findings. Much of this research implicitly argues that, in certain economic situations, by creating a stable environment it is possible that added defence expenditures may stimulate higher rates of investment, technological progress, technology transfer and hence increased overall growth.

Frederiksen and myself[15] also used Benoit's sample countries. However, our study grouped countries largely on the basis of foreign exchange earnings, import elasticity and productivity of investment. Again, relatively unconstrained countries experienced positive impacts on growth stemming from defence expenditures, while the countries that were relatively constrained in terms of foreign exchange showed a statistically insignificant but negative impact. Using a later time period, 1965–73, and again grouping developing countries on the basis of their relative savings and investment,[16] we found that the relatively unconstrained countries enjoyed a positive impact from defence expenditures.

These initial studies examined only the impact of defence expenditures on growth. More recent analysis in the area has been more sophisticated, employing more elaborate statistical devices and/or more subtle country groupings. For example, Third World military producers[17] during the period 1970–82 experienced positive impacts from military expenditures on growth, investment and savings, but declines in productivity.[18] Non-producers experienced declines in growth and investment. In recent years, analysis has branched into more complex issues, and utilized both time-series[19] and simultaneous-equation models estimated by two and three-stage least-squares regression techniques. These studies introduced the demand for military expenditures into the analysis to allow for feedback from the macroeconomy to defence.[20] Interestingly, the results[21] produced by these techniques tended to confirm the results obtained from the simpler, more naive models.

In short, the existing body of research demonstrates a consistent pattern whereby certain groups of Third World countries – usually the more successful economically, the more stable politically, or those engaged in military production[22] – derive positive impacts on investment and growth from military spending. Those countries less successful economically, more politically unstable or lacking a domestic arms industry fail to derive any positive economic impacts from defence expenditures.

Some studies have also identified a number of adverse effects that stem from defence expenditures which come at the expense of other forms of national expenditure. Such effects obtain even in those countries experiencing higher overall rates of growth from increased allocations to defence. In particular, countries with an indigenous arms industry may suffer a deterioration in the distribution of income from added defence expenditures. The same may also occur in military regimes as the authorities shift income from urban consumers to industrial groups.[23] A major limitation of these studies is that, by their nature, cross-sectional studies are very aggregative, such that applying them to specific countries is hazardous at best.

Obviously they are also incapable of capturing the dynamics associated with time.[24] Lebovic and Ishaq's[25] study of defence spending in the Middle

East attempts to overcome these deficiencies. Using a pooled time-series, cross-sectional analysis on various groupings of Middle Eastern states, they found that higher military spending tended to suppress economic growth in the non-oil states of the Middle East during the 1973–84 period. However, while Lebovic and Ishaq drew on time-series data, they were not able to incorporate the potential effects of lags between the time defence expenditures occur, and the period of maximum economic impact.

In this regard, Babin[26] has noted that incorporating the time variable into the analysis can be critical because some relationships that may exist over time disappear in the short run and vice versa. This implies that, at the national level, development usually requires a series of changes that occur through systems, which involve organizations, agencies, economic structures and technological variables. Consequently, as Babin concludes, it unjustifiable to assume that a country's defence spending will have an immediate, or even short-term, effect on national economic performance. Babin's main finding was that while short-run economic impacts of defence expenditure may be nil or even negative, the longer- term effect on growth is likely to be positive.

Along these lines, Kick and Sharda's[27] analysis suggests that an increase in the military manpower ratio has a significant positive effect on infrastructure and social welfare. This impact occurs with a long (12-year) time lag. Kick and Sharda also found that the relationship over a 12-year period is positive. Militarization, whether measured by expenditures or size of the military, does contribute to development.

Finally, recent work at the International Monetary Fund[28] suggests positive gains from reduced allocations to the military. The most recent of these studies[29] identified a substantial long-run "peace dividend" in the form of higher capacity output. This, in turn, may result from: (1) markedly lower military expenditure levels achieved in most regions during the late 1980s; and (2) further military spending cuts that might become possible in the future if global peace is sustained and deepened over time.

THE ISSUE OF CAUSATION

Nearly all of these studies have implicitly assumed a pattern of causation: defence expenditures are either politically and/or strategically driven and hence exogenous; or, instead, allocations to the military may simply reflect the underlying resource base (the ability to finance) and are hence endogenous. This is an important point, since many of the contradictory findings on militaries' economic impacts stem from differences in model construction, while the act of model construction in itself implicitly assumes that defence expenditures are either endogenous or exogenous.

It follows that before drawing any definitive conclusions as to the impact of defence expenditures, one must satisfactorily address the issue of causation. Fortunately several statistical tests are gaining wider acceptance for this purpose. To date, the original and most widely used causality test is one developed by Granger.[30]

The Granger Test

Granger defines causality such that *X* causes (G-C) *Y* if *Y* can be predicted more accurately in the sense of mean-square error, with the use of past values of *X* than without using past *X*. Based upon the definition of Granger causality, a simply bivariate autoregressive model for defence and gross domestic product (GDP) can be specified as follows:

$$GDP(t) = c + \sum_{i=1}^{p} a(i)GDP(t-i) + \sum_{j=1}^{q} b(j)DEF(t-j) + u(t) \qquad 6.1$$

$$DEF(t) = c + \sum_{i=1}^{r} d(i)DEF(t-1) + \sum_{j=1}^{s} e(j)GDP(t-j) + v(t) \qquad 6.2$$

where *DEF* = defence expenditures; *p*, *q*, *r* and *s* are lag lengths for each variable in the equation; and *u* and *v* are serially uncorrelated white-noise residuals. By assuming that error terms (*u*, *v*) are "nice", ordinary least-squares (OLS) becomes the appropriate estimation method.[31]

Within the framework of unrestricted and restricted models, a joint F-test is appropriate for causal detection:

$$F = \frac{RSS(r) - RSS(u) / (df(r) - df(u))}{RSS(u) / df(u)} \qquad 6.3$$

where *RSS*(*r*) and *RSS*(*u*) are the residual sum of squares of restricted and unrestricted models, respectively; and *df*(*r*) and *df*(*u*) are, respectively, the degrees of freedom in restricted and unrestricted models.

The Granger test detects causal directions in the following manner: first, unidirectional causality from *DEF* to *GDP* if the F-test rejects the null hypothesis that past values of *DEF* in equation (6.1) are insignificantly different from zero, and if the F-test cannot reject the null hypothesis that past values of *GDP* in equation (6.2) are insignificantly different from zero. That is, *DEF* causes *GDP*, but *GDP* does not cause *DEF*. Unidirectional causality runs from *GDP* to *DEF* if the reverse is true. Second, bidirectional causality runs between *DEF* and *GDP* if both F-test statistics reject the null hypotheses in equations (6.1) and (6.2). Finally, no causality exists between DEF and GDP if we cannot reject both null hypotheses at the conventional significance level.

Joerding[32] has tested the defence-growth hypothesis using Granger causality methods. That is, he tested for the assumed exogeneity of defence budgets. Using a pooled sample containing 15 observations from each of 57 countries, Joerding employed a multivariate model which also included investment and government spending and concluded that defence expenditures are not strongly exogenous and that previous studies were flawed.

While Joerding's work provides insight into the nature of the relationship between defence and growth, there are three issues that merit further attention, as suggested by LaCivita and Frederiksen.[33] First, Joerding lumps all countries into one sample. This suggests a commonality of causal relationships across diverse economic environments. As Frederiksen and myself have demonstrated, splitting a pooled sample into separate groups (in their case based on the level of relative resource constraints) can lead to quite different results.[34] Second, by aggregating the sample, Joerding assumed a common lag structure for all of the countries in the sample (in his study, four years on the defence and growth variables). It seems reasonable to hypothesize that if a causal relationship does exist (either defence to growth or growth to defence) one could expect the time lags to differ from country to country. And finally, Joerging's method for choosing lag length was *ad hoc*.

The results of Granger causality tests depend critically on the choice of lag length.[35] If the chosen length is less than the true lag length, the omission of relevant lags can cause bias. If the chosen lag is greater than the true lag length, the inclusion of irrelevant lags causes estimates to be inefficient. While Joerding chose his lag lengths based on preliminary partial autocorrelation methods, there is no *a priori* reason to assume lag lengths equal for all of our sample countries. For example, in a study of the Philippines, Frederiksen and LaCivita[36] found no statistical relationship between growth and defence when both variables had a lag equal to four. With a lag length of two periods, however, growth caused defence. Since both lag lengths are arbitrary, one cannot form an objective conclusion as to the direction of causation.

The Hsaio Procedure

To overcome such difficulties noted above, Hsaio[37] developed a systematic method for assigning lags. This method combines Granger causality and Akaike's final prediction error (*FPE*), the (asymptotic) mean-square prediction error, to determine the optimum lag for each variable. In an article examining the problems encountered in choosing lag lengths, Thornton and Batten[38] found Hsaio's method to be superior to both arbitrary lag length selection and several other systematic procedures for determining lag length.

The first step in Hsaio's procedure is to perform a series of autoregressive regressions on the dependent variable. In the first regression, the dependent variable has a lag of one, and this increases by one in each succeeding regression. Here, we estimate M regressions of the form:

$$G(t) = a + \sum_{i=1}^{m} b(t-1)G(t-i) + e(i) \qquad 6.4$$

where the values of m range from 1 to M. For each regression, we compute the *FPE* in the following manner:

$$FPE(m) = \frac{T+m+1}{T-m-1} ESS(m) / T \qquad 6.5$$

where: T is the sample size, and $FPE(m)$ and $ESS(m)$ are the final prediction error and the sum of squared errors, respectively. The optimal lag length, m^*, is the lag length which produces the lowest *FPE*. Having determined m^*, additional regressions expand the equation with the lags on the other variable added sequentially in the same manner used to determine m^*. Thus we estimate four regressions of the form:

$$G(t) = a + \sum_{i=1}^{m^*} b(t-1)G(t-1) + \sum_{i=1}^{n} c(t-1)D(t-1) + e(i) \qquad 6.6$$

with n ranging from one to four. Computing the final prediction error for each regression as:

$$FPE(m^*,n) = \frac{T+m^*+n+1}{T-m^*-n-1} ESS(m^*,n) / T \qquad 6.7$$

we choose the optimal lag length for D, n^* as the lag length which produces the lowest *FPE*. Using the final prediction error to determine lag length is equivalent to using a series of F-tests with variable levels of significance.[39]

The first term measures the estimation error and the second term measures the modelling error. The *FPE* criterion has a certain optimality property[40] that "balances the risk due to bias when a lower order is selected and the risk due to increases in the variance when a higher order is selected." As noted by Judge *et al.*,[41] an intuitive reason for using the *FPE* criterion is that longer lags increase the first term but decrease the *RSS* of the second term, and thus the two opposing forces are optimally balanced when their product reaches its minimum.

Depending on the value of the final prediction errors, four cases are possible:

(1) *Defence causes growth*. This occurs when the prediction error for growth falls when the equation includes defence. In addition, when growth is added to the defence equation, the final prediction error increases;

(2) *Growth causes defence*. This occurs when the prediction error of growth increases when defence is added to the regression equation for growth, and is reduced when growth is added to the regression equation for defence;
(3) *Feedback*. This occurs when the final prediction error decreases when defence is added to the growth equation, and the final prediction error decreases when growth is added to the defence equation; or
(4) *No relationship*. This occurs when the final prediction error increases when defence is added to the growth equation, and also increases when growth is added to the defence equation.

METHODOLOGY[42]

Several conceptual problems remain. Most economic time-series are non-stationary. Stationarity is an important property as it guarantees that there are no fundamental changes in the structure of the process that would render prediction difficult or impossible. To overcome this problem, I have used the rates of growth of each variable in the estimated equations.[43] Regressing these transformed series on a constant and time produced coefficients that were different from zero for all countries. Similar regressions of the untransformed levels indicated the presence of a trend.

The region's recent defence expenditures show great diversity (see Table 6.1) with few generalizations possible. Clearly, progress in the Arab–Israeli peace process has yet to be reflected in the region's attitude towards defence issues.[44] In many countries weapons systems are being upgraded and expanded, and gaps in national defences are being filled with new acquisitions. Across the Middle East, defence budgets account for anything from 3.3 per cent to 14 per cent of GDP: the European average is 1.85 per cent of GDP.

Of course one must be wary of over-generalizing. Israel's economy is fundamentally different from those of other countries in the region; it is more akin to some of the European economies. Within the Arab Middle East there are important differences between the major oil-exporting countries and those with far less or no oil, and there are also important country differences aside from oil.[45] In the sections below, the analysis has been confined to the economies of Israel Saudi Arabia, Egypt, Syria and Jordan, where, as Eliyahu Kanovsky notes, the relationship between economic stagnation and other socio-economic ills, along with the growth of Islamic fundamentalism, together constitute a grave threat to the longer-term durability of Arab–Israeli peace agreements.[46]

Table 6.1 Defence spending: Middle East and North Africa, 1985–95 (US$ million)

Country	*1985*	*1993*	*1994*	*1995*	*Growth Rate*	
					1985/95	*1993/95*
Sample Countries						
Saudi	23 603	16 450	14 275	13 200	–5.6	–10.4
Egypt	3 400	2 480	2 710	2 960	–1.4	9.2
Israel	6 640	6 200	6 700	6 900	0.4	1.9
Jordan	791	430	433	448	–5.5	–24.7
Syria	4 580	2 380	2 460	2 620	–5.4	–24.4
GCC						
Bahrain	198	251	248	253	2.5	0.4
Kuwait	2 360	3 010	3 090	2 910	2.1	–1.7
Oman	2 834	1 920	1 900	1 590	–5.6	–9.0
Qatar	394	330	302	326	–1.9	–0.6
Other Middle East						
Iran	18 700	4 860	2 300	2 460	–18.4	–28.9
Iraq	16 910	2 600	2 700	n/a	n/a	n/a
Lebanon	263	275	310	343	2.7	14.2
Yemen	1 041	355	318	345	–10.5	–42.4
North Africa						
Algeria	1 250	1 360	1 130	1 330	0.6	8.5
Libya	1 775	1 090	967	960	–6.0	–26.5
Morocco	850	1 090	1 230	1 210	3.6	19.3
Tunisia	550	231	225	262	–7.1	44.9

Source: *The Military Balance, 1994–95* (London: International Institute for Strategic Studies), 1995.

RESULTS

The results show great diversity across the sample of countries. In fact, no one pattern dominates the findings, suggesting that generalizations about the economic motivations for increasing or decreasing defence expenditures are of little value. The alleged peace dividend may be high for the region as a whole, but for several individual countries it is problematic that a reduction in defence expenditures would provide a major boom to their economies.

Israel

The patterns for Israel are particularly interesting and in many respects are more complex than for the other countries examined. The dominant pattern is one of feedback, whereby increases in defence expenditures impact positively on the economy (equation 1, Table 6.2). In turn, economic growth tends to generate additional resources to allow a further expansion in defence. The same pattern also holds for the defence burden (equation 2, Table 6.2). That is, an increase in the growth of the share of defence in GNP tends to increase the subsequent rate of growth in GDP. Here however the link between increased defence burdens and GDP is considerably weaker than the simple Defence → GDP linkages. This pattern seems to hold mainly when defence is not increasing its budgetary share (more specifically the growth in defence share of the budget). When this occurs (Equation 3, Table 6.2) there is a weak reduction in the growth of GDP. Finally, a particularly strong linkage occurs between increases in armed forces (per 1000 population) and GDP. Here, increases in the growth of the armed forces exert a strong (Equation 4, Table 6.2) stimulus to GDP. This stimulus occurs quickly, with the optimal lag around one year.

These findings suggest that defence expenditures in Israel have acted as a positive stimulus to overall economic expansion, but the precise nature of these links is unclear. However, it appears that the government has little incentive from a purely economic point of view in reducing defence expenditure. Presumably the reduction in defence expenditures would have to be replaced by some other type of expenditure to avoid increased unemployment and a slowdown in economic activity.

The ability of defence expenditures to stimulate the economy is consistent with a model of foreign aid recently developed by McGuire,[47] in which foreign aid creates several price and income movements in the recipient country. For Israel, aid from the United States has created an indirect stimulus to investment via the complementarity between investment and defence. In addition, the aid provides significant resources via tax relief to the private sector. Subsequently these resources flow into capital formation: "It appears in summary, that a significant fraction of United States aid goes to support capital formation in Israel via this diversion of resources."[48] In short, United States military grants to Israel have not only allowed the country to increase military expenditures rapidly in the short run, but, perhaps more importantly, to increase them in a way not detrimental to investment and economic growth.

Jordan

In contrast to Israel, Jordanian defence expenditures have tended to respond to an expanding resource base; that is, they have been passive in that they

Table 6.2 Defence expenditure, causal linkages with the macroeconomy: Israel, Jordan and Syria

Causal Relationship	*Time Period*	*Direction of Causation*	*Optimal Lag (years)*	*Optimal Lag strength*
Rates of Growth: Measures of Defence and GDP				
Israel				
1. Defence/GDP	1970–93	[Feedback]		
		MILX→GDP (+)	(3)	Moderate
		GDP→MILX (+)	(1)	Weak
2. Defence burden/GDP	1970–93	[Feedback]		
		MILX→GDP (+)	(3)	Weak
		GDP→MILX (+)	(1)	Weak
3. Defence budget share/GDP	1970–93	MILX→GDP (–)	(1)	Weak
4. Armed forces/GDP	1970–93	AF→GDP (+)	(1)	Strong
Jordan				
5. Defence/GDP	1970–94	GDP→MILX (+)	(3)	Strong
6. Armed forces/GDP	1970–93	AF→GDP (–)	(1)	Weak
7. Arms imports share of total imports/GDP	1970–93	No Relationship		
Syria				
8. Defence/GDP	1970–90	MILX→GDP (–)	(1)	Weak
9. Defence burden/GDP	1970–90	MILX→GDP (–)	(1)	Weak
10. Armed forces/GDP	1970–90	GDP→AF (+)	(1)	Weak
11. Defence budget share/GDP	1970–90	MILX→GDP (–)	(1)	Moderate

Note: Summary of results obtained from Granger causality tests using a Hsaio procedure to determine the optimal lag; i.e., a four-year lag indicates that most of the impact from the expenditures or GDP in any one year tends to be distributed over four successive years.

have tended to respond to underlying economic trends rather than initiating or modifying those trends. On an overall basis, increases in the armed forces have had a fairly negative impact on GDP. While one could only speculate as to the cause of this pattern, the lost output stemming from shifting workers from civilian to military activities would seem to be a logical place to start. However, it is clear that the country could significantly reduce its allocations to defence without incurring the risk of deflation. Conceivably in Jordan's case the major problems associated with a lasting Middle East peace agreement would be what to do with the resources that do not have to be earmarked for defence. In a recent assessment of the Jordanian economy the World Bank argued that in the short run, while peace may offer Jordan some immediate benefits arising primarily from an investment-led boom in the West Bank and Gaza Strip, it also carries substantial risks to macroeconomic stability.[49] The real question then is whether the country has the capacity to manage these increased risks through improved macroeconomic management and further efforts to strengthen the financial system.

Syria

In contrast to the patterns found in Israel and Jordan, defence expenditures have had a generally negative, albeit weak impact on the Syrian economy. On the one hand, this impact has tended to be short, averaging one year, but it is consistent across defence expenditures, the defence burden and the share of defence in the central government budget. On the other hand, the increased economic growth appears to provide additional resources to expand the armed forces.

Egypt

The dominant pattern in Egypt (Table 6.3) over this period is one of no statistically significant links between defence expenditures and the overall economy. It appears that increased defence expenditures tend to produce a stimulus for increased capital formation, but these linkages are weak. The ensuing link between investment and GDP is rather strong, making the overall impact of defence expenditures difficult to assess.

Saudi Arabia

Saudi Arabian patterns (Table 6.4) are more complex in that it is necessary to distinguish between total GDP and that of non-oil GDP. Given its high oil component, it is safe to assume that GDP could be affected by defence only under highly unusual circumstances. Therefore, it makes sense to test the impact defence may have had on the non-oil component of GDP. That is, did

Table 6.3 Defence expenditure, causal linkages with the macroeconomy: Egypt

Causal Relationship	*Time Period*	*Direction of Causation*	*Optimal Lag (years)*	*strength*
1. Defence expenditures/GDP	1970–90	No relationship		
2. Defence burden/GDP	1970–90	No relationship		
3. Armed forces/GDP	1970–90	No relationship		
4. Defence expenditures investment	1970–93	MILX→Investment (+)	(2)	Weak
5. Defence burden/investment	1970–93	MILX→Investment (+)	(2)	Weak
6. Armed forces/investment	1970–93	[Feedback]		
		Investment→MILX (+)	(4)	Weak
		MILX→INVEST (+)	(4)	Moderate
7. Investment/GDP	1970–93	Investment→GDP (+)	(2)	Strong

Note: See the note to Table 6.2.

Table 6.4 Defence expenditure, causal linkages with the macroeconomy: Saudi Arabia

Causal Relationship	*Time Period*	*Direction of Causation*	*Optimal Lag (years)*	*Optimal Lag strength*
Gross Domestic Product				
1. Defence/GDP	1970–91	GDP→MILX (+)	(1)	Weak
2. Defence burden/GDP	1970–91	GDP→MILX (+)	(1)	Weak
3. Armed forces/GDP	1970–91	No relationship		
Non-Oil GDP				
4. Defence/non-oil GDP	1970–91	MILX→GDP(+)	(2)	Moderate
5. Defence burden/non-oil GDP	1970–91	MILX→GDP (+)	(1)	Moderate
6. Armed forces/non-oil GDP	1970–91	Armed forces→GDP (+)	(2)	Moderate
7. Goverment investment/non-oil GDP	1970–91	[Feedback]		
		Investment→GDP (+)	(2)	Weak
		GDP→Investment (–)	(1)	Weak
8. Private investment/non-oil GDP	1970–91	[Feedback]		
		Investment→GDP (+)	(1)	Strong
		GDP→Investment (+)	(1)	Weak
Private Investment				
9. Defence expenditure/private investment	1970–91	MILX→Investment (+)	(3)	Weak
10. Government investment/private investment	1970–91	[Feedback]		
		Private→Public (+)	(1)	Moderate
		Public→Private (+)	(1)	Weak

Note: See the note to Table 6.2.

defence create linkages with the local economy or was it in competition with the private sector for resources? The results are as follows.

As anticipated, causation is largely from GDP to defence; that is, an increased resource base is used to fund additional allocations to the military. The impact here is quick, but not necessarily strong (Equations 1 and 2, Table 6.4). This may be due in part to the volatility of oil revenues and the stability in defence procurement contracts, once signed. That is, during periods of high oil revenues, contracts may be let that require expenditures over multiple years. Fluctuations in oil revenues would then mask this underlying linkage.

For non-oil revenues the pattern is largely one of defence expenditures providing a mild stimulus to the economy. Again, this stimulus occurs fairly quickly with an average lag of about two years. In the Saudi Arabian case the impact of private investment and government investment on GDP were also examined. Here it was found that private investment had a strong impact on non-oil GDP, with public investment a much weaker linkage. Of the three, defence expenditures were stronger than government investment as a stimulus to the domestic economy, but weaker than private investment.

While the actual Saudi Arabian defence expenditures appear to be linked to oil revenues and can be expected to decline, the country does appear to derive some domestic benefits from increased allocations to the military. Whether these are linkages with the country's offset programme are unclear. The fact is, these linkages appear stronger than they would be with government investment, for instance. Clearly the main problem for the Saudis will entail finding ways to replace defence expenditures (which are not likely to increase due to budgetary constraints) with other types of expenditures, such as private investment. This is a goal of both the current and the prior development plans. However, given the low productivity of capital investment, the country would apparently gain little from diverting expenditures from the military to further expansion in infrastructure.

CONCLUSION

These results suggest the difficulties in generalizing over possible peace dividends or even the willingness of countries to reduce defence expenditures as part of a Middle East peace process. Israel and Saudi Arabia probably have the least to gain from reduced defence expenditures; they were the only countries to experience a consistently positive linkage from defence to GDP, although the Saudi links are from defence to non-oil GDP. Egypt does not appear to gain any direct growth benefits from defence expenditures; however, there is some evidence that increased defence may stimulate capital investment. That country might benefit from a more detailed analysis to discern the nature of this linkage and whether or not other types of government expenditure might provide a stimulus of the same order of magnitude. Jordan would be the next most likely country to gain from reduced defence expenditures. As noted, this effect would not be a true peace dividend, since defence expenditures do not impact negatively on the economy. However, it is clear that Jordanians have many opportunities to productively use the resources that might have ordinarily gone to the military. Syria appears to be the country with the greatest economic stake in a lasting Middle East peace. Syria was the one country that derived negative impacts on economic growth from defence expenditures, and as a result it is the only candidate for a true peace dividend.

In general, these findings support Kanovsky's contentions[50] that (1) there is very little likelihood of any further significant reductions in regional military expenditures; and (2) that even if such reductions were to take place, there are many other impediments to economic growth in the Arab Middle East: in particular, adverse economic policies and poor political processes. His feeling is that peace agreements, however desirable in their own right, will not solve the basic economic problems of these countries. Only far-reaching changes in economic policy can extricate them from stagnation, unemployment and underemployment, debilitating poverty and a widening and dangerous gap between the few rich and the many poor.

APPENDIX: TESTING FOR UNIT ROOTS AND CO-INTEGRATION

As noted above, the time series must be stationary to yield valid Granger tests.[51] In this regard the finding of a unit root in a time series indicates non-stationarity.

In a well-known paper, Dickey and Fuller[52] suggested a method for computing a test for a unit root in a time series, and presented critical values for their proposed tests with and without the trend variable included. Dickey– Fuller tests were performed using PCGive Version 7. In a simple case where:

$$xt = a + bxt - 1 + et$$

where $b = 1$, which generates a random walk (with drift if a not equal to 0). Here, the autoregressive coefficient is unitary and stationarity is violated. A process with no unit or explosive roots is said to be $I(0)$; a process is $I(d)$ if it needs to be differenced d times to become $I(0)$. The Durbin–Watson statistic (*DW*)for the level of a variable offers one simple characterization of this integrated property. For example, if xt is a random walk, *DW* will be very small. If ^{xt} is white noise, *DW* will be around 2. Very low *DW* values thus indicate that a transformed model may be desirable, perhaps including a mixture of differenced and disequilibrium variables.

The tests[53] consisted of first performing the Dickey–Fuller procedure on the logs of all variables: Here, the t-test on the lagged value is the relevant statistic, with critical values provided in MacKinnon,[54] and Davidson and MacKinnon[55]. As noted above, these tests indicated non-stationarity. Next, tests were performed on the first differences of the log values. In all cases these were significant at the 95 per cent level (and often at the 99 per cent level).

Notes

1. Peter Kemp, "The Challenges of a Changing World: Middle Eastern Political and Economic Trends", *Middle East Economic Digest* 38(51) (23 December 1994), p. 2.
2. Francis Tusa, "New Prospects Make Waves in the Gulf: Naval Equipment Procurement in the Middle East", *Middle East Economic Digest* 39(49) (8 December 1995), p. 12.
3. Peter Kemp, "In the Age of Peace, Security Starts at Home", *Middle East Economic Digest* 39(49) (8 December 1995), p. 8.
4. Steve Chan, "Military Expenditures and Economic Performance", in United States Arms Control and Disarmament Agency, *World Military Expenditures and Arms Transfers, 1986* (Washington: United States Arms Control and Disarmament Agency, 1987); and S. Deger and Robert West, "Introduction: Defense Expenditure, National Security and Economic Development in the Third World", in S. Deger and R. West, *Defense, Security and Development* (London: Francis Pinter, 1987).
5. Emile Benoit, "Growth and Defense in Developing Countries", *Economic Development and Cultural Change* 35 (1978), pp. 271–80.
6. P.C. Frederiksen and Robert E. Looney, "Defense Expenditures and Growth in Developing Countries", *Journal of Economic Development* 7 (1982), pp. 113–26.
7. K.W. Rothschild, "Military Expenditure, Exports and Growth", *Kyklos* 30 (1977), pp. 804–13.
8. David Lim, "Another Look at Growth and Defense in Less Developed Countries", *Economic Development and Cultural Change* 31 (1983), pp. 377–84.
9. S. Deger and S. Sen, "Military Expenditure, Spin-Off and Economic Development", *Journal of Development Economics* 12 (1983), pp. 67–83.
10. W. Leontief and F. Duchin, *Military Spending: Facts and Figures* (New York: Oxford University Press, 1983).
11. R. Faini, P. Annez and L. Taylor, "Defense Spending, Economic Structure and Growth: Evidence Among Countries and Over Time", *Economic Development and Cultural Change* 32 (1984), pp. 487–98.
12. B. Biswas and R. Ram, "Military Expenditures and Economic Growth in Less Developed Countries: An Augmented Model and Further Evidence", *Economic Development and Cultural Change* 35 (1986), pp. 361–72.
13. L. Grobar and R. Porter, "Benoit Revisited: Defense Spending and Economic Growth in LDCs", *Journal of Conflict Resolution* 33 (1989), pp. 318–45.
14. C. Wolf, "Economic Success, Stability and the 'Old' International Order", *International Security* 6 (1981), pp. 75–92.

15. P.C. Frederiksen and Robert E. Looney, "Defense Expenditures and Economic Growth in Developing Countries", *Armed Forces and Society* 10 (1983), pp. 633–46.
16. P.C. Frederiksen and R.E. Looney, "Another Look at the Defense Spending and Development Hypothesis", *Defense Analysis* 1 (1985), pp. 205–10.
17. S. Neuman, "International Stratification and Third World Military Industries", *International Organization* 38 (1984), pp. 172–3.
18. Robert E. Looney, "Impact of Arms Production on Third World Distribution and Growth", *Economic Development and Cultural Change* 38 (1989), pp. 145–54.
19. Robert E. Looney, "Factors Underlying Venezuelan Defense Expenditures 1950–83: A Research Note", *Arms Control* (May 1986), pp. 74–108; Robert E. Looney, "The Impact of Defense Expenditures on the Saudi Arabian Private Sector", *Journal of Arab Affairs* 6 (1987), pp. 198–229; and Robert E. Looney "The Role of Defense Expenditures in Iran's Economic Decline", *Iranian Studies* 21 (1988), pp. 52–83.
20. K. Giymah-Brempong, "Defense Spending and Economic Growth in Sub-Saharan Africa, An Econometric Investigation", *Journal of Peace Research* 30 (1989), pp. 79–90.
21. R.E. Looney and P.C. Frederiksen, "Defense Expenditures, External Public Ddebt and Growth in Developing Countries", *Journal of Peace Research* 23 (1986), pp. 329–86; N. Mohammed, "Defense Spending and Economic Growth in Sub-Saharan Africa, Comment on Giymah-Brempong", *Journal of Peace Research* 30 (1993), pp. 95–6; and N. Mohammed, "Economic Growth and Defense Spending in Sub-Saharan Africa, Benoit and Joerding Revisited", *Journal of African Economies* 2 (1993), pp. 145–56.
22. Robert E. Looney, "Military Keynesianism in the Third World: An Assessment of Non-Military Motivations for Arms Production", *Journal of Political and Military Sociology* 17 (1989), pp. 43–64; and Robert E. Looney, "A Post-Keynesian Analysis of Third World Military Expenditures", *Rivista Internazionale di Scienze Economiche e Commerciali* 38 (1991), pp. 779–98.
23. Robert E. Looney, "The Economic Impact of Rent Seeking and Military Expenditures in the Third World", *American Journal of Economics and Sociology* 48 (1989), pp. 11–30.
24. P.C. Frederiksen and R.E. Looney, "Budgetary Consequences of Defense Expenditures in Pakistan: Short-Run Impacts and Longer-Run Adjustments", *Journal of Peace Research* 31 (1994), pp. 11–18.
25. J. Lebovic and A. Ishaq, "Military Burden, Security Needs, and Economic Growth in the Middle East", *Journal of Conflict Resolution* 31 (1987), pp. 106–38.
26. N. Babin, "Military Spending, Economic Growth and the Time Factor", *Armed Forces and Society* 15 (1989), pp. 249–62.
27. E. Kick and B.D. Sharda, "Third World Militarization and Development", *Journal of Developing Societies* 2 (1986), pp. 49–67.
28. Dan Hewitt, "Military Expenditures 1972–1990, The Reasons Behind the Post–1985 Fall in World Military Spending", IMF Working Paper WP/93/18, March 1993; and Dan Hewitt, "Military Expenditures Worldwide, Determinants and Trends, 1972–1988, *Journal of Public Policy* 12 (1992), pp. 105–52.
29. Malcolm Knight, Norman Loayza and Delano Villanueva, "The Peace Dividend, Military Spending Cuts and Economic Growth", International Monetary Fund Working Paper WP/95/53, May 1995.

30. C.W.J. Granger, "Investigating Causal Relations by Econometric Models and Cross-Spectral Methods", *Econometrics* 37 (1969), pp. 424–38; and C.W.J. Granger "Some Recent Developments in a Concept of Causality", *Journal of Econometrics* 39 (1988), pp. 199–211.
31. If the disturbances of the model were serially correlated, the OLS estimates would be inefficient, although still unbiased, and would distort the causal relations. The existence of serial correlation was checked by using a maximum likelihood correlation for the first-order autocorrelation of the residuals [AR(1)]. The comparison of both OLS and AR(1) results indicated that no significant changes appeared in causal directions. Therefore, we can conclude "roughly" that serial correlation was not serious in this model.
32. W. Joerding, "Economic Growth and Defense Spending: Granger Causality", *Journal of Development* 21 (1986), pp. 35–40.
33. C.J. LaCivita and P.C. Frederiksen, "Defense Spending and Economic Growth: An Alternative Approach to the Causality Issue", *Journal of Development Economics* 35 (1991), pp. 117–26.
34. P.C. Frederiksen and Robert E. Looney, "Defense Expenditures and Economic Growth in Developing Countries", *Armed Forces and Society* 10 (1983), pp. 633–46; and Frederiksen and Looney, "Another Look at the Defense Spending and Development Hypothesis, *op. cit.*
35. A.R. Chowdhury, "A Causal Analysis of Defense Spending and Economic Growth", *Journal of Conflict Resolution* 35 (1991), pp. 80–97.
36. P.C. Frederiksen and C.J. LaCivita, "Defense Spending and Economic Growth: Time Series Evidence on Causality for the Philippines 1956–1982", *Journal of Philippine Development* 26 (1987), pp. 354–60.
37. C. Hsaio, "Autoregressive Modelling and Money–Income Causality Detection", *Journal of Monetary Economics* 6 (1981), pp. 85–106.
38. D.L. Thornton and D.S. Batten, "Lag-length Selection and Test of Granger Causality between Money and Income", *Journal of Money, Credit and Banking* 17 (1985), pp. 164–78.
39. Since the F statistic is redundant in this instance they are not reported here. They are, however, available from the author upon request.
40. Hsaio (1979), *op. cit.*, p. 326.
41. R.C. Judge, W. Hill, H. Griffiths, H. Lutkephol and T.C. Lee, *Introduction to the Theory and Practice of Econometrics* (New York, John Wiley, 1982).
42. The data for military expenditures used to carry out the Hsaio tests are from the United States Arms Control and Disarmament Agency, *World Military Expenditures and Arms Transfers, 1993–1994*. Annual data on GDP is from various issues of the International Monetary Fund, *International Financial Statistics Yearbook*. When consistent price deflators were not available, I have introduced the growth of the defence burden (the share of defence in GDP) in the regression equations. Saudi Arabian macroeconomic data is from the Saudi Arabian Monetary Agency, *Annual Report*, various issues. In the case of Saudi Arabia the non-oil GDP deflator is used to obtain constant price series.
43. The Dickey–Fuller method, first published in 1979, was used to address the issue of non-stationarity and co-integration aspects of the time series used. See the Appendix for a full discussion of the method.
44. Peter Kemp, "Arms Rise as Risks of War Recede", *Middle East Economic Digest Special Report: Defense* 38(49) (9 December 1994), p. 9.
45. Edmund O'Sullivan, "In Search of New Growth Strategies: Middle East Economies", *Middle East Economic Digest* 38 (17 January 1994), p. 2.

46. Eliyahu Kanovsky, "Middle East Economies and Arab–Israeli Peace Agreements", *Israel Affairs*, 1(4) (Summer 1995), pp. 22–39.
47. M.C. McGuire, "Foreign Assistance Investment and Defense: A Methodological Study with Application to Israel, 1960–1979", *Economic Development and Cultural Change* 35 (1987), pp. 847–73.
48. *Ibid*, p. 867.
49. World Bank, *Peace and the Jordanian Economy* (Washington: World Bank, 1994), p. 1.
50. Kanovsky, "Middle East Economics", *op. cit.*
51. A full discussion of these issues is given in C.W.J. Granger, "Some Recent Developments in a Concept of Causality", *op. cit*.
52. D.A. Dickey and W.A. Fuller, "Distribution of the Estimators for Autoregressive Time Series with a Unit Root", *Journal of the American Statistical Association* 74 (1979), pp. 427–31. See also Dickey and Fuller, "Likelihood Ratio Statistics for Autoregressive Time Series with a Unit Root", *Econometrica* 49 (1981), pp. 1057–72.
53. For a full description of the tests – the selection of lags and the process of differencing – see J.A. Dornik and D.F. Hendry, *PCGive Version 7.0: An Interactive Modelling System* (Oxford: University of Oxford 1992), pp. 111–12.
54. J.G. Mackinnon, "Critical Values for Cointegration Tests", in R.F. Engle and C.W.J. Granger (eds), *Long Run Economic Relationships* (Oxford: Oxford University Press (1991), pp. 267–76.
55. R. Davidson and J.G. Mackinnon, *Estimation and Inference in Econometrics* (Oxford: Oxford University Press, 1993).

7 Would Islamic Banks Help Lessen the Decline of Palestinian Banking?

J.W. Wright, Jr.[1]

INTRODUCTION

Palestinians have lived in the Israeli-occupied territories as a severely disadvantaged majority,[2] and the economic conditions in the West Bank and especially in the Gaza Strip have dramatically worsened since Arafat and Rabin's famous handshake. Rather than opening a new stage in the Middle East peace process, the economic agreements that have been signed seem to be using Palestinian capital flows to promote Israeli and Jordanian business interests in the region rather than promoting employment development among the Palestinians themselves. In no area of the economy is this more true than in the banking sector which, after three decades of steady decline, has little capital left to offer the small- and medium-sized business owners who are most likely to create employment opportunities quickly and productively. At the same time it is becoming increasingly clear that mortgage banking in these areas is not a workable option for distributing capital; there is no real facility for valuing capital on a long-term basis. The intensified restrictions Israel has placed on the movement of Palestinian goods and people also makes it nearly impossible for Palestinian businesses to borrow or for their Israeli partners to accurately write cash flow projections. Under such a legally unbalanced trade regime, banks fear lending on a property-collateral basis; this regime has made many bank portfolios in the area unsafe.[3]

Fortunately, the World Bank and other groups seem to have realized that the employment situation in the West Bank and Gaza is at a crisis point. As for the United States, the Wye Accord's pledge of an additional $400 million in emergency assistance shows their recognition of the seriousness of this situation. Unfortunately, the effects were limited and there was neither enough time nor funds available to attack the real problem: lacking capital mobilizations. The current answer to this critical problem is a social investment fund which would likely be funded by the World Bank. The problem with this approach is that there are still too few Palestinian institutions in the occupied territories that would be able to administer these fund distributions. Those best organized for the job are the Jordanian and Egyptian banks which have opened branches, but they have not been willing to reinvest locally. This situation helps the Jordanians and Egyptians to raise capital, while the Palestinian situation is made worse. Negotiations to stop these practices have already taken place, but the effectiveness of post-negotiations implementation remains a question.

These situations mean that controversies about solving the finance-gap problems revolve around both the means for distributing foreign aid funds and the development of viable financial networks. This chapter examines the agendas of social investment funds as compared to the aims and goals of Islamic banks and concludes that, if they were to be granted licenses by the Israeli authorities, Islamic banks might be able to provide an effective means for distributing funds while at the same time promoting regional trade.

Moreover, negotiators wanting to use economic means for promoting regional peace must also realize that Palestinians could easily be left out of developing financial and trade regimes. Jordan has signed a peace treaty with Israel and agreed to open its borders to regional trade. In return, Jordanian banks will be allowed to open their doors in some Palestinian communities. But the real agenda seems to be fostering Jordanian–Israeli trade, or by using Jordan rather than Palestine as a conduit for Israeli–Gulf trade. Certainly these agreements have not led to the interchange of more Palestinian labour into either Jordan or Israel,[4] or to the Gulf[5] (which had been predicted as part of the regional peace dividend, and this is not to mention a number of shifting intra-Levantine economic alliances)[6].

At the same time,the Palestinians are faced with an international community that does not look its way. Nearly $6 billion of development projects were proposed at the Amman economic summit, many of which will receive international aid funding, but the Palestinian firms received many fewer pledges for partnership funds than did the Egyptians, Jordanians or Israelis. The possible development of a Bank for Economic Cooperation and Development in the Middle East and North Africa that will "offer no concessionary financing and will provide a forum for high level dialogue" is meant to facilitate combining Gulf investment capital with highly-capitalized Arab–Israeli joint venture projects.[7] This plan would not only further redirect the flow of goods in the region in less-than-free market directions, but would also leave small Palestinian employers with few financial outlets.

Therefore, if the goal of the Central Bank of Palestine, for example, is to make a real Palestinian financial system possible, then its administrators will have to recognize the factors that constrain the flow of finance and investment into and within the occupied territories.[8] Chief among these are religion, regulation and repression.

There are numerous economic reasons why international aid agencies should consider using financial instruments that are compatible with Islamic economics when dealing with Palestinian businesses. Such an approach would be effective in helping to develop small and medium-sized Palestinian enterprises (SMEs) in the PA-controlled territories. There are also several reasons why collateral-based financing arrangements cannot work in the West Bank and Gaza, a fact which makes it imperative that alternative means for capital distribution be developed. In this context, Islamic banks could become vehicles for distributing development funding and import–export financing, or as effective administrators of social funds.

THE DECLINE OF MORTGAGE BANKING FOR SME FINANCING IN THE WEST BANK

The debate over SMEs has a special note of appeal for people wanting to encourage development of Palestinian businesses, and for firms that wish to increase trade between US and Arab manufacturers and retailers. There are several reasons. The first is that the current Palestinian economy has an inordinately strong base of small, family-owned, service-oriented businesses. This is partially due to an Arab culture that seems to gravitate towards mercantile commercial activities. Several Middle East historians, including Albert Hourani, Charles Issawi, Bernard Lewis and others, point out that Arab commerce has for centuries been built on caravan and mercantile trade. A number of economists and political-economists have likewise noticed that family-owned, merchant-oriented centres of influence meld into a uniquely Arab form of corporate conservatism.[9] This services-based mentality inhibits mortgage-based lending.

Another reason for the lack of property-based financing in the West Bank revolves around the migration of Palestinians to the Gulf states in the 1970s, which created a lack of industry-specific human resources. A significant "brain drain" took place as oil prices rose and the Arab Gulf states imported substantial quantities of labour from Palestine. For over a decade remittances flowed from the Gulf-financed family businesses throughout the Arab world.[10] No reliable sources exist on the amounts of money transferred to Palestine via worker remittances. However, it is known from the experiences of Jordanian migrants in the Gulf that remittances provided the sole source of income for millions of people, and that they were the source of start-up capital for 70 per cent of SMEs.[11] It was also the SMEs that bore the brunt of absorption costs associated with the expulsion of Palestinians from the Gulf states in the late 1980s and throughout the 1990s.[12]

However, the most compelling explanations for the service-dominated Palestinian economy in the territories are not cultural or social, but political. The preference of Palestinians for small-scale service businesses is more importantly a reflection of the uncertain and erratic commercial and regulatory environments that prevail because of countervailing government oppression.[13] The Israeli government has obstructed most attempts by Palestinians under occupation to develop their land into productive industrial facilities, and has denied whenever possible licenses to Arabs wanting to start businesses. These formal and informal prohibitions are not limited to Palestinians but are applied as well to non-Jewish American and European firms. This is done via Israeli legislation that supports what the Knesset Finance Committee calls "a strategic interest group".[14] Committee rulings require that foreign investors wishing to buy "strategic properties" must file affidavits that prove their commitment to Zionism, a proof which generally consists of documentation that a firm is a Jewish majority-owned firm.

More lessons about the costs of economic restrictions placed on the Palestinians by the Israeli government can be learned from the financial raids on Beit Sahour during the *Intifada*. The Israeli government imposes separate and higher tax structures on Palestinian-Arab businesses than it does on Israeli-Jewish businesses. The vigour of tax collection, moreover, varied widely and arbitrarily from property to property. One business owner was required to pay taxes ten times his annual revenues for the preceding year. One hundred per cent of a firm's annual earnings was not an unusual tax.[15] The way these taxes were levied became an issue in 1975 and 1976 when a value-added tax was imposed on Palestinian consumers in the West Bank and Gaza. However, in 1987, as a measure of civil disobedience, 90 per cent of the residents of Beit Sahour refused to file tax forms.

The Israeli reaction was unexpected and severe. In September 1989 the military government imposed a 42-day curfew on the residents and merchants of the town, enforced by the closure of streets and businesses by Israeli army units. Many Palestinian business owners suffered personal injury during this siege, and others lost their lives. In a series of expeditions that were conducted at times when all Palestinian electrical and communications devices had been shut down, the Israeli banking system removed millions of dollars from the individual bank accounts of Palestinians, and an additional 350 families suffered the seizure of their commercial and personal property by the Israeli military. During the six-week curfew an estimated $7.5 million in cash and capital were taken from Arab families and businesses.[16]

It is important to remember that the raid on Beit Sahour began some 20 years after the initial Israeli assault on the Arab banking system in 1967. With the occupation of the West Bank and Gaza Strip came the forcible shutdown of eight Arab banks and their 32 branches. Deposits of major accounts were frozen, records of investments were either destroyed or transferred to the Bank of Israel, and the balances of persons active in the resistance movement were confiscated. It was not until 1981 that the Bank of Palestine reopened in Gaza, and it was only in 1992 that this bank was allowed to deal in foreign currency exchanges. Until 1994 the Bank of Palestine in Gaza and a branch of the Cairo-Amman Bank in Nablus were the only Arab banks allowed to operate in the occupied territories. In contrast, over 30 Israeli bank branches operate in the West Bank.[17]

There is no doubt that Israeli aggressions have stifled business development efforts,[18] and that they continue to plague Palestinian trade and development.[19] To these must be added the socio-economic costs suffered by "administrative detainees" (political prisoners held without formal charge or trial) at the Ansar detention camps and elsewhere.[20] Finally, Arab-owned businesses in the occupied territories have no long-term assessable property values, trends of cash flows remain at the whim of the Israeli tax authority, and the Israeli banking system cannot be entrusted to protect Arab investors' deposits or to maintain vital confidentiality. Nor are these situations changed in any way by the current peace agreements.

The effects of these economic messages, then, are four-fold.

- First, Palestinian businesses under occupation have gravitated toward the service sector because these types of businesses require less capital investment.
- Second, Palestinians have avoided the reinvestment of earnings in capital goods because these are always subject to confiscation; they have, therefore, either hoarded money or invested in grey market institutions and offshore banks.
- Third, Palestinians have, as a means of non-violent protest, resisted the use of Israeli banks for credit or for savings.
- Fourth, the perception prevails among Palestinians that there is little hope that a legal, indigenous bank will be established, driving local money market exchanges underground. Moreover, history has taught Palestinians and other non-Israelis that too much profitability leaves them susceptible to physical detention and their properties as likely candidates for confiscation.

The net result is that mortgage banking will not work as a means for distributing capital to SMEs in the occupied territories: asset values are indeterminable, service-based skills are not mortgageable, and property rights and legal representation do not exist for Palestinian business owners in any meaningful sense. Therefore, if the objective is to develop markets in the West Bank and Gaza Strip, then the use of venture capital and equity-partnership financing arrangements for Arab businesses must be facilitated. If it is desirable for Arab business owners to be able to use and trust new financial institutions, then facilities not associated with Israeli banks must be promoted. I propose that the World Bank's lead be followed: the situation should be approached from a "social investment fund" perspective. Furthermore, the use of an Islamic bank as a social investment fund administrator for Muslim-oriented SME financing contracts should be considered.

WILL THE NEW BANKING AGREEMENTS REVERSE THE DECLINE?

There are fewer banks in the West Bank and Gaza today than there were in the last days of the Ottoman Empire.[21] The financial system in the territories has indeed declined to levels lower than 100 years ago. The primary effort to date to stem the decline of the Palestinian financial base has been the development of the Palestinian Monetary Authority (PMA). In this section I rely heavily on quotes from Annex V: Protocol on Economic Relations, signed in Washington DC on 28 September 1995, and on reports from the European Union's *Peace Media* series.[22] The premise of these negotiations was to further define and facilitate implementation of the economic agreements reached in the Paris Protocol a year earlier, to enhance "the notion of 'limited autonomy' for the Palestinians".[23] According to the annex: "The PMA will act as the Palestinian Authority's official economic and financial advisor."

However, what is most odd about this institutional arrangement is not its level of autonomy, but rather its lack of control over monetary policy. From the PA perspective, the PMA is only an advisory board. It does not, like the US Federal Reserve, have the right to conduct open market operations without approval from either the PA or the Israelis. Indeed, the PMA can specifically only "predict its supervision", but in the process it must, by treaty, "re-license each of the five branches of the Israeli banks operating in the Gaza Strip and the West Bank". It does not have the authority to act autonomously in matters of fiscal policy, it can essentially only approve of Arab bank expansion if this expansion is approved by both the "home authority and host authority", and it must allow Israeli bank expansion.

More troubling is the bank's lack of control over essential Central Bank functions. The following statements are primary examples of how control is established:

- First, all banks in the territories must accept the new Israeli shekel (NIS).
- Second, when the PMA collects the reserve requirements it set for banks under its jurisdiction, it must hold those reserves in Israeli shekels.
- Third, "[t]he liquidity requirements on the various kinds of NIS deposits in banks operating in the area will not be less than 4% to 8%"; and it will be only annually that the PMA and the Bank of Israel will meet to determine "the amount of convertible NIS during a calendar year".
- Fourth, the PMA must "supply temporary finance for banks operating in the region", including Israeli banks.
- Fifth, "[t]he clearing of money orders and transactions between banks operating in Israel will be done between the Israeli and the Palestinian

clearing houses on a same working day basis", but there is no reciprocal agreement that forces Israeli banks to process funds this quickly.

- Sixth, "the exchange of foreign currency for new Israeli shekels and *vice versa* by the PMA will be carried through the Bank of Israel Dealing Room"; however, "[t]he BOI [Bank of Israel] will not be obliged to convert in any single month more than 1/5 of the semi-annual amount", and, in addition, there will be "monthly ceilings on such conversions".

There are several problems with these arrangements. Foremost among them is that without control of reserve requirements, the PMA can neither set money supply policies nor regulate interest rates. Moreover, because it must provide a discount window to Israeli as well as Palestinian banks, it must ultimately target portions of its temporary fund accounts at lending to Israeli borrowers. This situation essentially forbids the PMA from reinvesting its entire portfolio in Arab-owned banks or institutions. And, because the PMA does not have a foreign currency dealing room, and because the Bank of Israel is only required to deal with the PMA in limited amounts, the PMA has no emergency borrowing facilities. This situation leads to the mobilization of informal-sector Palestinian capital into formal-sector Israeli institutions.

These agreements also take key profit centres away from the PMA. First, the delivery of money orders and other funds on a one-day basis without reciprocity leaves the PMA without standing moneys on which it cannot earn interest (while it is the Bank of Israel which is accruing this needed revenue). The lack of a foreign currency dealing room also takes away the PMA's ability to make trading profits in the international currency markets.

There are all sorts of requirements on the PMA, only a few of which are mentioned briefly here, that pose serious problems for the bank. One is that the primary control of its portfolio policy lies with administrators in the Bank of Jordan, and the requirement that a "special fund" be created by the PMA "to provide political risk insurance to the industrial estate", again without mention of reciprocity from the Bank of Israel. It is also interesting that the fastest growing bank in the occupied territories is the Arab Bank, an essentially Jordanian enterprise that is closely controlled by a predominately Arab Christian board and executive staff. This situation does not encourage the Palestinian Muslim majority to have faith in the new banking regime. Without control of interest policy, without the ability to run market operations or plan its own portfolio investment policies, without the means to create trading and processing profits, without the ability to even offer licenses without prior approval, the new Palestinian Monetary Authority does not seem to have the tools it needs to stem the decline of the Palestinian banking system. Indeed, evidence shows that the downward spiral continues.[24]

AN OUTLINE OF ISLAMIC FINANCE

This situation clearly calls for the development of an alternative system of banking that will both engender trust from majority patrons and break through established institutional barriers in ways that will get funds directly into the hands of entrepreneurs and small business owners. One alternative solution would be to promote the establishment of Islamic banks, institutions that by definition must make equity-based participatory investments.

Let me begin by discussing some of the basic tenets of Islamic economics that have led to the proposition of modern Islamic banking. The foundations of Islamic finance lie in the aim to protect tribesmen against "inimical self-interests and undue profiteering."[25] The *Qur'an* supports a free market system in which all resources, human and natural, are employed to full capacity, making it the duty of every Muslim to pursue productive and fair business activities.[26] Merchants are told, on the one hand, to "let there be amongst you traffic and trade, by mutual goodwill" (Sura 4:29), and on the other hand, to eschew hoarding, usury, monopolies, extortion, and pre-emptive or unfair foreclosure in bankruptcy.[27]

The dialogue over the adaptability of Islamic financial precepts to commercial business practices is relatively new. It has been only in the last 50 years that Islamic banks, or banks operating without "the interest rate mechanism",[28] have been formed. Modern Islamic banking originated in efforts to distribute capital to rural farmers and small-scale entrepreneurs in Muslim countries.[29] Today, the largest Islamic banks are found in the Arab Middle East, including the Islamic Development Bank in Saudi Arabia established in 1974, the Dubai Islamic Bank established in 1975, the Faisal Bank of Egypt established in 1977, the Kuwait Finance House in 1977, the Jordanian Islamic Bank, in 1978, the Bahrain Islamic Bank in 1979, and Al-Baraka in Saudi Arabia.[30] In addition, Islamic lending has become the only legal source of credit in Iran since 1983 and Pakistan since 1985.[31]

These institutions share a few common goals: to promote profit and loss financing or equity-based lending contracts, and to circulate capital to the Muslim community through investments that adhere to rules forbidding usury (*riba*) and the contracting of risk-free positions (*gharar*).[32] Therefore, borrowers from an Islamic bank must accept lending contracts that contain equity ownership agreements, and depositors must accept that the bank's portfolio risk is based on profit-sharing investments.[33] Unfortunately, attempts to use Islamic lending for consumer product credit have failed to develop dedicated patronage behaviour.[34]

For business development purposes, however, Islamic banks can open the monetary bottlenecks that often prevent financial intermediation and savings mobilization in many predominantly Muslim countries.[35] As the World Bank states in its 1989 report on the role of financial systems in development: "It is not savings only that are required, but a channel of communication between potential savings and potential real investment."[36] It is worth noting that finance-gaps in other Arab countries are often caused by the reluctance of business owners to use state-sponsored banks in the formal sector; the same is true for financial structure instability.[37] This is certainly true in the West Bank and Gaza Strip, just as it is true that Palestinians avoid Israeli banks as a form of non-violent protest. This situation leaves a great deal of potentially productive capital – which could be recycled into development – hidden away in homes.

The establishment of indigenous Islamic banks or the penetration of a regional Islamic bank into the Arab Palestinian and mostly Muslim population of the occupied territories could facilitate the cycling of immobile capital into formal sector production and employment. Islamic banks might also be used as administrators of social funds or of social investment funds intended to develop local commerce and employment by investing and reinvesting capital into small enterprises usually considered riskier than large industrial projects. In addition, an indigenous Islamic bank could bring capital into the country. Chandra and Khan's study of "segmented economies" shows that foreign investment also tends to grow at increasing rates when unproductive capital saved in the informal sector is transferred to formal sector credit-distributing facilities.[38] And, because capital flight is usually a response to perceived political interference, establishing an Islamic financial institution could facilitate the repatriation of capital from the Palestinian diaspora.

ISLAMIC FINANCIAL AND PARTICIPATORY DEVELOPMENT

What follows now is a short accounting of contracts that are generally acceptable for use by Islamic banks. A noticeable part of the Islamic economics agenda is a required level of community participation. On the savings side, Islamic banks offer deposit accounts that function in basically the same way as the commonly-known checking accounts, savings or demand deposit accounts, investment accounts and trust accounts. The major differences in these Islamic deposit accounts and those offered by Western-style banks is that fixed-rate interest is not paid on deposits. Depositors are treated as equity investors in an Islamic bank, much as an American might participate in a credit union, cooperative or mutual fund shares, with depositors participating in profit-sharing earnings distributions through shareholder interests.

However, just as deposits into Islamic banks are considered equity investments, loans from Islamic banks are written as partnership contracts rather than as mortgages or secured credit arrangements. Just as Islamic banks cannot guarantee rates of return to depositors, they also cannot require a stated rate of return on money distributed. Partnership contracts fall into two categories, *sharikah* partnerships, where capital and labour are jointly provided and where profits are distributed according to a fixed ratio agreed upon before moneys are transferred, and *mudaraba* partnerships, where silent partnerships provide capital and a managing partner provides expertise. In this latter form, profits are shared according to a predetermined ratio, but losses are assumed by the silent partner.[39]

In order for a *sharikah* or informal business partnership to be formed, a joint capital or mutual labour expenditure must take place, either by a voluntary and planned agreement initiated by the partners – for example the joint purchase of property or a joint venture in business – or through an involuntary event like an inheritance. Commercial partnerships (*sharikah al-aqd*) are usually more specific in the contract's organization. Forms of *sharikah al-aqd* include *sharikah al-amwal*, those based on limited monetary investments; *sharikah al-amal*, those based on labour; and *sharikah al-wajuh*, those based on the expertise of the managing partner.

The financing of *sharikah al-aqd* can be divided into three types of contracts: *musharaka/mufawadah* or unlimited investment partnership,[40] the *inan* or limited investment partnership, and the *mudaraba* contract which is a hybrid of *musharaka* and *inan* contracts. In order for the *musharaka* form to be used, the partners must share equally in their monetary investment, their right of disposal for jointly held capital, their right to profit distributions, and in their responsibility towards debt reduction. *Musharaka* partners serve as agents (*wakil*) for each other, but *inan* partners base their relationship on the principle of agency. In a *musharaka* contract, both partners stand to share in the profits and in the financial losses, and one partner can contract debts for the business for which both partners may be held liable. The second key feature of a *musharaka* contract is the level of participation. Under the *musharaka* contract, the lender can intercede in the management process if the anticipated results are not achieved.

The advantages of loans and joint ventures are combined in *sharikah al-aqd* or *mudaraba* contracts, for they cannot be strictly classified in either category.[41] The primary difference between *mudaraba* and *musharaka* contracts is the degree of agency given to the managing partner. The investing partner shares in the venture's risk because there is no guarantee the money will be returned, and the managing partner stands to lose time, effort and reputation. But, unlike the *musharaka* investor, the person investing money in a *mudaraba* contract cannot be held liable for losses beyond the amount invested. The managing partner has complete freedom under normal business conditions, but the lender can assume a managerial position in cases of financial exigency or when a partner is deemed to be incompetent. The lender in a *musharaka* contract is a beneficial owner in the venture via the purchase of shares in the company. During the term of the contract the limited partner receives a set percentage of the profits. The length of the contract can be definite or indefinite.

The spectrum of lending contracts goes beyond the straight *mudaraba* and *musharaka* contracts, including effective equivalents of leases, account receivables, agricultural loans, consumer loans and investment leverage accounts. Indeed, Islamic financial contracts are analogous to a variety of funding vehicles commonly used in international capital markets. Muslim investors can create a limited partnership defined as an undivided interest in a commercial entity where a general partner assumes ultimate liability and where a set of limited partners supply the bulk of capital and risk a maximum of their total investment. By this reasoning, a limited partner has signed a *musharaka* investment agreement, while the general partner has signed a *mudaraba* borrowing agreement.

There are several versions of *mudaraba* contracts depending on the bank and the country under study, not all of which can be discussed here. However, most venture capital firms offer contracts where investors receive shares in a newly-formed corporation in exchange for an infusion of capital. Under American commercial law, the investor is limited to losses equal to the amount invested in the entity as incorporated. In essence, equity or venture capital investments are *musharaka* contracts. Investment trusts, mutual funds, lease arrangements with repurchase agreements, and participating convertible bonds are essentially risk sharing/profit sharing contracts that fall under the rubric of financial instruments approved by most *sharia* councils.[42]

It is also important to look at arrangements for financing direct exports. The premier agency for financing international trade in the United States is the Export–Import Bank, or Eximbank. Several important aspects of the foreign affairs part of Eximbank's agenda have been illustrated by previous researchers.[43] First among them is that Eximbank is an arm of the US government used to facilitate market development in foreign countries; second, if viewed from my current perspective, they illustrate how some Eximbank contracts could be construed as Islamic. Eximbank has facilities for financing purchase/repurchase agreements, which are analogous to a *salaf* or post-production contract. Arrangements such as these, referred to by Dunn and Bradstreet as the "new deal at Eximbank",[44] are part of a range of products meant to enhance trade between SMEs and to promote participation and free market operations in markets where American businesses stand to compete.[45]

However, the major factor in Islamic banking is the equity-basis or risk-sharing provision that must be involved in both depositing and borrowing contracts. Savers must make deposits into a direct investment account if they wish to receive a return on their money. Borrowers must accept the lender as a partner that holds equity rights in the business. It is the key question of participation that leads me to believe Islamic banks could be used as social funds to enhance development of local business enterprises in Palestine.

To my knowledge, the link between Islamic finance and the development of small businesses has not been made in development literature, at least not in American or European academic journals. However, two major reports have been written that recognize the unique features of SMEs in member nations of the Organization of Islamic States. One of these is a 1987 United Nations Industrial Development Organization (UNIDO) report that illustrates how SMEs facilitate "employment generation, poverty eradication, improving the distribution of incomes, fulfilling basic needs, etc" in developing Muslim countries.[46] The report does not address the Palestinian situation directly, though some parallels can be drawn from the section on Jordan. According to this report, 90 per cent of Jordan's industrial base and 41 per cent of its total employment come from small-scale employers. UNIDO's 1980 report on Jordan confirms and extends this claim by stating that the SMEs are the source of the kingdom's wealth of entrepreneurial ability.[47] The tie between small business development and the broader agenda of economic development is not new.[48] Neither is the link between small business development and venture capital financing entirely novel, although this notion has not been as widely accepted by economists as one might think.[49]

SOCIAL FUNDS AND ISLAMIC LENDING

Moving on to a discussion of social investment funds, I comment here on Mary E. Schmidt's discussion of social funds in her section of a report published by the World Bank.[50] Schmidt defines a social fund as an organization that provides:

> funding to local level organizations, such as community-based NGOs [nongovernmental organizations], and local governments in a more flexible and rapid way than line ministries. They are demand-driven funding mechanisms...that respond to requests generated at the local level. Social funds are typically set up as autonomous institutions that are transparent and have flexible funding, procurement and distribution procedures....[They] prioritize selection of microprojects according to the intensity of participation...[and] provide for capacity building of intermediary and community organizations as early as possible.[51]

Social investment funds bring money into private sector development more quickly than most other systems of aid and capital distribution; they are particularly responsive to the demand-driven funding needs of the private sector. Social investment funds require participation of both the borrowers and the lenders in the fund's decision-making processes, and they provide for the planned and strategic repayment of funds. Although long-term administration of the loan collection has been a problem with some funds that have used a revolving credit approach, others, like the project that began in Albania in 1993, seem to be having a very positive effect on the community, and their payment/profitability experiences have been positive. Another fund that has had a positive experience is the Egypt Social Fund Project which began in 1991. New funds are also in operation in Armenia and Georgia.

When the mandates of Islamic finance and the objectives of the World Bank's social investment fund projects are laid side-by-side, five common principles arise:

(1) that capital should be distributed into demand-driven projects that will create maximum community-level employment, particularly at the SME level;
(2) that financing should be made available as directly as is possible to entrepreneurial concerns and local producers and that funding mechanism be creative, "flexible, simple, and transparent";
(3) that lenders and borrowers share in the decision-making process, and sometimes in the management process;
(4) that institutions be chosen that "maintain a commitment to participation"; and
(5) that the fund operate in a way that reflects culture-conscious planning that builds integrity and trust between participants.

Social funds can also facilitate local-level import and export trading. I further propose that the problems social investment funds have had in managing long-term collections could be solved in Muslim countries by using Islamic banks as the fund administrators; community, moral and religious suasion has considerable power.

INVOLVING THE ARAB-AMERICAN COMMUNITY

Returning to the agenda set out at the beginning of this chapter, real links can be drawn between the potential for using Islamic banks as a means for developing markets for financial transfers into the occupied Palestinian territories. Since the summer of 1993 I have been conducting research on Arab-American businesses; one concern of this research is whether or not Islamic banking could enhance the US economy. Over 3000 Arab Americans were contacted through a survey questionnaire via organizations such as the American Arab Anti-Discrimination Committee (ADC) and the Council for the National Interest (CNI), among others. The questionnaire asked individual Arab Americans to detail a variety of socio-economic data about their careers and businesses. Seventeen per cent of those contacted responded. Forty-nine per cent of respondents indicated that they practice Islam in some form, and 46 per cent identified their religion as Christian.

This research reveals that the Arab American community provides a natural link for trade between American and Arab firms. The responses indicated that an inordinately high proportion of the sample group is involved in international trade. Eighteen per cent of the CNI sample and 16 per cent of the ADC sample work in positions that "facilitate export trade for US produced goods that are sold in Arab countries". In analysing these responses, I found that these "export facilitators" were not only naturalized citizens who had moved to the United States from the Middle East, but also second and third generation citizens who had specialized in fields related to the Arab world. Eighteen per cent of respondents from CNI and 22 per cent of respondents from ADC who were born in the United States indicated that they had worked in an Arab country. Of these export facilitators, 45 per cent of our group of business owners reported annual sales in excess of $500 000, and 15 per cent reported sales in excess of $2 million. Seventy-four per cent of Muslim Arab Americans felt an SME finance gap exists in their community that impedes business expansion, and 47 per cent said they would make 60 per cent of their credit transactions through an Islamic bank if one were available in the United States.

Gillespie *et al.* have been studying the attitudes of specifically Palestinian Americans towards homeland investment.[52] Their findings are summarized as follows:

> In total, 42 percent of respondents indicated a current interest in Palestinian investment, while 47 percent reported a potential interest in such a venture. Such positive response is very high, and it implies that the Diaspora is indeed a good target for homeland investment....investors indicated interest in manufacturing for export (71 percent), manufacturing for domestic sale (67 percent), investment in services (67 percent), and purchasing mutual funds consisting of companies based in Palestine (61 percent)....67 percent of those interested in investment in Palestine claimed to be interested in real-estate for personal use....
>
> In addition, 50 percent of the respondents indicated that they were Christian, and 48 percent responded that they were Muslim.

Gillespie *et al.* point out that their sample is not a random sample because of the nature of the demographics list they used in their survey, and I realize that the members of CNI and ADC may not be representative of the entire Arab American community, and they are certainly not a mirror for the Muslim American community. But, for our purposes – to reach business owners and find out whether a network could be constructed to enhance and finance trade through them – the responses to both of these studies indicate real networking opportunities for Palestinian and Palestinian American businesses.

However, we also found that this community will require access to participatory financing if it is to facilitate trade with the Middle East. This indicates that support of Islamic banks in the Middle East and in the US could create mutually beneficial financial networks for enhancing Palestinian investment. In addition, the network that Islamic banks themselves offer could provide an important link in the international trade dynamic between the US and Muslim countries. Using the 30-nation network that has been established by owners of Islamic banks could create a certain competitive advantage. Most of these institutions operate in oil-rich countries in the Muslim world, rentier-by-proxy states, or in states with huge populations such as Egypt, India and Malaysia. These countries represent accessible, wealthy, large and potentially lucrative markets for US products.

CONCLUSION

So where, then, does this tying-in of so many disparate ideas take us with regard to the topic I have set forth in this chapter? My answer is not for development officers to sponsor the setting up of Islamic banks around the world, although there certainly might be some facility in that idea. Rather, I propose that we simply change our view of financial instruments already available and repackage them for use by and with our Muslim trading partners in the Middle East, and especially in the occupied West Bank and Gaza Strip. In addition, US and European companies should take advantage of the financing arrangements that are available through existing Islamic banks. These institutions are eager to support import–export trade. Furthermore, I believe that communities in the Palestinian and other Israeli-occupied territories need to establish indigenous Islamic banks in order to spur growth. Under the current financial agreements it seems certain that mortgage or collateral-based lending will not be operable. This leaves equity finance as the only viable option.

This leads to several suggestions. One is to encourage efforts by the large international funding agencies like the World Bank, the IFC, the IMF and others to pursue social investment funds that offer participatory financing contracts to Muslim-owned SMEs in Palestine. Although these funds are not Islamic from a Western point of view, they can serve as Islamic-appropriate lenders to customers and agents in Muslim countries and particularly in the West Bank and Gaza. However, these agencies should insist on accountability such that foreign aid investments actually reach Palestinian SMEs. This has been a problem in the past with economic and financial assistance delivered through Israel. In addition, US aid funds should be earmarked to make purchases by the SMEs of products bought by American firms.

Second, these organizations would be well-served by hiring fund managers from existing Islamic banks to serve as distributors of equity-based capital. It would be appropriate to establish a Palestine Enterprise Fund, for example, that would funnel US Agency for International Development funds to Arab and Muslim businesses interested in buying and selling American-made products. This too would encourage cooperation among various world agencies, which is my third point. Cooperation among US agencies, international non-governmental organizations and the major Islamic development banks should be encouraged to a much greater extent than it is today. The Islamic Development Bank in Saudi Arabia, with resources in billions of dollars, has been wholly overlooked in discussions on Palestinian development credit arrangements, as have the Islamic banks in the United Arab Emirates. This may be because the Israeli government has dismissed all applications for opening branches of Islamic banks in the West Bank and Gaza. However, this position could be changed through political pressure in peace negotiations or outside them, especially if it is realized that the strong network of Islamic banks in the Gulf is a link for tapping oil-produced financial capital.

Fourth, American businesses should explore the possibilities for gaining client financing through Islamic banks. This is especially important in the Gulf Cooperation Council (GCC) states, but it could also open markets in Egypt, Jordan and other Arab countries. Moreover, American agents that represent US business interests such as Eximbank should pursue development of financing arrangements that are Muslim-approved contracts. What may seem like a rhetorical device to a Western banker is seen as fair and practical to many Muslims. It must be remembered that the goal of American export agencies is to increase trade. With this in mind, it seems clear that the development of Islamic financial instruments becomes an important service to American clients. Trade could also be encouraged if Muslim Americans could operate Islamic banks. No full-service Islamic banks exist in the US, and to date the Federal Reserve and the Comptroller of the Currency have not taken applications seriously. I believe a change in this stance would help mobilize savings that are dormant in the US.

In conclusion, evidence supports the idea that the United States could profit from trade in the Arab Middle East in general, and in the West Bank and Gaza Strip in particular, if it were to facilitate the use of equity-based lending and the establishment of social funds throughout the occupied territories. Moreover, it is apparent that branches of Islamic banks which are already operating in the Gulf, Jordan and Egypt could serve as logical distributors of this equity capital to Palestinians. However, discussion of Islamic banks in the foreign policy/commercial development equation must then be included. This need not be difficult. The changes needed to support an Islamic economics agenda are more semantic and visionary than they are structural or regulatory. Unfortunately, my point that American businesses will want renewed assurances that their trading patterns will not be shut down by the Israelis through prejudicial taxes, civil and human rights violations, and legal inequities can only be addressed through changes in Israel's own posture and/or power relationship *vis-à-vis* the Palestinians. These businesses, at any rate, are the American institutions that need protection. Following the handshake there was new hope that the Israelis would change their economic policies and allow free trade for Arab and American businesses in Palestine. If this could ever be made to happen, then implementing policies towards increasing American trade and establishing Islamic banking would become complementary agendas.

Notes

1. The author would like to thank Karen Pfieffer, chair of the Economics Department at Smith College for inviting me to lecture on Islamic finance as a means for distributing funds in Palestine. Her suggestions allowed me to expand and develop the themes discussed in this and one other article. This chapter is an expanded and revized edition of my lecture at Smith College and my article "American Trade and Islamic Banking in the Former Israeli Occupied Territories," *International Journal of Commerce and Management* 5(4) (1995), pp. 71–94.
2. Noah Lewin-Epstein and Moshe Semyonov, *The Arab Minority in Israel's Economy: Patterns of Ethnic Inequality* (Boulder, Col.: Westview Press, 1993).
3. April Wright, "Are Middle East Banks Safe?", *International Journal of Commerce and Management* 5(3) (1995), pp. 90–105.
4. Radwan A. Shaban, Ragui Assaad and Sulayman Al-Qudsi, "The Challenge of Unemployment in the Arab Region", *International Labor Review* 134(1) (1995), pp. 65–82; see also Sami Aboudi, "Palestinian Industrial Parks", *Peace Economics* (2nd quarter 1995), pp. 8–14.
5. Sharon Stanton Russell and Muhammad Ali Al-Ramadhan, "Kuwait's Migration Policy Since the Gulf Crisis", *International Journal of Middle East Studies* 26(4) (1994), pp. 569–87.
6. Laurie A. Brand, "Economics and Shifting Alliances: Jordan's Relations with Syria and Iraq, 1975–1981", *International Journal of Middle East Studies* 26(3) (August 1994), pp. 393–413.
7. Ghadeer Taher, "Amman Economic Summit Launches Middle East Development Bank", *Peace Economics* (4th quarter 1995), pp. 16–19.
8. For an important series of essays on the continuing effects of Israeli economic policies in the occupied territories, and the real impact of the economic agreements reached by the Israelis and the Palestinian Authority, see the European Union's *Peace Media* series, Valerie York (ed.).
9. Louis Cantori, "Corporate Conservatism in the Middle East", lecture delivered at the Center for Contemporary Arab Studies, School of Foreign Service, Georgetown University, Washington DC, 1993.

10. Mohammed S. Amerah, *Major Employment Issues in Some Arab Countries* (Amman: Economic Research Center for the Royal Scientific Society, 1990).
11. A.Y. Abu-Ayyash, *Absorption of Returnees in Small Industrial Enterprises: The Case of the Development and Employment Fund* (Amman: Economic and Social Commission for Western Asia, 1991).
12. Several recent reports address this issue in Jordan and to some extent in the occupied territories. Readers should see J.W. Wright, Jr, "Islamic Banking in Practice: Problems in Jordan and Saudi Arabia", University of Durham Centre for Middle Eastern and Islamic Studies, Occasional Papers Series, no. 48, 1995; Christopher M. Vaughn, "Jordan's Rentier-by-Proxy Economic Agenda: Recent Changes, Observations and Prospects for the Future", Proceedings of the British Society for Middle East Studies Conference on Democracy in the Middle East, St Andrews University, 1992, pp. 644–56; Economic and Social Commission for Western Asia, "The Return of Jordanian/Palestinian Nationals From Kuwait; Economic and Social Implications for Jordan", Amman, 1991; and ESCWA, 1992.
13. Sandra Samaan, "Small and Medium Enterprises and their Potential in Palestine", Address at the Center for Contemporary Arab Studies, School of Foreign Service, Georgetown University, Washington DC, 1994.
14. This term is used here in the same context that it is used in Emma C. Murphy, "Structural Inhibitions to Economic Liberalization in Israel", Proceedings of the British Society for Middle East Studies Conference on Democracy in the Middle East, St Andrews University, St. Andrews, Scotland, 1992, pp. 217–34. It should also be noted from this discussion that structural problems within the Israeli banking system prevent efficient capital markets from developing even within the Green Line. Murphy discusses in detail how the Knesset Finance Committee's "strategic importance" policy censors direct foreign investment. This policy led Shamir's economic privatization programme to fail because it prevents investment by non-Jews in industrial and manufacturing concerns. Because it has veto power over sales towards privatization, the committee has effectively blocked development of competitive and stable money markets inside Israel and in the territories it occupies. The gross result is that neither Arabs nor Westerners are allowed to invest in producing enterprises in the West Bank and Gaza. Properties that could be used as collateral for capital distribution through mortgage lending either do not exist or cannot be used.
15. Norman Finkelstein, "Bayt Sahur in Year II of the Intifada: A Personal Account", *Journal of Palestine Studies* 19(2) (Winter 1990), pp. 62–74.
16. Anne Grace, "The Tax Resistance at Bayt Sahur", *Journal of Palestine Studies* 19(2) (Winter 1990), pp. 99–107.
17. People wanting a more detailed analysis of the Israeli withholding of banking services from Palestinians should consult Policy Research, Inc. and the United States Agency for International Development, "Development Opportunities in the Occupied Territories: Finance and Credit"; and "Annex III: The Financial Sector", in "Developing the Occupied Territories: An Investment in Peace", Washington, World Bank, Vol. 3.
18. Samaan, *op. cit.*
19. Emma C. Murphy, "Israel and the Palestinians: The Economic Rewards of Peace", University of Durham Centre for Middle Eastern and Islamic Studies, Occasional Paper Series, no. 47, 1995; and Rodney Wilson, "The Palestinian Economy and International Trade", University of Durham Centre for Middle Eastern and Islamic Studies, Occasional Paper Series, no. 45, 1994.

20. Jad Isaac, "A Socioeconomic Study of Administrative Detainees at Ansar 3", *Journal of Palestine Studies* 18(4) (Summer 1989), pp. 102–9.
21. Christopher Clay, "The Origins of Modern Banking in the Levant: The Branch Network of the Imperial Ottoman Bank, 1890–1914", *International Journal of Middle East Studies* 26(4) (1994), pp. 589–614.
22. "Special Supplement to Annex V: Protocol on Economic Relations", Israeli–Palestinian Interim Agreement, cited in *Palestine Report*, December 1995, pp. 15–25; and European Union, *Peace Media*, *op. cit.*
23. "Developing the Palestinian Economy: An interview with George T. Abed", *Journal of Palestine Studies* 23(4) (Summer 1994), pp. 41–51.
24. See the section on the financial system in a special report prepared for UNCTAD by Fadle Naquib entitled "Prospects for Sustained Development of the Palestinian Economy: Strategies and Policies for Reconstruction and Development", 1995.
25. A. Pervez Imtiaz, "Islamic Finance", *Arab Law Quarterly* 5(4) (1990), pp. 259–81; and Wilson, 1994.
26. Radi El-Bdour, "Problems of Research in Islamic Economics (with emphasis on priorities and application)", Symposium of The Islamic Research and Training Institute and the Islamic Development Bank on Problems of Research in Islamic Economics, Jeddah, Saudi Arabia, 1986, pp. 110–44.
27. Key scriptures that outline these mandates include the following:

> Those that live on usury shall rise up before Allah like men whom Satan has demented by his touch; for they claim that usury is like trading. But Allah has permitted trading and forbidden usury. (2; pp. 275–276)
>
> Give up what remains [due to you] from *riba* [usury], if ye are [in truth] believers. And if ye do not, then be warned of war [against you] by Allah and his messenger. And if ye repent then ye have your principal [without *riba*]. (2; pp. 278–279)
>
> Proclaim a woeful punishment to those that hoard up gold and silver and do not spend it in Allah's cause. The day will surely come when their treasuries shall be heated in the fire of hell. If your debtor be in straits, grant him a delay until he can discharge his debt; but if you waive the sum as alms it will be better for you, if you but knew it.
>
> No profit without toil and no money without labour. Man hath only that for which he has put forth effort. (Sura 53: 39-40)

There is also a need to differentiate three important constructs: one originating in the *Qur'an* and *sharia* advocating sound financial relations among people, the ban of instruments that use *riba* and support for charity-oriented giving through *zakat*. According to many Muslim scholars these became financial relations traditionally promulgated and practiced in early Islamic culture, especially at its political and economic zenith. These are different in the minds of some *sharia* councils from translations from European and other nations pertaining to finance and trade. As the second reader of this chapter pointed out, a mere translation into Arabic of trade and financial constructs which are equally prevalent in Western civilization does not make them Arabic or Islamic. In fact, I have used some of that reader's words in this footnote. This view, while true, represents a conservative approach to the analysis of Islamic lending contracts. I mention this here because it frames much of the debate currently taking place over the applicability of Islamic economics in the modern financial world. A further argument is that while it is true that some Islamic nations have substituted profits made through interest-based fees with profits from services charges of floating rate flat fees, these changes are platitudinous and demagoguery. I take no position on this issue. However, I believe that most Arab Muslims will behave in what they believe is an economically ethical manner when given the option to do so; therefore, the establishment of a system of Islamic banks should have a high level of market appeal in the predominantly Muslim West Bank and Gaza Strip.

28. Zubair Iqbal and Abbas Mirakor, "Islamic Banking", International Monetary Fund Occasional Paper no. 49, Washington DC, 1987.
29. A.S.M. Kahn, "Islam and Modern Banking", *Thoughts on Economics*, 9(1) (1988), pp. 63–6; and Volker Nienhaus, "Islamic Banking: Microeconomic Instruments and Macroeconomic Implications", *Thoughts on Economics* 9(1) (1988), pp. 66–86.
30. Moustafa Abdel-Magid, "The Theory of Islamic Banking: Accounting Implications", *International Journal of Accounting* 17(1) (1982–83); pp. 79–102.
31. Muhammad A. Khan, "Islamic Banking in Pakistan", *International Journal of Islamic and Arabic Studies* 2(2) (1985), pp. 21–34; and David Cobham, "Finance for Development and Islamic Banking", British Society for Middle Eastern Studies Conference, St. Andrews, Scotland, 1992, pp. 619–37.
32. Nabil Saleh, *Unlawful Gain and Legitimate Profit in Islamic Law: Riba, Gharar and Islamic Banking* (Cambridge, UK: Cambridge University Press, 1986), pp. 49–50.
33 A.H.M. Sadaq, "Islamic Perspectives on Monetary and Fiscal Policies and their Implications for Development", *International Journal of Islamic and Arabic Studies* 5(1) (1988), pp. 1–16. Also see M. Umar Chapra, *Toward a Just Monetary System* (Leicester, UK: The Islamic Foundation, 1985); Ma'en Mardi Al-Qatamin, "Islamic and Conventional Banks: A Comparative Study", MBA. thesis, University of Nottingham, 1990; and S.R. Khan, "Profit and Loss Sharing: An Economic Analysis of an Islamic Financial System", Ph.D. dissertation, University of Michigan, 1983.
34. Cengiz Erol and Radi El-Bdour, "Conventional and Islamic Banks: Patronage Behavior of Jordanian Customers", *International Journal of Bank Marketing*, 1990.
35. Bernhard Fischer, "Savings Mobilization in Developing Countries: Bottlenecks and Reform Proposals", *Savings and Development* 13(2) (1989), pp. 117–31.
36. World Bank, *World Development Report* (New York: Oxford University Press, 1989), as reviewed by Rodney St Hill, in "Stages of Banking and Economic Development", *Savings and Development* 16(1).
37. J.W. Wright, "Islamic Banking in Practice: Problems in Jordan and Saudi Arabia", University of Durham Centre for Middle Eastern and Islamic Studies, Occasional Papers Series, no. 48, 1995; and J.W. Wright, Bandar Al-Hajjar and John Presley, "Structural and Attitudinal Impediments to Effective Capital Distribution in Saudi Arabia's Islamicizing Economy: Implications for Financial Sector Training", in Ehsan Ahmed, *Economic Growth and Human Development in Islamic Perspective* (Herndon, Va: International Institute for Islamic Thought, 1992), pp. 87–95.
38. Vandana Chandra and A. Ali-Khan, "Foreign Investment in the Presence of an Informal Sector", *Econometrica* 60 (1993), pp. 79–103.
39. Most articles about Islamic lending and capital distribution contain some discussion of *musharaka* and *mudaraba* contracts. Most useful for providing

definitions on Islamic financial instruments is Radi El-Bdour, "Economic of Profit Sharing Contracts: Conceptual and Theoretic", Workshop of the Islamic Research and Training Institute and the Islamic Development on Investment Strategy in Islamic Banking: Applications, Issues, and Problems, Jeddah, Saudi Arabia, 1987, pp. 57–88. Unless otherwise noted, the discussion here comes closest to his, with his permission. The econometric model presented in that article and others are not, however, germane to the discussion at hand. Another article that should be consulted is Rodney Wilson, "Islamic Financial Instruments", *Arab Law Quarterly* 6(2) (1991), pp. 205–14.

40. The terms *mufawada* and *musharaka* are used interchangeably. However, readers should recognize that a variety of transliteration styles exist for Islamic financial terms. For example, the spelling and pronunciation of some concepts such as *vakil* rather than *wakil*, or with a glottal sound, *reba* rather than *riba*, and so on, are different in non-Arab Islamic countries. I would like to thank the second reader of this chapter for articulating these distinctions during the review process. Additionally, the term *mudaraba* can be used interchangeably with *qirad* and *maqarada*.
41. A.M. El Gousi, "Riba, Islamic Law, and Interest", PhD dissertation, Temple University, 1982, pp. 215–216.
42. Another noteworthy area for potential profits is in the insurance market. *Takaful* funding pools are Islamic equivalents to a mutual insurance fund reserve; a risk management account that is funded collectively by investors and borrowers and managed by an Islamic bank. Investments are made from the fund through *mudaraba* arrangements, but profits serve as reserves against unexpected capital losses.
43. For more detail on the foreign affairs part of Eximbank's agenda readers should consult Warren Glick, "Financing Foreign Trade and the Future of the U.S. Export–Import Bank", *Journal of European Business*; Dean Alexander, "The Export-Import Bank of the US Battle against Subsidized Export Credits", *Dickson Journal of International Law*; and Bobby Apostolakis, "Concessionary export subsidies and the U.S. Export-Import Bank", *International Review of Applied Economics*. There is also a 17 May 1993 State Department release regarding President Clinton's intentions to use Eximbank and most-favoured nation status to promote US foreign policy.
44. Dunn and Bradstreet, "Report on the Export–Import: A New Deal at Eximbank", *Dunn and Bradstreet Reports* 41(5) (1992), pp. 44.
45. This comes from "Eximbank Can Help Exporters Get Working Capital", *Business America* 8(16) (27 August 1991); 12. However, there is a series of short but helpful articles in *Business America* entitled "Sources of Export Financing". See these issues: 114; p. 22; 114; p. 13; 114; p. 1; 113; p. 5; 111; p. 21; 111; p. 16.
46. United Nations Industrial Development Organization, "The Role of Small and Medium Scale Industries in OIC Member States", *Journal of Economic Cooperation Among Islamic Countries* (1987), pp. 1–54.
47. United Nations Industrial Development Organization, "Country Industrial Development Profile of Jordan: Problems and Prospects", UNIDO/ICIS.159, 1980.
48. For a short review of literature on this subject, the reader is referred to Donald C. Mead, "Small Enterprises and Development", *Economic Development and Cultural Change* 39(2) (1991), pp. 409–20.
49. For an introduction to this subject readers should consult Richard Kitchen, "Venture Capital: A New Approach to Financing Small and Medium Enterprises in Developing Countries", *Savings and Development* 13(3) (1989),

pp. 287–313; and John Samuels and Michael Theobald, "Equity Finance in Developing Countries", *Savings and Development* 13(4) (1989), pp. 337–49.

50. Mary E. Schmidt, "Chapter on Social Funds", *World Bank Participation Handbook* (Washington DC: World Bank, 1994).
51. *Ibid,* pp. 165–6.
52. Kate Gillespie, Liesle Riddle, Edward Sayre and David Sturges, "Financing Palestine: The Attitude of Palestinian-American Toward Homeland Investment", in Faith M. Hanna (ed.), *Middle East Banking and Finance: A Collection of Essays* (New York: The Arab Bankers Association of North America, 1996), pp. 67–87.

8 Will the Arab–Israeli Peace Process Generate Increased Portfolio Investment in the Middle East?

Rodney Wilson

INTRODUCTION

Although the Middle East, especially Israel and its immediate Arab neighbours, has benefited from more official aid than any other region of the developing world for over two decades, flows of private capital into the region remain disappointingly small.[1] To a large extent direct and portfolio investment have been inhibited by the perceived political risks. The peace process might be expected to reduce these risks and increase the involvement of both multinational companies and Western fund managers in the region. Yet much of the multinational company involvement continues to be confined to the oil sector, and none of the capital markets is regarded as significant in relation to emerging markets elsewhere in Asia or Latin America. This chapter examines whether that situation is likely to change with respect to portfolio investment flows if the peace process succeeds in reducing political risk.

DEVELOPMENT FAILURES AND AID DEPENDENCY

The failure of capital markets to develop in the Middle East has increased dependency on foreign aid and decreased the supply of domestic savings. In comparison to the rapidly growing economies of East and Southeast Asia, growth rates in the Middle East are poor, with the per capita gross national product growth figures being negative for much of the region for the last decade, or a mere 1 or 2 per cent (Table 8.1). This can be partly explained by the fall in oil prices that accompanied the decline in OPEC power, but the earlier rapid increases in oil revenues during the 1970s might have been expected to encourage the development of regional capital markets that could have protected many of the economies in the subsequent slump.

Table 8.1 Basic growth and development indicators

Country	*GNP growth, 1985–94, %*	*Nominal GNP per capita, 1994, $*	*Real PPP GNP per capita, 1994, $*
Algeria	–2.4	1 690	5 330
Egypt	1.6	710	3 610
Israel	2.5	13 880	15 690
Jordan	–6.3	1 390	4 290
Kuwait	–1.3	19 040	24 500
Morocco	1.1	1 150	3 440
Oman	0.6	5 200	9 150
Saudi Arabia	–1.2	7 240	N/A
Tunisia	1.8	1 800	4 960
Turkey	1.5	2 450	4 610

Note: Nominal GDP figures are calculated at official exchange rates, and real purchasing power parity figures (PPP) figures are adjusted for relative prices.
Source: *World Bank Atlas*, 1996.

The newly-industrializing countries in East and Southeast Asia have high domestic savings ratios, in excess of 30 per cent of GDP in the case of Muslim countries such as Malaysia and Indonesia. This high saving is used to finance investment, which brings economic growth. However, in the Middle East both savings rates and growth rates are much lower. Savings rates are especially low in Egypt and Jordan: the figures for 1994 being 5.9 per cent and 3.3 per cent, respectively.[2] These rates could have been much higher if the governments had provided incentives to encourage savings, such as increasing the attractiveness and perceived stability of bank deposits. There have been some moves in this direction, encouraged by the IMF, but bank deposits remain fairly static overall after an allowance is made for inflation. The main change in Egypt has been a substitution of domestic currency deposits for foreign currency deposits as interest rates on the former were finally raised and the currency stabilized.

To a considerable extent the deficiency in domestic savings in Jordan and Egypt has been compensated for by inflows of foreign assistance and remittances, although the future of the latter has become more uncertain as Arab workers have returned home from the Gulf. The evidence from Jordan suggests a revival of remittances immediately after the substantial drop in 1991 that resulted from the Gulf war, which itself may have been followed by a post-1993 decline in both Jordan and Palestine (see Chapter 7 in this volume). The trends for remittances into Egypt likewise saw a rise in 1992 as workers returned to the Gulf, followed by a further decline in 1993.[3]

The literature on dual-gap analysis suggests that aid flows can be a complement as well as a substitute for domestic saving.[4] In the cases of Egypt and Jordan it is the returns on the substantial aid flows that can be questioned. Equivalent savings rates might have produced higher economic growth if there had been efficient financial intermediaries to channel the funds to productive uses. It is doubtful if the governments of Egypt and Jordan, or indeed the aid agencies themselves, were effective intermediaries. Arguably, equivalent private savings or private financial inflows would have resulted in higher rates of economic growth. Given how low growth rates actually were, it is doubtful if governmental inflows increased the efficiency of the utilization of private sector flows. The erratic nature of government financial flows cannot have helped, as the uncertainty from one year to the next regarding political outcomes meant that official finance could not be regarded as a reliable complement to private savings. Much depended on decisions taken in the US, the main supplier of funds, rather than in Jordan or Egypt.

Much of the American funding was related to the peace process, commitments being essentially politically determined. Disbursements did not necessarily arrive at the points in the business cycle when they could be used most effectively, and indeed were unrelated to economic conditions. Jordan benefited from American aid only after it showed its willingness to negotiate with Israel, and the West Bank and Gaza were included once negotiations with the PLO proceeded. As Table 8.2 illustrates, Egypt and Israel received the major share; indeed these two states accounted for much of the US global foreign aid budget and not only the spending in the Middle East.

Much of the American aid is for military procurement (Table 8.3 shows how the amounts have varied since 1990). Disbursements of military

Table 8.2 United States economic assistance to the Middle East (US$ million)

Country	*1985*	*1990*	*1991*	*1992*	*1993*
Egypt	1 065	901	783	893	748
Israel	1 950	1 195	1 850	1 200	1 200
Jordan	100	4	31	—	65
Lebanon	20	8	9	9	10
Morocco	38	31	50	41	33
Oman	20	13	16	30	—
Tunisia	23	14	4	4	5
West Bank/Gaza	—	—	—	6	30
Yemen	28	23	3	3	4
Regional	23	12	8	17	28
Total	3 270	2 199	2 754	2 205	2 124

Source: *Statistical Abstract of the United States*, 1995, p. 812.

Table 8.3 United States military assistance to the Middle East (US$ million)

Country	*1985*	*1990*	*1991*	*1992*	*1993*
Egypt	1 177	1 296	1 302	1 302	1302
Israel	1 400	1 792	1 800	1 800	1800
Jordan	92	70	21	21	10
Morocco	50	44	44	23	41
Oman	40	—	3	1	1
Tunisia	67	31	12	11	3

Source: *Statistical Abstract of the United States*, 1995, p. 813.

assistance tend to be more stable than those for economic assistance as they are normally tied to contracts to supply armaments. The amounts quoted in Table 8.3 are in addition to the economic assistance shown in Table 8.2. These flows can be regarded as financing consumption rather than production, and only in the case of Israel has the aid assisted in the establishment of an indigenous armaments industry with export capability.

It can be argued that the high levels of foreign aid to the Middle East have resulted in a dependency culture, with the economies displaying rentier characteristics in the sense of being consumption- rather than production-driven. As governments have been the immediate recipients of the aid, this has increased their powers of patronage and leverage over the private sector. One result is that the local private sectors require state support, but the governments do not need the support of the private sector. Entrepreneurial activity becomes directed at how to gain as much as possible from government largesse, rather than towards competing in the market for private custom. As a consequence, businesspersons in the region have become adept at dealing with governments and bureaucracies but are less able to plan effectively for the development of their own businesses. Even in oil-rich states like Saudi Arabia, the private sector seems unable to plan without consulting government agencies. The macroeconomic consequence of this microeconomic failure is that few of the economies in the Middle East are able to pay their way in the world. Despite three decades of rhetoric about the need to reduce dependence on primary production, especially oil, there is little evidence of any real diversification and privatization is slow.

Manufacturing has been largely oriented to protected domestic markets, with state-run industries now reaching an impasse as costs are often relatively high and the quality of output low, yet with management still resisting any attempt at reform through privatization. Much of the manufacturing sector has become a liability rather than an asset for the state, although continuing protection at least reduces demands for funding for restructuring. Self-sustaining growth seems more elusive than ever, and none of the countries in the region have export industries that can compete effectively in global markets.

The lack of competitiveness of the economies of the Middle East, especially in manufactured goods, is demonstrated through revealed comparative advantage figures which have been calculated for the countries of the region.[5] Revealed comparative advantage refers to a product's share in a country's exports as a proportion of its share in world trade, an index of greater than one implying a revealed comparative advantage. Egypt, Syria and the oil-exporting countries of the Gulf would appear to have a revealed comparative advantage in refined fuels, and Jordan in chemicals, mainly phosphates.[6] Israel, Lebanon, Syria and Turkey have a revealed comparative advantage in foods, the value for Egypt being 1.07. Saudi Arabia and Qatar have a revealed comparative advantage in petrochemicals. None of the countries of the region, including Israel, has a revealed comparative advantage in machinery or vehicle production, and in the broad and important "other manufacturing" category only Turkey, and surprisingly, Lebanon, appear to have an advantage.

Given just how ill-equipped the economies of the Middle East and North Africa are to profit from the international trade liberalization which is being implemented under the Uruguay Round accords, it is not surprising to find that World Bank predictions of the gains for the region are especially disappointing. The model developed by the World Bank to quantify the outcome of the Uruguay Round predicts that the short-term gains to the region as a whole will be a mere $800 million for manufacturing, while world agricultural reform will cost the region $300 million as the prices of imported foodstuffs rise with the reduction of export subsidies by the European Union.[7] In the longer run farmers in the Middle East may gain, but the World Bank is pessimistic about the extent of the gain, which is estimated at only $100 million for the entire region.

The phasing out of the multifibre arrangements which restrict imports of textiles into the European Union and the United States is expected to benefit Far Eastern producers at the expense of those in countries such as Tunisia, Morocco, Israel and Turkey. The short-term loss for the period up to the year 2000 for the textile and clothing industry in the countries of the Middle East and North Africa is estimated at $400 million. Overall, the Uruguay Round will cost the countries of the region 0.1 per cent of their GDP in the short run, and bring possible long-term gains of 0.3 per cent of GDP. In contrast, the overall long-term gains for Malaysia, the Philippines and Thailand, are 8.8 per cent, 4.4 per cent and 10.9 per cent of GDP, respectively.[8]

THE GROWTH OF PRIVATE SECTOR COMPANIES IN THE MIDDLE EAST

The failure of government industrialization policies have implications for the private sector throughout the Middle East. Government interventions through nationalization and regulation in the 1950s and 1960s were taken in response to market failure, as private entrepreneurs were unwilling to invest in the type of import-substitution ventures which it was believed at the time were crucial for economic self-reliance. When the governments themselves failed, this merely compounded the problems. Having crowded out the private sector and made what was left of it very dependent on government, there was little chance of it playing a leading role in development.

As a consequence of the nationalization policies adopted by the governments of Egypt, Syria and Iraq, there are no entries from these important countries on the list of leading companies in the Middle East. Eight of the top-20 Middle Eastern companies are based in Saudi Arabia, four are Israeli, three are Turkish and a further three are based in the smaller Gulf states (see Table 8.4). Of the remaining two, one is the Lebanon-based real estate

Table 8.4 Top-20 Middle Eastern companies, by capitalization (US$ million)

Rank	*Company*	*Country*	*Capital*	*Profit*
1	SABIC	Saudi Arabia	10 586	1 075
2	Etisalat	UAE	4 424	338
3	Saudi American Bank	Saudi Arabia	3 136	270
4	Riyadh Bank	Saudi Arabia	2 976	155
5	Al-Rajhi Bank	Saudi Arabia	2 784	260
6	National Bank of Kuwait	Kuwait	2 603	185
7	Bezeq	Israel	2 197	167
8	Solidere	Lebanon	2 172	18
9	Teva Pharmaceuticals	Israel	2 087	98
10	Bank Hapoalim	Israel	2 083	271
11	Bank Leumi	Israel	2 047	219
12	Sceco-Central	Saudi Arabia	2 005	–205
13	Petkim Petrokimya	Turkey	1 920	171
14	Sceco-West	Saudi Arabia	1 677	–259
15	Akbank	Turkey	1 554	253
16	Arab National Bank	Saudi Arabia	1 497	108
17	Arab Bank	Jordan	1 496	142
18	Turk Hava Yolian	Turkey	1 481	68
19	Saudi British Bank	Saudi Arabia	1 378	93
20	Arab Banking Corporation	Bahrain	1 285	136

Note: Market capitalizations were valued in December 1994.
Source: *Financial Times 500*, 25 January 1996, p. 43.

development company, Solidere, which is rebuilding Beirut after the Lebanese civil war, and the other is the Arab Bank, a Palestinian institution with a long and honourable reputation, based in Amman.[9] Eleven of the companies listed are banks. The list includes the Saudi Arabian Basic Industries Corporation (SABIC), one of the world leaders in petrochemical production, which is by far the largest company in the region. Etisalat and Bezeq are the major telephone companies, located in the United Arab Emirates and Israel, respectively, and Sceco Central and West are the electricity companies for the cities of Riyadh and Jeddah respectively. The leading Turkish company, Petkim Petrokimya, is an oil refiner and distributor, and Turk Hava Yolian is the privatized Turkish airline.

Apart from utilities and oil-related companies, there is only one industrial undertaking represented in the top-20 Middle East company list, Teva Pharmaceuticals of Israel. Koor Industries, the Israeli holding company which controls many domestic manufacturing establishments, has a market capitalization of just $1.28 billion; this places it outside the list in 21st position. Koc Holding of Turkey, which has similar manufacturing interests, is in 25th position with a market capitalization of $1.07 billion. The other major Israeli holding company, Cial, had a market capitalization of under $800 million, while its smaller rival, IDB Development, had a capitalization of $775 million.

Given the prominence of Israeli companies on the list of the largest Middle East companies, it might be tempting to surmise that the peace process and the normalization of relations between Israel and the Arab states might result in a gradual one-way penetration of Israeli commercial interests throughout the region. Such a scenario seems unlikely, however, not merely because of political risk factors but also because of the nature of the Israeli holding companies. Most are mere financing umbrellas covering businesses largely oriented to the Israeli domestic market, the only exception being the armaments industry where Israel has enjoyed some success in penetrating the markets of developing countries, mainly in Latin America. The possibility of Israeli banks or holding companies taking over companies in neighbouring countries is remote, not least because of the lack of suitable businesses to buy up, or indeed capital markets that could be vulnerable to corporate raiders. More likely would be some modest joint ventures, possibly in fields such as pharmaceuticals, where there is a significant market in many Arab countries.

There is a notable absence of indigenous Middle Eastern multinational companies, apart from in the area of banking, where institutions such as the Arab Bank have a significant presence in several Middle Eastern countries. The nationalization of most of the leading private companies in Egypt, Syria and Iraq in the 1950s and 1960s not only curbed private initiative, but also created state companies which were nationally rather than regionally or internationally oriented. As the companies were dependent on government, there was no possibility of their being permitted to expand activities away from the home base. The most these companies could aspire to was to become national champions, not significant international players able to compete with freer and more flexible multinational companies. There was a failure to recognize the link between foreign direct investment and export success, the state companies being inward-looking with respect to sales and insular with regard to product development and process innovation.

An enormous boost to the private sector could come through privatization measures in Middle Eastern countries, but although governments have not rejected such measures partly as a result of IMF enthusiasm for privatization plans, progress has been painfully slow. Turkey is the only country to have privatized significant public enterprises, notably the state airline, but even there significant obstacles remain.[10] The UAE has also made considerable progress. Still, Arab governments have been reluctant to confront the vested interests in their state-sector industries, fearing the reaction from managers concerned about their own positions.[11] There is also the fear that privatization could result in significant reductions in the work-forces of the industries involved, resulting in widespread discontent from those made redundant or those who face future job uncertainty.[12] There are some economists, notably in Egypt, who are sceptical about the merits of privatization, fearing the consequences for income distribution.[13] Even in Israel there is considerable opposition to privatization, there are powerful vested interests that oppose it, as well as a widespread feeling that the existing semi-socialist economic structures serve the country well enough without the need for painful restructuring.[14]

EQUITY MARKET DEVELOPMENT

One of the major advantages that private companies have over their nationalized counterparts is their ability to raise equity capital. Nationalized industries in the Middle East are invariably underfunded, as even when governments have allocated the initial investment, there has been a reluctance to finance further funding for modernization and upgrading of plant and equipment. The region's banks have mostly funded stock-holding and provided trade financing facilities rather than the long-term capital injections required for business development. Surveys of business interests in the region reveal that even private sector enterprises identify finance as a severe constraint, citing both the lack of access to finance and its high cost as major problems inhibiting expansion.[15]

Middle Eastern equity markets are very underdeveloped, and to a considerable extent the region has lost out on the growing investment by Western fund managers in emerging markets. Only the stockmarkets in Istanbul and Tel Aviv are large enough to be classified as emerging markets, while the exchanges in Amman, Cairo and Casablanca are still very limited in terms of the number of companies quoted, share turnover and the value of the stock. In 1994, cross-border equity flows into emerging markets worldwide exceeded $40 billion, but less than $300 million was attracted into the Middle East.[16] Portfolio investors from outside the Gulf Cooperation Council (GCC) states are not permitted to purchase shares in private or quoted companies in Saudi Arabia, Kuwait or the United Arab Emirates,[17] although foreign direct investment in joint ventures is permitted as long as there is a majority GCC shareholding. Portfolio investors from GCC states are permitted to invest worldwide, and there are no currency restrictions, but those from the northern Arab states cannot invest in Western markets, or indeed in other markets in the region, due to restrictions on capital movements.

There are, however, no restrictions on Western portfolio investors purchasing equities in Cairo, Amman, Casablanca or Istanbul, but few fund managers appear to be interested. Lebanese expatriates, including those living in the US and Europe, invested in the construction company Solidere when it was floated in 1994, but there is little involvement by Westerners. Nevertheless, the initial share offering of $650 million in Solidere was 42 per cent oversubscribed, which demonstrates the substantial resources of the Lebanese expatriate community, their interest in equity investment and their confidence in the future of Beirut.[18] Similarly, Palestinian and Jordanian expatriates are major investors in the Amman market, and Egyptian expatriates, to a lesser extent, in Cairo and the much smaller exchange in Alexandria. These Arab expatriates have the advantage of greater knowledge of the markets, especially the personalities involved, as much as the companies themselves. However, most rely on local brokers and do not actively manage their own portfolios. The same applies to Jewish investors from the United States and Europe who have portfolios on the Tel Aviv exchange, although there are a few notable investment analysts in New York with some knowledge of the companies quoted on the Tel Aviv exchange.

Egypt has the oldest stockmarket in the Arab world, the history of the Alexandria exchange dating from 1883.[19] A separate exchange was established in Cairo, and by the 1920s this was flourishing. Indeed, for a while it was the fifth busiest securities market in the world, with business channeled into a number of quoted holding companies. It was Bank Misr, founded by Tal'at Harb, that owned a stake in each of these companies, Bank Misr itself being a quoted company. Although the cross-holding structures can be criticized as serving the interests of a narrow business clique, the successful growth of the textile industry in Egypt was entirely financed by private capital in the 1920s and 1930s, with modern plant and equipment installed without any calls on government funding.[20] Indeed much of the machinery was still working when the industry was nationalized by President Nasser, along with Bank Misr; it was arguably the lack of subsequent investment that resulted in the industry stagnating and becoming totally dependent on a heavily protected domestic market.

Although there has been some revival in the Cairo stockmarket in the 1990s, Tables 8.5 shows the components listed in terms of shares and capitalization, with share dealings worth around $30 to $40 million a month by 1995, this is a very small amount for an economy of Egypt's size.[21] Most transactions are in local currency, but around 10 per cent of the total are in US dollars (the dollar functions as a type of parallel currency in Egypt, although its role is being reduced). Dealings on the Alexandria exchange are less than 10 per cent of the value of those in Cairo, with few dollar transactions. Most dealing is through floor trading in both exchanges, although there is a small over-the-counter market through Egyptian banks. The volume of transactions is minuscule in comparison to most emerging markets, seldom exceeding 5000 deals per month in Cairo. Furthermore, the market is at a virtual standstill during the month of Ramadan, as many of the traders are devout Muslims.

The majority of companies listed on the Cairo exchange are closed, which precludes the issue of new shares. Most interest, however, has recently been centred on the joint stock companies, as the Capital Market Act of 1994, which has improved regularity procedures, is encouraging existing companies to raise fresh equity capital and new companies to seek market quotations.

Before the Act there were only 12 stockbrokers, but by 1995 there were over 40, and settlement procedures have been speeded up.[22] Four mutual funds with an initial capital of $150 million have been established by the state-owned National Bank of Egypt, Bank of Alexandria, Bank Misr and the partially private Egyptian American Bank. Privatization would, of course, result in a substantial boost to stockmarket activity, but although there are 314 companies on the government's privatization list, so far only limited tranches have been offered on the stockmarket for a handful, the most

Table 8.5 Companies listed on the Cairo stock-market

Type of Company	*Joint Stock*	*Closed Company*
Number of companies	154	526
Number of shares	291 900	153 100
Capital £E million	1 372	2 995
Capital $US million	390	631

Source: Central Bank of Egypt, *Economic Review, 1994/95*, p. 123.

notable being the 10 per cent stake in the Paints and Chemical Industries Company.[23]

There is little Western involvement in the Cairo stock-market, with not more than 2 per cent of the $70 million in assets which are actively traded being held by European or American fund managers. Foreign and Colonial, Merrill Lynch, Robert Fleming and Framlington all have regional funds which include Egypt, but the extent of their future involvement will clearly depend on market conditions. The incentives are already in place, and the 2 per cent capital gains tax is unlikely to deter Western funds. However, much depends on share price performance. Share price-to-earnings ratios average 17 for the 20 most-traded companies on the Cairo stock-market, which is lower than in many emerging markets. Share prices rose by 24 per cent in 1994 but marked time in 1995, with a stagnant performance over the year as a whole.

The future outlook for share prices, and the willingness of Western fund managers to include Cairo and other Middle East markets in their portfolios, will largely depend on the political climate in the region. There is no profit to be made in setting up special mutual funds or investment trusts for Middle Eastern markets if the expensive advertising necessary to bring such funds to the attention of the Western investing public is undermined by adverse political developments and news coverage. The Middle East peace process could potentially help the flow of equity capital into the region, but investors are well aware that peace between Israel and the Arab states would resolve only one of the several conflicts in the Middle East, albeit the most serious and long-standing one. Politicians may suggest that by solving one conflict others would also begin to be resolved, but investors are more cautious and ultimately it is the markets that will provide the verdict.

So far the omens do not look good. Share price information on the Cairo exchanges is not available on-line through financial information services such as Datastream, but the prices of some Israeli funds, as well as the major traded stocks on the Amman, Istanbul and Casablanca exchanges, are included. The Israel Fund, which was launched in 1994 in anticipation of growth in the value of quoted companies on the Tel Aviv stockmarket, has proved very disappointing to date. The price fell by almost 40 cents in the first few months after the launch (see Figure 8.1); since then it has fluctuated between 60 and 80 cents, well below the $1 issue price. Not only has the trend been downward, but technical analysis shows that the price in early 1995 was above a three or four-month moving average, suggesting that buyers might be better to defer any purchase plans.

Technical analysts can interpret when to buy and sell in various ways, and if the first two months' prices are omitted, the trend for the Israel Fund is only slightly negative. Fund managers are more concerned with fundamental analysis, but the Middle East peace process has not done much to change

Figure 8.1 Israel Fund performance, $ price

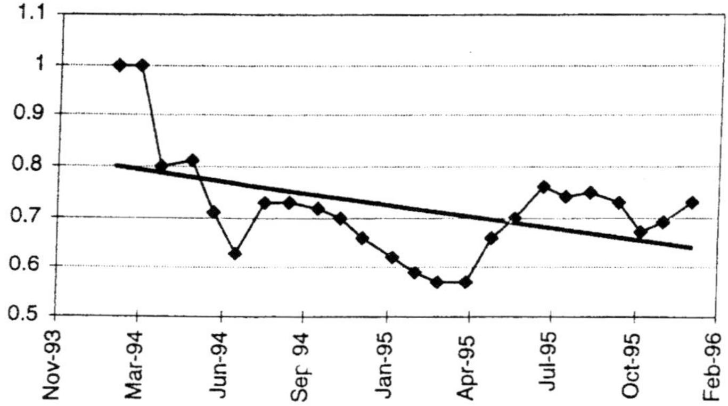

Source: Datastream International.

country risk perceptions. There remains the unquantifable effect of the continuing threat of violence from Islamists in both Egypt and the Israeli-occupied territories. Jordan's private sector benefited throughout the 1970s and 1980s from Iraqi business, as its main regional trade was with Baghdad, but the continuing economic embargo and the uncertain political future for Iraq also affects investors' attitudes towards Jordan. Attempts by the Jordanian government to distance itself from Iraq may have impressed political actors and commentators, but financial analysts are more cautious. The peace treaty with Israel has not helped the prices of shares on the Amman market, and the trend ever since was downward despite the attempts by governments to project an optimistic picture regarding the economic outlook for Jordan (see Figure 8.2). As the market in Amman fell by 23 per cent in 1993, a better performance in the following two years might have been expected. However, Western fund managers placed less than $6 million in shares in Amman, a minute proportion of the $280 million which the Jordanian authorities had hoped to attract.[24]

Markets in the Middle East and North Africa which are distant from states directly involved in the peace process appear to have performed better than those of the three core countries that have signed peace treaties: namely, Egypt, Jordan and Israel (see Figures 8.3 and 8.4). In both Morocco and Turkey there is at least some uncertainty created by the growing influence of Islamists. In Turkey there has also been a long-time insurgency campaign by the Kurdish PKK, and to complicate matters even further there are the additional factors of instability within the coalition government and the indecisive elections that produced it. Yet in spite of these factors the stockmarkets in both Casablanca and Istanbul have fared comparatively well, and most Western portfolio investment has gone into the markets in these countries.

Figure 8.2 Amman financial market index

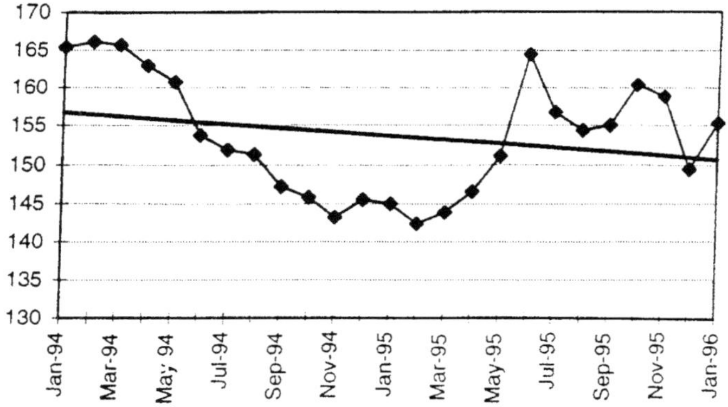

Source: Datastream International.

Figure 8.3 Casablanca leading-25 share index

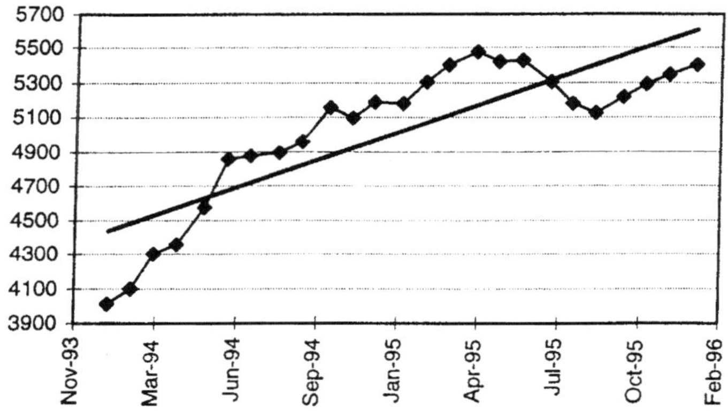

Source: Datastream International.

Framlington, one of the largest Western fund management groups, launched a Maghreb fund in September 1994 that initially placed $30 million in Morocco and Tunisia.[25] The civil war in neighbouring Algeria does not seem to have affected the fund's performance.

CONCLUSION

The tempered optimism in political circles generated by the peace process between Israel and the Arab cordon states does not seem to be matched by

Figure 8.4 Istanbul all-share index

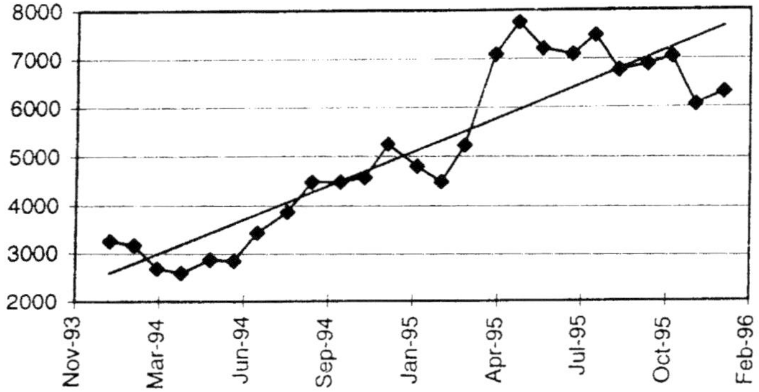

Source: Datastream International.

changing perceptions of the impact of political risk on financial markets. Western fund managers who know the region and are in a position to appraise fundamental risks remain extremely cautious. This trend will likely be reinforced during the Netanyahu term of government in Israel. Financial markets in countries affected only marginally by the peace process but subject to some of the same political risks appear to be performing much better than those of the core countries. If future private portfolio investment is limited or minimal, which seems likely, international aid flows will be the only financial gain from the peace process, especially for its Arab participants. These aid flows have not produced positive long-term benefits in the past, and there is no reason to expect this to change in the future. Continuing dependence on external governments may continue or even increase as a result of the peace process, with privately funded self-sustaining development more elusive than ever.

Notes

1. Ishac Diwan and Lyn Squire, "Private Assets and Public Debts: External Finance in a Peaceful Middle East", *Middle East Journal* 49(1) (1995), pp. 69–88. These World Bank economists estimate the net inflows of governmental capital as averaging 16 per cent of GNP for the Arab Mashreq and 14 per cent of GNP for Israel for the 1970–90 period.
2. Nemat Shafik, *Claiming the Future: Choosing Prosperity in the Middle East and North Africa* (World Bank, Washington DC, 1995), pp. 92, 100.
3. International Monetary Fund, *International Financial Statistics* (Washington DC, February 1995), pp. 216, 326.
4. Two-gap analysis is explained in most economic development texts, drawing on the original work by Hollis Chenery in the 1960s. See for example Michael

Todaro, *Economic Development*, 5th edn (London: Longmans, 1994), pp. 543–5; and Gerald M. Meier, *Leading Issues in Economic Development*, 6th edn (Oxford: Oxford University Press, 1995), pp. 215–16.

5. Alexander Yeats, "Export Prospects of Middle Eastern Countries: A Post-Uruguay Round Analysis", International Economics Department, International Trade Division, World Bank, Washington DC, 1995.
6. Nemat Shafik, *op. cit.*, P. 67.
7. Glenn Harrison, Thomas Rutherford and David Tarr, "Quantifying the Outcome of the Uruguay Round", *Finance and Development* (December 1995), pp. 38–42. A fuller version of the findings is presented in Will Martin and L. Alan Winters (eds), "The Uruguay Round and Developing Economies", World Bank Discussion Paper no. 307, Washington DC, 1995.
8. *Ibid.*, p. 39. For further discussion of these issues see Raed Safadi and Maarten Smeets, "The Impact of the Uruguay Round Agreement on the Countries in the Middle East and North Africa", *Newsletter of the Economic Research Forum for the Arab Countries, Iran and Turkey* 1(4) (1994), pp. 3–5.
9. For a brief financial history of this bank see Rodney Wilson, *Banking and Finance in the Arab Middle East* (London: Macmillan, 1983), pp. 43–9.
10. Maurice J. Patton, "Constraints to Privatisation in Turkey", in lllya Harik and Denis J. Sullivan (eds), *Privatisation and Liberalisation in the Middle East* (Bloomington: Indiana University Press, 1992), pp. 106–22.
11. Ibrahim Helmy, Abdel-Rahman and Mohammed Sultan Abu Ali, "The Role of the Public and Private Sectors with Special Reference to Privatization: The Case of Egypt", in Saad El-Naggar, *Private and Structural Adjustment in the Arab Countries* (Washington DC: International Monetary Fund, 1968), pp. 141–81.
12. Marsha Pripstein Posusney, "Labour as an Obstacle to Privatisation", in lllya Harik and Denis J. Sullivan, *op. cit.*, pp. 81–105.
13. Galal A. Amin, *Egypt's Economic Predicament: A Study in the Interaction of External Pressure, Political Folly and Social Tension in Egypt, 1960–1990* (Leiden: E.J. Brill, 1995), pp. 96–8.
14. Julian Ozanne and Quentin Peel, "An Economic Vision Israelis are Ignoring", *Financial Times*, London, 30 January 1996; p. 5.
15. See for example Hamid Alavi, "International Competitiveness of the Private Industry and the Constraints to its Development: The Case of Morocco", Middle East and North Africa Discussion Paper no. 6, World Bank, Washington DC, June 1993, pp. 40–3.
16. James Whittington, "Equity Souk Opens for Foreign Business", *Financial Times Survey of Emerging Markets*, 20 February 1995, pp. 7–8.
17. James Whittington and Mark Dennis, "Middle East: Most Markets Restrict Foreign Investment", *Financial Times FT500 Survey*, 25 January 1996, p. 43.
18. Nasser Saidi, "Lebanon's Future: A Regional Capital Market", *Newsletter of the Economic Research Forum for the Arab Countries, Iran and Turkey*, 1(3)1(994), pp. 7–8.
19. Mona Qassem, "Developments in the Stock Market in Egypt", *Newsletter of the Economic Research Forum for the Arab Countries, Iran and Turkey* 1(3) (1994), pp. 8–9.
20. Marius Deeb, "Bank Misr and the Emergence of the Local Bourgeoisie in Egypt", in Elie Kedourie (ed.), *The Middle Eastern Economy: Studies in Economics and Economic History* (London: Frank Cass, 1976), pp. 69–86.

21. Estimated from figures in the Central Bank of Egypt, *Economic Review*, 1994–95, 35(1), pp. 24–5.
22. James Whittington, "Cairo Stock Exchange: the Market Wakes Up", *Financial Times Survey of Egypt*, 15 May 1995; p. 2.
23. *Ibid*.
24. James Whittington, "Equity Souk Opens for Foreign Business," *op. cit.*, pp. 7–8.
25. *Ibid*., p. 8.

9 The Middle East Peace Process: How is it Affecting Planning in the Cities and Regions in Jordan?

Peter L. Doan

INTRODUCTION

The effects of international agreements and formal treaties on domestic planning and policy-making are not clearly understood. Treaties between governments provide a framework for maintaining social and economic ties and establishing trade policy, but assessing their actual impact is far more challenging. The acrimonious debate and uncertain overall effects of the North American Free Trade Agreement (NAFTA) between Canada, the United States and Mexico illustrate the difficulties of predicting short-range effects and for anticipating subsequent long-term policy shifts.

Peace treaties can reduce uncertainty and establish the overall direction of political ties between countries formerly at war, but treaties in and of themselves cannot guarantee the quality of the social, political and economic interactions that will evolve between countries. These exchanges are based on decisions of individuals which are difficult to control through government intervention. Accordingly, it is difficult to predict the local-level impacts of a given treaty which, in turn, generates additional uncertainty for planners and policy-makers concerned with regional development. During "normal" periods, decision-makers in less developed countries struggle to stretch insufficient resources to meet a myriad of pressing problems, but unanticipated impacts can contribute to an atmosphere of crisis which may exacerbate uncertainty over appropriate policy remedies.

This chapter examines the state of local-level planning in Jordan in the wake of the peace treaties and protocols that have been signed by Jordanian–Israeli diplomats. It focuses in particular on the ability of planners in cities and regions outside the Amman metropolitan area to respond to increased development pressures resulting from the peace process. Amman has received a disproportionate share of urban investment and economic activity, and is likely to receive a good deal more as a result of the Wye Accord. Whether these treaty-related benefits will exacerbate the growth of

Amman or have a more dispersed effect on outlying areas is a key question for planners in Jordan. Because the technical capacity to deal with rapid growth is quite limited outside of Amman, the chapter considers the constraints on planning institutions and their ability to cope with such growth.

PLANNING INSTITUTIONS AND CRISIS MANAGEMENT

Uncertainty in planning is by no means a novel concept, but Western uncertainty is moderate in comparison to Third World uncertainty, the problems with the latter being often exacerbated by high levels of political and economic instability. Uncertainty in the Jordanian context is dominated by a long series of crises starting with the Arab–Israeli wars in 1948 and 1967, the 1970 civil disturbances of Black September, the 1973 Arab–Israeli war, less directly by the Lebanese civil war beginning in 1975, the 1982 Israeli invasion of Lebanon, and extending to the recent 1990–91 Gulf war. Jordan's experience in dealing with these crises has had a profound effect on the development of its planning institutions and practice.

Jordan's first experience with planning dates itself from King Hussein's order for the formulation of a national development plan for the years 1962–67. Because this development plan did little more than project economic growth and present a prioritized list of projects, it was abandoned after two years and replaced by a Seven-Year Plan for 1964–70,[1] which was, in turn, interrupted by the 1967 war. A Three-Year Plan for 1973–75 was drafted to provide a bridge to more organized national development planning, but this plan was influenced by the 1973 war. That conflict carried several indirect benefits to Jordan, including large quantities of Arab investments and assistance to Jordan resulting from the windfall of the Arab oil embargo, and increased employment opportunities for skilled Jordanian (and Palestinian) workers.

The next two national development plans from 1976–80 and 1981–86 were conceived and implemented during a period of unprecedented growth in the Jordanian economy. That growth was largely due to the high levels of remittances from Jordanians working abroad and the large volumes of foreign assistance which Jordan continued to receive. The 1981–85 plan cited the population dominance of Amman as a problem, but contained few concrete or corrective policy measures. The 1986–91 plan for the first time included substantial participation from residents in less-developed regions[2] and incorporated separate sections on regional development objectives.[3] Unfortunately, the financial crisis of 1988[4] interrupted the implementation of this latter plan and undermined efforts to increase local participation in the planning process.

The need for more effective regional planning and policies to address the spatial distribution of urban population remains clear in the wake of King

Hussein's death,[5] but the means through which King Abdullah's court can achieve a more meaningful redistribution of population and economic activities is less obvious. The planning function in Jordan has been a predominately national-level activity and only within the past ten years has it been extended to the sub-national regional level.[6]

The vision and overall strategic direction for planning purposes come from Jordan's royal family, and will likely continue to be so. While the technical skill levels of bureaucrats and planners in Jordan are quite high,[7] the specific skills needed to implement these development initiatives are heavily concentrated in Amman. As a result planners in Jordan tend to be reactive and, although quite creative, have not developed the strategic planning skills necessary for dealing with the post-peace treaty conditions.

While the signing of the formal peace agreement between Israel and Jordan did not technically constitute a crisis, it does represent an important strategic opportunity with potentially very large consequences. Teams of high-level negotiators have worked hard to anticipate and iron out some of the most probable difficulties which may arise, but for the vast majority of Jordanians the treaty was a surprise and is still a very large unknown. Even now, to take advantage of this opportunity Jordan must move beyond its traditional reactive planning mode and engage in a broad-based strategic discussion of planning goals and objectives. If not, the economy and population will be at a considerable disadvantage *vis-à-vis* their more advanced neighbours who have already begun a far-sighted strategic planning process.[8]

After more than five years, there is an even greater need for local-level planning and policy initiatives in areas likely to experience large tourism and other cross-border impacts. Development pressures in these regions are likely to be intense, with a range of associated problems such as congestion, pollution, environmental degradation, inefficient urban growth patterns and skewed income distribution. It is not clear if traditional models of centralized planning and decision-making can cope with the rate and variety of decisions required at the local level in such circumstances. Given the complexity of many of these development issues, a planning and decision-making model which incorporates local perspectives and emphasizes learning from experience may be needed. In the next section we examine existing planning processes in Jordan and evaluate the effect of post-treaty development pressures on those processes.

POST-TREATY PLANNING ISSUES

Jordan's ability to plan effectively for future development depends on whether its leadership is able to adapt its existing planning institutions to cope with longer-term strategic planning issues. The crisis-management skills developed over the past four decades may still be needed in the near term because of the fragile state of the peace process itself, the ultimate success of which is tied to the resolution of the Israeli–Palestinian conflict.[9] However, the need for a strategic approach which articulates and enhances Jordan's central location in the Middle East region and its skilled labour force is of critical importance for the economic survival of the country over the long run. Several areas in which these skills are most likely to be needed are explored below.

The Rapid Growth of Tourism

The tourism sector is likely to show the largest direct effects from the peace process and to make a significant contribution to economic development in this region in the short and medium term. The dramatic growth of tourism revenues has captured the interest of the popular media[10] and the careful attention of domestic and international investors. As illustrated in Table 9.1, total tourist visits to Jordan have increased steadily from a low point just after the Gulf war; by 15 per cent from 1992 to 1993, and by 10 per cent from 1993 to 1994. From the first six months of 1994 to the first six months of 1995 tourist visits increased by a staggering 40 per cent. The largest group of tourists is from the Arab Gulf states, but increasing numbers of Europeans and Americans are visiting Jordan. In addition, during the first half of 1995 there were more than 52 000 Israeli tourists.[11] The likelihood of continued increases is high as tourists have come to realize that Jordan is no longer a "hot-spot" to be avoided.

An increase in tourist visits is usually translated into economic gains for the country experiencing that growth. Table 9.2 shows that during this period both receipts and expenditures from the tourism sector have increased steadily. More importantly, the contribution of tourism to gross national

Table 9.1 Tourist arrivals in Jordan, by nationality, 1992–5

	1992 (Jan–Dec)	*1993 (Jan–Dec)*	*1994 (Jan–June)*	*1994 (Jul–Dec)*	*1995 (Jan–June)*
American	39 250	52 512	27 388	42 490	49 716
European	120 898	151 475	88 930	101 352	141 894
Other	12 804	15 607	12 806	17 247	17 159
Gulf States	490 629	547 006	187 207	356 843	184 753
Israel	0	0	0	0	52 144
Total (semi-annual)			317 331	526 932	445 666
Total (annual)	663 581	765 600	844 263		

Source: Ministry of Tourism, Statistics Department.

Table 9.2 Increase in tourist expenditures, receipts and percentage contribution to GNP

	1992	*1993*	*1994*
Expenditures	238.1	239.1	296.8
% increase from previous year	24%	0.4%	19%
Receipts	314.3	390.2	582.0*
% increase from previous year	46%	24%	49%*
Tourism contribution to GNP	10%	11%	15%*

*Revised figures for 1994 based on a statement of the Minister of Tourism as reported by the *Jordan Times*, 12 December 1995.
Source: Ministry of Tourism, Statistics Department.

product has also increased steadily from 10 to 15 per cent, indicating the increasing importance of that sector to the Jordanian economy. While this growth emphasizes the economic benefits of tourism, it is important to also consider how those benefits are distributed. First one must consider the spatial distribution of tourism benefits to outlying areas, which may have few other sources of income. In addition, it is important to consider the effects of these benefits on the distribution of income within the kingdom as a whole. To the extent that only the elite derive benefits from tourism, the long range prospects for the sector may be limited by increasing hostility towards an invasion of foreign tourists, especially when a portion of these tourists are from Israel.

At this point it is difficult to make a concrete assessment of the distributional impacts of tourism. However, to the extent that hotels are owned and operated by international capital and tend to employ non-Jordanian workers, the profits and employment prospects are likely to be limited within Jordan. Furthermore, if the five-star hotels purchase goods and services that are imported from outside the country or local-regional area, there is likely to be even greater leakage of benefits outside the local economy. Data are not currently available on these patterns of investment and employment.

A tourism masterplan has been prepared by the Japan International Cooperation Agency (JICA) which highlights the potential of the sector until the year 2010. While this report presents a basic analysis of the infrastructure and local services needed to attract Western tourists, it does not address the longer-term economic and social impacts of large tourists flows in and out of previously remote rural areas. Traffic-demand models are useful to predict the demand for highways, but do little to gauge the more sensitive aspects of the rapid changes likely to occur at the ground level.

Projections of as many as 2000 tourists per day have prompted substantial new investments in hotels in the vicinity of the ancient city of Petra, but little planning has been done to ensure that development occurs in an orderly fashion, with a view to avoiding problems in areas such as sanitation, solid waste disposal, safe drinking water, as well as the possible degradation of fragile historic sites. The environmental crisis occurring in Wadi Musa and the greater Petra region due to rapid growth has forced the World Bank and the US Agency for International Development to make substantial investments in water and sanitation systems for this area. This kind of belated infrastructure provision is not a good model for careful planning: some sort of development oversight in this special region is essential.[12]

Other Issues

Transport linkages. The fanfare accompanying the signing of the transportation accords between Israel and Jordan[13] indicate the importance of post-treaty linkages. The agreements which allow Jordanian trucks to transport goods across the Wadi Araba and Sheikh Hussein border crossing points for transit to Israel's Mediterranean sea ports are clearly the result of careful negotiations. However, the effects of the increased traffic on land-use patterns through the already congested Aqaba region and the northern Jordan Valley have not been specified.

These developments are likely to require substantial local planning inputs as well as an integrated regional planning mechanism to protect the environmentally sensitive Wadi Araba region, the cities of Eilat and Aqaba, the Red Sea coastline along the Gulf of Aqaba, as well as the northern Jordan Valley and nearby cities. In addition, the Jordanian government has announced plans to construct a rail line between Irbid and Haifa which will accelerate these effects. The regional importance of railways is well-recognized in Jordan,[14] but such large projects are likely to have local impacts which merit careful consideration by local planners and officials concerned with stimulating and guiding the development process.

Potential population movements. Although issues related to the repatriation of the Palestinian refugees and other displaced persons have been postponed until the final status negotiations, there are clearly a number of complex planning issues involved. Infrastructure planners in Jordan who already struggle to accommodate the rapid growth of the existing population need to have a clearer idea of the scope of any return movements of population, if any. The question of who will return and who will be allowed to return is the subject of many private and public conversations in Jordan, but there is little official guidance.

There are a range of possibilities. One extreme scenario would include a large percentage of Jordanian citizens of Palestinian origin eventually returning to claim citizenship in a future Palestinian state. The effects of such out-migration would be tremendous for Jordan, resulting in a depletion of manpower and a surfeit of basic infrastructure built for a much larger population. An equally extreme scenario in the opposite direction would include no return migration and possible population movements away from a Palestinian economy which is so constrained by the dominant Israeli economy that investments and employment are severely curtailed. The implications of this scenario are equally grim for a Jordanian economy already severely stretched to absorb 300 000 returnees after the Gulf war. Reality will probably fall somewhere in between these extremes, but there appears to be little strategic consideration of the possible consequences.

It is too early to analyse the full range of peace-related problems and planning issues. Only the rapid growth of the tourism sector has had a measurable impact to date on development patterns. The protracted negotiations over the transportation sector were concluded relatively recently, in January 1996. The even more delicate negotiations over the "right of return" for Palestinians in Jordan (and elsewhere) have been put off until the final status phase. The impact of these other issues will be determined in the future. Therefore, the rest of this chapter focuses on the tourism sector and uses it as a lens through which to view the evolution of planning procedures. The study includes six secondary cities in Jordan where there are likely to be modest to very large effects in this sector.

METHODS

The method used to evaluate the evolution of planning in secondary cities in the wake of the peace treaty includes a review of previous census documents as well as the National Village Survey conducted by the Ministry of Planning in 1985 and the preliminary results of the 1994 census. These figures were used to assess changes in the spatial distribution of the population between these smaller urban centres prior to the advent of the peace process. Information on projected tourist flows gathered by the Ministry of Tourism was employed; also included were data drawn from structured interviews with leaders in six municipalities, as well as informal interviews with a variety of government officials. The analysis focuses on the development impacts of tourism, which has become one of Jordan's leading sources of foreign exchange and which appears to be the most significant area for peace-related growth.

To assess the capacity and constraints of planning at the local level, I have examined six municipalities which are either currently facing "development pressure" or are likely to face such pressures in the short term. A structured interview was conducted in each municipality with the newly-elected mayors and local council members. The questions addressed the extent of local development pressure, the existing capacity for planning within the municipality, and the effectiveness of existing planning procedures.

The six intermediate-sized cities chosen for this study represent a range of smaller urban centres where local planning capacity is likely to be scarce, and where local development impacts are likely to be high.[15] Wadi Musa is Jordan's most important tourist destination. Jarash and Madaba are secondary tourist destinations of considerable importance. Umm Qeis, Karak and Salt are other cities whose tourism potential has not yet been fully realized.

CITY COMPARISONS

To understand the tourism potential of these cities it is necessary to understand something of their history. Jordan's historical role as a crossroads in the cradle of urban civilization[16] makes it attractive to tourists interested in history and the evolution of civilization. Jordan's unique geological features, such as Wadi Rum and the Dead Sea, are also sources of attraction for some more environmentally-aware tourists. Although this chapter focuses on the impacts of the former kind of tourists on existing cities, there will clearly be significant impacts resulting from the latter kind of tourists in the fragile desert areas and environmentally-sensitive Dead Sea zone.

Each of the cities selected for this survey has a long and fascinating history. Salt was an Ottoman administrative centre for the region and contains some excellent examples of Ottoman architecture from the late nineteenth century. Its status as a thriving commercial centre predates the founding of the modern state. In 1921, then-Emir Abdullah decided against establishing the capital of Transjordan in Salt and moved instead to the small village of Amman to the east. In 1995, the Japan International Cooperation Agency completed a feasibility study for investing JD 10 million to transform the old city centre into a tourist area by renovating many buildings and establishing tourist facilities.[17]

The city of Karak is located on what was once a walled hilltop, dominated by a massive castle built during the Crusades. During the latter years of the Ottoman Empire the people of Karak actively resisted the imposition of imperial authority, until 1894, when an Ottoman military expedition pacified the region and established Karak as the administrative centre of the *mutasariffiyya*.[18] By 1921, this city was well-established as a key administrative centre for the southern region. The modern city has spread onto several adjacent hills, but the old walled city remains a fascinating blend of old and new architectural styles.

Modern day Jarash is located on the site of the Decapolis city of Gerasa, which was severely destroyed by an earthquake in AD 747.[19] The modern city of Jarash was resettled beginning in 1878 by Circassian refugees from the Caucasus Mountain area of Central Asia. The new city was built on the northern half of the Roman ruins; very little remains of this portion of the city with the exception of the Roman baths, several segments of the ancient wall and the excavations of several other buildings. In marked contrast, the southern half of the city consists of a set of extremely well-preserved Roman ruins, which constitute a major tourist attraction. However, the integration of tourist activities into the modern town remains a challenge for this city, since most visitors never venture beyond the ruins to explore the modern city and patronize the shops and restaurants located there.

Madaba is located not far from Mount Nebo, which is thought to be the site from which Moses viewed the promised land. Madaba was an important centre of Christianity during the Byzantine era and was known for the expertise of its craftsmen in creating beautiful mosaic floors in many churches throughout the city, many of which can still be seen today. After a period of abandonment the modern city was resettled by three Christian tribes who moved north from Karak in 1880.[20] Within a short time this resettled area was thriving, at least in part because of the rich agricultural land surrounding the city. The recent opening of the Madaba Archaeological Park and the Madaba Mosaic School, a specialized school for the design and reconstruction of mosaics, indicate that there is real potential for the growth of tourism in this area.[21]

Another major site with good potential for tourism development is the village of Umm Qeis in the northern-most area of the Irbid governorate. The city of Umm Qeis is located on and around the ancient city of Gadara (another city of the Decapolis). Umm Qeis was occupied intermittently during the eighteenth and nineteenth centuries by families engaged in agriculture in the region. However, the adoption of the Ottoman Land Code in 1858, stating that private ownership of land was to be based upon continuous cultivation, provided the impetus for formal land registration in this area. The town itself was settled by people from the nearby villages of Sama Rusan and Malka during the late 1870s and 1880s.[22] These new registrants built houses on the site of the ancient city and used many of the cut stones and statues in their houses, creating a vibrant mosaic of new and old architectural styles.

In 1985 the residents of homes built on the archaeological site were evicted in order to facilitate the excavation of the ruins. While the government built a new housing estate for the residents, this eviction has caused a long-standing dispute which is not yet fully resolved. The Ministry of Tourism has authorized hotel development in this region, but continuing problems with local residents have slowed project implementation. Residents feel that they should have the right to build and operate tourist-oriented facilities so that they might gain some benefit from the presence of the tourists.

The residents of the city of Wadi Musa historically viewed themselves as the guardians of the entrance to Petra. They were so successful that the Western explorer, J.L. Burkhart, thought he had "discovered" a lost city in 1806 when he visited the region. However, while the site was inhabited by local tribesmen, it was little more than a village serving as a stop on the Muslim pilgrimage route to Mecca, with virtually no urban infrastructure of its own. Over time, with gradual recognition of the attraction of Petra for archaeologists, geologists, geographers, as well as a growing number of intrepid tourists and travellers, the village grew into a small city.

Initially agriculture was the major revenue source for all of these cities, although over time Karak, Madaba, Salt and Jarash developed as regional market towns and trading centres. Umm Qeis and Wadi Musa remained considerably smaller and have grown primarily because of the archaeological significance of their sites.

POPULATION CHANGES

Population growth in most of these cities in recent years has been quite rapid, as shown in Table 9.3. Salt and Madaba have had the largest total population increases, with Salt adding 16 000 new residents and Madaba adding nearly 20 000. However, as illustrated in Table 9.3, when the rate of growth is considered, Wadi Musa has shown the fastest percentage growth of the six cities, increasing from 654 people in 1961 to 11 210 in 1994 – an increase of 1600 per cent over the 33-year period. Jarash grew by 460 per cent and Madaba grew by 400 per cent. Salt grew by 250 per cent and Umm Qeis and

Table 9.3 Case study: city populations, by year, and growth rates, by period

Name	*City Populations by Year*				*Growth Rates by Period*			
	1961	*1979*	*1985*	*1994*	*1961–79*	*1979–85*	*1985–94*	*1961–94*
Salt	16 176	33 037	40 847	56 296	104%	24%	38%	248%
Madaba	11 224	28 236	34 911	55 156	152%	24%	58%	391%
Jarash	3 796	9 978	12 266	21 244	163%	23%	73%	460%
Karak	7 422	11 941	14 425	18 587	61%	21%	29%	150%
Wadi Musa	654	5 432	6226	11 210	731%	15%	80%	1614%
Umm Qeis	1 196	2 485	2865	3 396	108%	15%	19%	184%

Sources: Census of Population and Housing 1961; Census of Population, 1979; National Village Survey, 1985; Preliminary Results of the Census of Population, 1994.

Karak have grown by roughly 150 per cent. These rates make Wadi Musa the third-fastest growing city in Jordan.[23] Jarash is the sixth-fastest growing city and Madaba is the seventh-fastest. Thus these cities represent urban locations with strong growth patterns.

The growth of Wadi Musa is clearly a function of its key location at the entrance to Petra, the most important tourist destination in Jordan. The growth of Madaba and Jarash can only partly be attributed to increasing tourism. Part of their growth is a function of the natural rate of increase and of in-migration from outlying areas. In June 1994, both cities were designated the administrative centres for two of four newly-created governorates, suggesting that they are likely to continue to provide a vital administrative link to their regions. Madaba is also developing as an industrial centre especially for food processing and bottling industries. The opening of a Coca-Cola bottling plant in Madaba is a direct result of the signing of the peace treaty; this company was previously unable to operate in any Arab country because of the Arab boycott of companies doing business with Israel.

Table 9.4 suggests that the spatial impact of the tourist visits is likely to be concentrated in certain geographic regions. In three of the cities for which data are available, the increase in tourist flows has been more than twice as high as the national increase. However in the older, more established cities the rates of growth appear to be much smaller; in the case of Karak it lags behind the national average. The rapid growth of Wadi Musa is expected, but the growth rates in Jarash and Madaba suggest that they have become part of the tourist circuit. The statistics for Umm Qeis do not permit an assessment of changes in visitor patterns, but the fact that visits to this site continue to exceed the number of visitors to Karak does suggest that there is considerable potential for tourism-related growth in this city as well.

Table 9.4 Visits by foreign tourists to selected municipalities in Jordan, 1994–5

	1994 (Jan–June)	*1994 (Jul–Dec)*	*1995 (Jan–June)*	*Rate of Growth*
Madaba	45 849	60 213	94 258	106%
Jarash	65 835	74 518	148 110	125%
Karak	18 862	34 950	23 650	25%
Wadi Musa	45 526	50 662	105 550	132%
Umm Qeis	n/a	n/a	28 990	n/a
Total	317 331	526 932	445 666	40%

Source: Ministry of Tourism, Statistics Department.

DEVELOPMENT PRESSURES

These data suggest that tourism has a significant peace-related effect in some of these cities. Wadi Musa is in a virtual state of crisis, while Madaba and Jarash are already experiencing large increases in tourist visits and may experience tourism-related development pressures if existing trends continue. Because both of these cities are within an hour's drive of Amman, the pressure to build large hotel complexes for tourists will be less than in Wadi Musa. However, poor planning in these cities is causing them to suffer the consequences of increased traffic and congestion, with little opportunity for increasing revenues to cover expenses. In the future, better planning to develop facilities which encourages tourists to spend more time visiting these cities would increase the economic benefits of tourism there. According to the tourism masterplan, other cities such as Umm Qeis, Karak and Salt are likely to see some growth, but the rate of growth is likely to be lower.[24] These cities will also need to develop strategies to maximize the economic development potential of tourist visits.

Table 9.5 presents a list of construction projects within each municipality which may be used as a proxy for development pressure. These measures suggest that Wadi Musa has seen a major construction boom over the past 18 months, both for new hotels and tourist facilities, but also for private homes. Direct observation of the construction process in Wadi Musa indicates that nearly every house has added an additional floor or floors, which has caused a large expansion of the construction sector and placed an even greater demand on existing infrastructure.

The tourism masterplan prepared by the Japan International Cooperation Agency has projected tourist flows which range from one million visitors in the year 2005 to more than two million by the year 2010, at the highest rate of growth. The report indicates that this number of tourists will require total

Table 9.5 Construction since January 1994

	Hotels	*Restaurants*	*Retail*	*Other Tourist*	*Private Homes*
Salt	0	1	70	4	446
Madaba	1	2	50	0	500
Jarash	0	2	30	0	0
Karak	1	3	25	6	405
Wadi Musa	17	14	250	20	700
Umm Qeis	1	0	0	0	50
Total	20	22	425	30	2101

Source: Interviews with Municipal Councils by the author, July 1995.

hotel rooms to increase from 16 354 in the year 2000, to 27 916 in the year 2010 for the highest growth case. This latter case suggests that 2773 hotel rooms will be needed in the Petra region by the year 2000 for an estimated 820 000 annual tourist visits. The report notes that 336 rooms currently exist in Wadi Musa and an additional 900 rooms are under construction, indicating that the city will need 1573 more rooms in the next five years. Other areas will also need considerable investments in hotel facilities to house increased numbers of tourists. For instance, by the year 2000 the Jarash tourism region is expected to receive 96 000 tourist visits per year with an estimated demand for 389 hotel rooms; currently there are 28 rooms in Ajlun, leaving a need for 361 more. The Karak–Dead Sea area is expected to receive 72 000 visitors by the year 2000, with a demand for 259 beds of which 24 rooms currently exist and 32 more are under construction, leaving a demand for 203 more rooms.

In spite of the projected demand for new hotels there appears to be a general lack of hotel construction in secondary cities other than Wadi Musa. There is a large current boom in hotel construction in Amman with six five-star hotels recently licensed for construction[25] and a major expansion of the Intercontinental Hotel underway.[26] In addition, there is a major tourist development for the Dead Sea area which will consist of four tourist-class hotels with 1600 rooms at a cost of $280 million.[27] Incredible as it may seem, according to the tourism masterplan the level of new investments will be insufficient to meet the growing demand for hotel beds, even in Wadi Musa. It is difficult to assess the accuracy of these tourist projections and thus to judge whether this level of investment represents an overinvestment in tourist beds in Wadi Musa, or whether it is an efficient use of scarce capital resources.

THE PLANNING PROCESS

During the interviews with municipal officials it was evident that there is little familiarity with the planning instruments available to local councils. A financial plan (budget) is recognized as critical by council members, but a land-use plan is simply a document imposed from outside. This perception stems from the fact that in most cases there was little or no local input into the land-use planning process. Most plans were drawn up by architects and engineers from the Ministry of Municipal, Rural Affairs, and the Environment (MMRAE) with a mandated local review period, but little substantive feedback in most cases. Although the MMRAE has established procedures for drafting masterplans for municipalities that explicitly include provisions for local input and comments, in practice the amount of input given appears to be quite limited. Many local officials were not even aware of the existence of the land-use plan. There appears to be little understanding of the utility of the planning process for predicting changes in population, tourist flows or economic impacts of these changes.

Most of the technical staff of this ministry are based in Amman, although there are some technical staff in each governorate administrative centre. The governorate-level staff are nominally charged with providing technical planning assistance to municipalities within each region, but these staff are largely drawn from the design professions with little social science or policy planning backgrounds. At the municipal level planners are rare to non-existent, except in the largest cities. Smaller cities like Wadi Musa and Umm Qeis have virtually no technical staff whatsoever.

The level of expertise at the local level is quite variable. The number of elected council members varies from seven to eleven. More importantly, the level of experience of these key decision-makers is also highly variable. The council in Karak has four members with government experience, and six who have professional or managerial experience. In contrast, in Umm Qeis there is one person with government experience and the rest are either retired military personnel or farmers. Madaba and Salt both have numerous council members with experience in business and trade because of the importance of the private sector in the two largest cities in the subset.

Table 9.6 presents the staff assignment areas of various municipal employees, indicating the large variation in their skills. The "public works" category is the single largest assignment area, suggesting that most municipal services are publicly provided in these cities. Madaba and Karak have the two largest total numbers of employees and also have more than a handful of planners on the staff. Other cities with a smaller overall payroll have considerably fewer planners on the staff, suggesting that any planning work will have to be done by outside consultants or by members of technical directorates either in the governorate or from Amman. The Planning Department of the city of

Table 9.6 Staff assignments of municipal employees

	Salt	*Madaba*	*Jarash*	*Karak*	*Wadi Musa*	*Umm Qeis*
Administration	15	56	n/a	20	5	3
Finance	13	13	n/a	15	7	2
Planning	0	9	n/a	5	3	2
Public works	33	29	n/a	190	12	4
Other	14	100	n/a	20	2	6
Total	75	207	n/a	250	26	17

Source: Interviews with Municipal Councils by the author, July 1995.

Wadi Musa has a very small staff that is overwhelmed by demands for the review of building permits and new development proposals. This lack of planning capacity is a major constraint on the ability of local governments to prepare rationally for the coming onslaught of foreign visitors.

CONCLUSION

A continued impediment to the peace process in Jordan will be how to conceptualize and implement a state of peace with Israel, and how to take advantage of the resulting possibilities for social and economic development. There is clearly a continued need for external support, especially in the form of financial assistance to support this process,[28] but many of the difficult decisions will have to be made locally. While the overarching dimensions of this process will undoubtedly be provided by the royal family, especially as a new king consolidates control, the availability of planning skills to implement that process at the local level is an important question.

The ability of Jordan's planning institutions to adapt to these changing conditions will influence the success or failure of the peace process. A reinvigorated planning process is needed to solicit local input and shape collective insights into a clear vision for the future. By necessity this kind of planning process will have to be more decentralized and more autonomous than ever before, in order to focus on the local concerns and potential problems resulting from the implementation of the peace treaty.

It is unlikely that the problems faced by Jordan as a result of the peace process will be like anything its people have experienced before. Resolving these kind of problems will involve a more experimental and innovative approach to problem-solving and policy-making. The question remains whether Jordan will be up to this task. While the human-resource base certainly has the required skills to make these adjustments, the real question is whether the institutional leadership will permit a more decentralized and innovative process.

Resolving these issues will require a different kind of planning response. Old methods which relied on centralized planning from Amman are not likely to provide timely decisions that are sufficiently informed about local conditions and requirements. A centralized bureaucracy, even an otherwise efficient one, will have difficulty coping because the rate of change is likely to be quite rapid, and the impacts of those changes will be rather localized. Furthermore, because the nature and intensity of development pressures are likely to be quite different from previous trends, central planners will be faced with a series of crises stimulated by decision-making with little relevant experience and few readily applicable decision models.

In short, although the potential economic benefits of peace are quite high, Jordan must begin a concerted planning effort to prepare its population and infrastructure for expanded linkages and trade across the Jordan Valley in order to receive maximum benefit from that peace. In this chapter I have argued that insufficient attention has been paid to the development of a local planning capacity and its critical role in shaping the post-treaty development process. Jordan has a well-trained and reasonably effective cadre of planners at the central level, but efforts must be made to expand the function and empower local planners to deal with regional issues. If such changes fail to materialize, it is possible that the inability of planners to keep up with the rapid pace of development may create substantial bottlenecks in the provision of key services and vital infrastructure. As a result, inadequate planning capacity may impede the successful implementation of the peace treaty.

Notes

1. Michael Mazur, *Economic Growth and Development in Jordan* (London: Croom Helm, 1979).
2. Rex Honey, Steve Nichols, Suleiman Abu Kharmeh, Musa Khamis, and Peter Doan, "Planning Regions for Regional Planning in Jordan's 1986–1990 Plan", in John Frazier, Bart Epstein and J.F. Langowski (eds), *Papers and Proceedings of the Applied Geography Conferences*, vol. 9, 1986.
3. Peter L. Doan, "Urban Centrality and Agricultural Productivity: Regional Development in the Hashemite Kingdom of Jordan", in R. May (ed.), *The Urbanization Revolution* (New York: Plenum, 1989).
4. Lamis K. Andoni, "The Five Days that Shook Jordan." *Middle East International*, 28 April 1989: 3–4.
5. Musa Samha, "Population Spatial Distribution Policies in Jordan," in *Population Spatial Distribution* (Amman: UN ESCWA, 1993).
6. The two regional authorities, the Jordan Valley Authority and the Aqaba Region Authority are special exceptions because these institutions have been given a substantial amount of control over planning processes and outcomes. However, there are two special cases in which authority has been delegated because of the perceived national interests at stake in developing the only port and ensuring adequate infrastructure (and water) for farming in the Jordan Valley. For these reasons they are not easily replicable.
7. Jamil Jreisat, "Managing Development in the Arab States", *Arab Studies Quarterly*, 14 (1992), pp. 1–17.
8. Rachelle Alterman, "Can Planning Help in a Time of Crisis? Planners' Responses to Israel's Recent Wave of Mass Immigration", *Journal of the American Planning Association* 61(2) (Spring 1995), pp. 156–77.
9. Don Peretz, *Palestinian Refugees and the Middle East Peace Process* (Washington DC: US Institute of Peace Press, 1993).
10. As a case in point a recent article in a major US news magazine highlights Jordan as an exciting tourist destination after the signing of the peace accords. The article even suggests that Jordan may be "safer" now than Israel. "Cooled-off hot spots", *US News and World Report*, 9 October 1995.
11. According to the Minister of Tourism, there were 84 859 Israeli tourists during the first ten months of 1995, and the total number of tourists from all countries

was expected to exceed 1 million by the end of the year. "Khatib Sees Jordan Earning Record $723 million from Tourism", *Jordan Times*, 10 December 1995.

12. The Greater Petra Region Authority was established in the spring of 1995 to address these issues.
13. "Jordan, Israel sign Transport Agreement", *Jordan Times*, 17 January 1996.
14. "Railway Transport Network is Key to Development in Arab World", *Jordan Times*, 20 November 1995.
15. The city of Aqaba is likely to see significant growth as a result of the peace treaty, but since it also functions as the only port in Jordan, the effect of the peace process is harder to determine; therefore it has been excluded. In addition there are likely to be large tourist impacts in the Dead Sea area, but these effects are not likely to be concentrated in a single city and have also therefore been excluded.
16. Barclay G. Jones, "Interregional Relationships in Jordan: Persistence and Change", in Adnan Hadidi (ed.), *Studies in the History and Archaeology of Jordan, II* (Amman: Department of Antiquities, 1985).
17. "Amman, Salt City Centres and Southern Madaba to be Turned into Touristic Areas," *Jordan Times*, 12 December 1995.
18. Kamal Salibi, *The Modern History of Jordan* (London: I.B. Tauris, 1993); Peter Gubser, *Politics and Change in Al-Karak: A Study of a Small Arab Town and its District* (New York: Oxford University Press, 1973).
19. The Decapolis cities were a loosely-knit coalition of ten cities in this region formed during the Hellenistic period, prior to the imposition of Roman rule in AD 106.
20. Michel Piccirillo, *Madaba, Mount Nebo, Umm Rasas: A Brief Guide to the Antiquities* (Amman: Al-Kutba Publishers, 1990); Raouf S. Abujaber, *Pioneers Over Jordan: The Frontier of Settlement in Transjordan, 1850–1914* (London: I.B. Tauris, 1989).
21. "Queen Inaugurates Mosaic School, Archaeological Park in Madaba", *Jordan Times*, 13 November 1995.
22. Seteny Shami, "Settlement and Resettlement in Umm Qeis: Spatial Organisation and Social Dynamics in a Jordanian Village", in J.P. Bourdier and N. Alsayyad (eds), *Dwellings, Settlements, and Tradition: Cross-cultural Perspectives* (Lanham, Md.: University Press of America and the International Association for the Study of Traditional Environments, University of California Berkeley, 1989); Thomas Weber, *Umm Qais: Gadara of the Decapolis* (Amman: Al-Kutba Publishers, 1990).
23. The two fastest growing cities – Russeifa and Wadi Sier – are virtual suburbs of Amman; they absorbed large numbers of returnees after the Gulf war. This information makes the growth of Wadi Musa even more remarkable.
24. Japan International Cooperation Agency, *The Study on the Tourism Development Plan in the Hashemite Kingdom of Jordan, Interim Report*, Amman, July 1995.
25. "Khatib Sees Jordan Earning Record $73 Million from Tourism This Year", *Jordan Times*, 10 December 1995.
26. "Jordan Inter-continental Announces $20m Expansion Plan", *Jordan Times*, 10 December 1995.
27. "Investors Formulate New Terms for Dead Sea Hotel Projects", *Jordan Times*, 16 January 1996.
28. World Bank, "Peace and the Jordanian Economy", World Bank Working Paper, Washington DC, 1994.

10 External Assistance to the Palestinian Economy: What Went Wrong?[1]

Barbara Balaj, Ishac Diwan and Bernard Philippe

INTRODUCTION

The historic breakthrough in the peace negotiations between the Israelis and Palestinians in Oslo, occasioned by the signing of the Declaration of Principles at the White House on 13 September 1993, brought with it euphoria and expectations of a blooming peace and bustling prosperity. The international community, anxious to demonstrate its solidarity and support, quickly stepped in to cement the peace pact with pledges of large amounts of economic aid. It was envisioned that donors would move quickly to rebuild a dilapidated infrastructure, with the private sector acting in tandem to create an investment boom. A new era, characterized by anticipation of rapid improvements and tangible benefits in the daily lives of Israelis and Palestinians alike, would begin.

Now, six years after the Declaration of Principles was signed, it is now acutely apparent that events did not measure up to political promises and popular expectations. Economic activity has remained stagnant at best. The flow of donor investments to rebuild the West Bank and Gaza Strip has not matched the scale of the original pronouncements. The private sector remains largely on the sidelines, deterred by the systemic risks related to the vagaries of the negotiation process. And the peace process is itself continuing in spite of economic difficulties, rather than being propelled forward as a result of strong economic performance, as was originally anticipated.

The goal of this chapter is limited yet important in understanding what went wrong. It develops two main theses: first, that the main reason behind the shortfall in donor financing for infrastructure lies in the unexpected ballooning of the Palestinian budget deficit; and second, that given the constraints imposed by the political environment, the external assistance process has functioned as well as could be expected. In effect, these arguments imply that the main reason for economic stagnation must be found in the political realm.

The chapter is organized in three sections. The first explains why the recurrent budget developed a much larger deficit than was originally predicted. The second section describes how the main actors adjusted to this unexpected event and shifted their priorities. Finally, the concluding section tries to assess what lies ahead.

AN UNEXPECTED PROBLEM: LARGE RECURRENT BUDGET DEFICITS

In the aftermath of the 1993 Declaration of Principles, donor pledges of assistance to the West Bank and Gaza totalled \$2.1 billion for 1994–98, which subsequently increased to \$2.6 billion. These pledges represent new assistance, above and beyond any funds that donors traditionally allocated to the West Bank and Gaza through non-governmental organizations, the United Nations system and other channels. The emergency assistance programme put in place by the World Bank projected that \$580 million would be disbursed by June 1995. Those expectations were well-founded: by the end of June 1995, \$542 million had been actually disbursed, falling short of the target by only about \$40 million (Table 10.1).

In comparing initial projections with actual disbursements, however, the composition of expenditures differs quite dramatically. In the original plan, investments in infrastructure were supposed to consume the lion's share of donor pledges, with smaller expenditures on recurrent items to help establish the new Palestinian Authority (PA), along with some technical assistance to put together the institutions and blueprints necessary for an infrastructure boom. However, two years later investments had consumed only about one-half of the originally projected amounts, while amounts allocated to the financing of recurrent expenditures were 2.5 times more than initially anticipated.[2]

While infrastructure investments could have been larger if conditions on the ground had been more conducive to development, an important reason for the shortfall lies in the unexpected ballooning of recurrent expenditures, the financing of which necessitated about \$150 million more than originally expected over the period under consideration. Donors were compelled to shift their pledges away from planned investments towards recurrent cost support. The large donors – especially the United States and the European Union – were required to devote scarce managerial attention to figuring out the instruments and modalities needed to bail out a new Palestinian Authority that was too impoverished to even cover salaries for its police force. And, as always, when the fiscal accounts were unbalanced, donors became very sensitive to transparency and accountability issues, looking

Table 10.1 Emergency assistance programme and actual performance (US$ million)

	Programmed			*Actual*
	1994	*1995*	*1994–mid-1995*	*1994–mid-1995*
Public investment (including private sector support)	217	306	370	206*
Recurrent and start-up budget	108	0	108	240
Non-governmental organizations	50	40	70	37
Technical assistance	18	33	35	59
Total	393	379	581	542

Source: World Bank, 1995.
*Disbursed to implementing agencies, not all of which has been yet translated into activities on the ground.

for institutions outside the control of the PA to use as vehicles for their investments.

What explains this tremendous discrepancy between expectations and the actual outcome? After the signing of the Declaration of Principles, the recurrent budget deficits of the new PA were expected to be small in scale and short-term in nature (amounting to $108 million in 1994). Several assumptions underpinned this notion:

- First, the Israeli Civil Administration had, over the years, maintained an essentially balanced recurrent budget in the West Bank and Gaza.[3] It was assumed that the core activities would be unaffected by the transfer of authority, at least in the early phase of Palestinian autonomy.[4]
- Second, the primary new expenditures involved the one-time set-up costs of the PA and the recurrent expenses associated with the newly-created Palestinian police force. Start-up costs were estimated at $112 million in 1994 and $30 million for 1995, excluding police equipment. The police force was expected to be 9000 members strong, with a price tag of about $100 million in 1994 and $130 million in 1995. Its equipment needs were estimated at $100 million, to be spread over the period 1994–95.[5]
- Third, these new expenses were assumed to be partially covered by transfers from Israel in the form of a return to the Palestinian treasury of taxes paid by Palestinians, which had previously accrued to the Israeli treasury. It was assumed that this "tax leakage" would cease soon after the PA had acquired political control in areas of the Gaza Strip, and a few months later, in several West Bank cities. The leakage was estimated by the World Bank at approximately 8 per cent of GDP, or, very roughly, $200 million per year.[6] Given the calendar of future events envisioned at the time,[7] this amounted to $135 million in 1994 and the full amount of $200 million in 1995. The projections allowed for an initial drop in tax collection by the PA, with a recovery starting in 1995, as it acquired the appropriate administrative mechanisms to carry out this function.

However, the situation on the ground evolved differently, and continues to do so. The autonomy phase has not come into full force in the entirety of the West Bank, but only within a handful of tiny and territorially discontiguous municipal enclaves. The "tax leakage" continues in the West Bank where most of the Palestinian economic activity is concentrated. Tax collection was also below expected levels and police expenditures larger, but this was largely offset by cuts in other planned expenditure items.[8]

The Economic Protocol, reached in April 1994, regulated the economic aspects of the evolving relationship between Israel and the PA.[9] This protocol called for the elimination of the tax leakage and for the return of "lost" tax and tariff revenues. But it only applied to areas under the authority of the PA, meaning that only the Gaza portion of the tax leak, about $50 million, would be returned in the first stage. The West Bank portion, the remaining $150 million, would be returned only when the protocol were applied in the West Bank, that is, after the beginning of the interim period following the redeployment of Israeli forces and the PA administrative council elections. This phase, which was expected to last for only six months according to the Declaration of Principles, began a year behind schedule, which translated into a loss to the Palestinian treasury of about $150 million for the period under consideration.

There were also other shocks, which were to a large extent eventually absorbed by cuts elsewhere in the budget, the running of arrears and some accumulation of domestic debts (about $70 million). The costs of the police force increased more than originally anticipated. Total costs for 1994 added about $60 million for the period January 1994–June 1995. The transfer of authority in Gaza was disorderly, and tax revenues dipped more and for longer than was expected, thus reducing Palestinian revenue by about $50 million compared to projected targets. The return of taxes paid by Gazans and accruing to the Israeli treasury as agreed by the protocol was slow, reducing the revenue at the PA's disposal in the early phase of the transition.[10] To cover the budget squeeze, the planned set-up "transitional projects" were deeply cut. Planned projects in the field of welfare – such as the compensation of those injured during the *Intifada*, work programmes in Gaza and the rehabilitation of prisoners – had to be delayed, scaled down or scrapped altogether, and police salaries were often not paid in full or in a timely manner.

The main obstacle to a balanced budget is a transitory problem rather than a structural one. With the small public sector inherited from the Israeli Civil Administration, in addition to the Palestinian police force, public expenditures, if contained, are not abnormally large. And for an economy such as the West Bank and Gaza, they could be stabilized at a reasonable 25–27 per cent of GDP (depending on the size of the police force). This will ultimately depend, of course, on the Palestinians extending their economic authority from the small enclaves into the larger portion of the West Bank. The PA might then be in a position to collect taxes at levels at least as great as the Civil Administration, that is, about 15 per cent of GDP. With the added 8 per cent of GDP in taxes returned by Israel, the remaining structural deficit would be manageable at about 2–4 per cent of GDP, perhaps a bit more if the police force were to expand above 20 000. And there is much room for improvement in tax collection over the poor performance of the Israeli Civil Administration. Because of its greater political legitimacy, the PA could do much better over time.[11]

Ultimately, then, any solution to the current fiscal fragility of the Palestinian Authority necessitates more favourable arrangements with Israel.

This does not necessarily involve a renegotiated Economic Protocol. It has been said that this protocol was a deal between Palestinian businesspersons and Israeli politicians, in the sense that Palestinian businesspersons would gain by obtaining access to the large Israeli market, while Palestinian politicians would lose a strategic advantage by retaining unbalanced trade relations with Israel.[12] This strategic choice complicates fiscal matters because fiscal independence is also largely lost. However, this does not necessarily make fiscal balance an impossible task, as argued above, and the fiscal situation should improve now that the Economic Protocol has been extended into the West Bank and the Palestinian treasury has started receiving the customs revenues paid by West Bank Palestinians. Further improvements are contingent on the development of a workable system to collect value-added tax within the occupied territories, and to refund Palestinians for the purchases made in Israel. And, assuming an end of closure policies toward the West Bank and Gaza, the structure of imports should shift away from Israel. With the opening of the West Bank bridges to Jordan and the completion of the Gaza port, tariff revenues should also rise.

However, as long as the current problems are not resolved, the Economic Protocol will remain under attack. By establishing a customs union between the Israeli and Palestinian economies, the protocol limits the amount of trade taxes that can be raised. Tariff revenues are the easiest tax to collect in poorer countries with weak institutional systems, even though an estimated total import bill of $1.5 billion, perhaps as much as 90 per cent comes from Israel and is not subject to tariff because of the existing customs union arrangements.[13] The potential for greater tariff revenues were the Palestinian economy to exit Israel's customs unions is enormous.[14] But on the other side of the ledger the ability to export freely to a $65 billion economy would also be very valuable as a locomotive for economic growth and would provide an important strategic advantage over Jordan.[15] If the closures – which reduce the value of the union to Palestinians – and fiscal pressures ultimately seal the fate of the customs union, this will represent one important victory for the logic of politics and its zero-sum game to the detriment of economics and its promise for more favourable positive-sum games.

REACTIONS TO THE BUDGET CRISIS

The nature, magnitude and duration of the Palestinian budget problem caught the three key actors – the donors, Israel and the Palestinians – unaware and unprepared. They forced a major change in the content of the West Bank and Gaza assistance programmes away from traditional donor-financed investment and technical assistance projects towards atypical support for start-up and recurrent expenditures. Initially, none of the three actors are particularly well-equipped to deal with this predicament. The situation was further complicated by political difficulties, interdependencies and interactions between the key players. However, after some initial fits and starts, the three parties responded quite well. Ultimately, they succeeded in arriving at a tripartite agreement which would help the nascent Palestinian Authority meet its start-up and recurrent costs and begin assuming its governing responsibilities and functions.

The Political Backdrop

Delays in the peace process caused by the delicate and protracted nature of the bilateral negotiations, and the violence occasioned by those forces most vehemently opposed to it, slowed completion of the various building blocks of peace. This led to delays in the implementation of the Declaration of Principles, the Israeli–Palestinian Economic Protocol, the Gaza–Jericho redeployments and the "early empowerment" in the West Bank cities. These political delays had a major impact on the Palestinian budget problem, and of course, on the investment programme as well.

Funding start-up and recurrent expenditures for the Palestinian Authority posed a number of special problems for the donor community. Donors normally prefer to provide development financing in the form of specific investment and/or technical assistance projects. In historical terms, it has been virtually unprecedented for a large group of donors to finance recurrent costs, mostly salary costs that are unrelated to project or adjustment operations, and particularly on the scale provided to the PA. Defending such assistance to their home parliaments proved difficult for many donors. Further, issues of burden-sharing had to be addressed. Donors also had to deal with the problems of transparency and accountability, which are more difficult than for project financing. This is especially true in the case of the West Bank and Gaza which does not have a central bank that can provide the usual control mechanisms or a workable budget mechanism in the Ministry of Finance (see Chapter 7 in this volume for more on banking issues in the West Bank and Gaza). Related to these concerns, new channels of assistance through which donor funds could flow had to be created.

The large number of donors involved in the aid process has been both a source of strength and weakness for the budget effort. While the large number of donors has helped to raise the requisite funds in tough times of fiscal restraint, it has also made the process of aid coordination and delivery more complicated and cumbersome. For example, there are 27 donors contributing $411 million to recurrent costs, a large number of donors relative to pledges.

In reviewing the aid process to the West Bank and Gaza Strip, a comparison with the 1979 Egyptian–Israeli peace treaty is instructive. In the case of Camp David there was one, large committed donor, the United States, which guaranteed the economic and security requirements of both Egypt and Israel. American aid stemming from Camp David continues today at a rate of more than $5 billion annually, with approximately $2 billion going to Egypt and $3 billion to Israel. The result has been 16 years of peace, chilly perhaps, but peace nonetheless.

However, in the case of the Oslo agreement between Israel and the PLO, no single donor or group of donors has emerged to fully guarantee the economic, development or other requirements of the Palestinians under occupation, or to ensure security between them and the Israelis.

Israeli domestic political concerns and security interests have dominated the economic aspects of the peace process in many ways. The signing of the Declaration of Principles was followed by recurrent outbreaks of violence on both sides that have continued, on and off, ever since. Increasingly, Palestinian opposition attacks have been launched within Israel's pre-1967 borders. The Israeli government has taken tough measures in reaction to these incidents, tightening the closure and reducing the number of Palestinian work permits issued after each violent episode, and slowly loosening the closure and its associated restrictions to a degree after periods of relative quiet (though never eliminating it entirely). These restrictions have complicated public and private sector transactions in the West Bank and Gaza, with attendant budgetary implications.[16]

After some initial delays the Israelis delivered on the fiscal agreements it reached with the PA: namely, transferring taxes and administrative records, and providing training to Palestinian tax officials. With respect to the devolution of economic functions such as taxation and regulation of financial markets, there was resistance within the Israeli establishment to changes that would affect Israeli regulations. Israeli officials worried that transferring responsibility to the PA for the value-added tax or customs systems could open up ways for Israeli firms to escape taxation. Similarly, giving up controls over financial transactions could allow for capital flight from Israel and the laundering of illegal transactions.[17]

But economic relations remained well within the logic of the political transformations taking place. The speed at which the Economic Protocol was implemented on the ground was adjusted to the speed at which the Palestinians were able to deliver on security as well as other political demands, from suppressing opposition to the peace process to advancing negotiations on other fronts. The resolution of the tax leakage in the West Bank, because it is embedded in the extension of the Economic Protocol, was made hostage to the resolution of the political negotiations for the interim arrangements.

On the Palestinian side, the PLO faced the challenge of transforming itself from an outside revolutionary movement based in Tunis, into an inside civilian governing authority based in Gaza. The transition period was also made particularly difficult given the many dilemmas confronting the Palestinian leadership in dealing with its own constituency, Israel and the donors.

With respect to internal Palestinian politics, the problems between "inside" and "outside" Palestinians, and strategic differences between those supportive of the peace process and those opposed, surged to the surface. Underlying political conflicts had an impact on economic choices as well. The PA did not collect taxes early on in order to lengthen the "honeymoon" period, thereby garnering greater public support and suppressing latent and blatant forms of opposition.

Palestinian relations with donors were also tinged with divergent political interests. The PA experienced a dilemma between delivering the kind of financial transparency requested by the donors and the centralizing tendencies dictated both by PLO organizational reflexes and the need to retain control over critical economic choices. This was magnified by the tight resource constraint, which meant that there was a need for day-to-day decisions about the allocations of scarce resources among many competing requirements. Further, Palestinian political infighting and institutional weaknesses posed an impediment to the ability of the PA to absorb donor aid and rapidly construct a system of checks and balances acceptable to the donors.

Finally, in its relations with Israel, the PA came to appreciate the importance of reducing security risks if the peace process were to move forward. Thus, the PA began to constantly increase the size of the Palestinian police force. Expectations were that the force would eventually go as high as 30 000 members in order for the Palestinians to be able to deliver on their security commitments, that is, in the event of a general withdrawal of the Israel Defence Forces from the West Bank.

Response to the Budget Crisis: Formation of the Tripartite Architecture

Politics has played a role in the dynamics of the response to the budgetary crisis as well. The aid coordination process with respect to the mobilization of donor funding for recurrent costs was characterized by two distinct phases: (1) a "technical" phase in which the World Bank assumed a leading role; and (2) a more political phase with the formation of a tripartite arrangement.

The first phase began shortly after the December 1993 Consultative Group (CG) meeting,[18] when the urgent need for immediate donor support for PA expenditures was recognized. The World Bank organized a special conference for donors in January 1994, which set the stage for the creation of a critical channel through which donors could contribute funds. The Johan Jurgen

Holst Fund for Start-Up and Recurrent Costs,[19] a World Bank-administered trust fund, provided an important means through which donors could make funds available to the new PA. Initially envisioned as a transitional, short-term administrative mechanism, it assumed a longer life due to the unresolved Palestinian budgetary crisis. With time, the Holst Fund has attracted ever-increasing numbers of donors and volumes of funds. By mid-1995 some 20 donors had committed $180 million to the Holst Fund, $136 million of which was then disbursed to the PA for salaries and operating costs. The European Union represents the single largest contributor to recurrent costs.

While the Holst Fund is now the main channel, donors responded to pressing calls for recurrent cost support via other channels as well. For example, the European Union has acted as an important complementary channel to the Holst Fund for aid to the universities. Several donors also contributed direct bilateral aid to separate so-called "transitional projects", complementing multilateral aid channelled through the Holst Fund. More importantly, a separate channel for donor support to the Palestinian police force was also needed. While recognizing the critical importance of the Palestinian police in keeping law and order and enforcing security, many donors found it particularly difficult to provide financing in this area. There were disputes over the actual number of Palestinian policemen required to do the job, and concerns over the possibility of a diversion of resources for para-military purposes in the event of intra-Palestinian and/or Israeli-Palestinian conflict. Even after donor monies were made available to pay police salaries,[20] there were still problems in finding mechanisms and channels to deliver payments to the police because the matter proved too politically sensitive for most governments and organizations to handle. Eventually a solution was found: donor funds which were initially transferred on a bilateral basis are now administered by the United Nations through the local UNRWA offices.[21]

In the months that followed the 1994 donor conference, informal and formal Ad Hoc Liaison Committee (AHLC)[22] meetings and consultations were called with great frequency and urgency to deal with the slippage in the negotiating agenda and the resulting budget crisis. Each round of meetings required the solicitation of numerous donors in order to piece together a new tranche of funds to help meet Palestinian transitional and budgetary expenditures.

With time, tensions began to mount among the donors as the recurrent budget problem came to be seen as an open-ended commitment without a foreseeable resolution. In other words, donors were asked to finance budget deficits without definitive indications as to when the need for financing recurrent costs might finally cease. The 1994 "early empowerment" agreement for the West Bank cities was contingent on the availability of donor financing.

However, donors were simply called upon to provide funding without being given the opportunity to comment on the negotiated political agreements. The European Union was particularly insistent that the fiscal situation not be indefinitely separated from the overall political context.

The second phase began with the postponement of the September 1994 CG meeting on account of a dispute between the Israelis and Palestinians over the issue of proposed investments in East Jerusalem. The World Bank, which has economics as its mandate, was not equipped to deal with the types of political issues raised at the CG. The Bank was also not in a position to impose conditions on the three parties of the type desired by the European Union.

The United States was very active in putting together the first understanding between donors, Israel and the Palestinians to help solve the deficit issue. The underlying rationale was to achieve agreement on funding for the budget, particularly with respect to financial requirements for "early empowerment" in the West Bank cities as well as the ongoing needs for Gaza and Jericho. The new understanding covered the period of October 1994–March 1995. Donors were asked to provide aid within this limited time frame to help meet Palestinian budget requirements estimated at $125 million.[23] Some conditions were placed on the Israelis and Palestinians to address the tax situation and expenditure controls in an effort to raise more revenues to cover the budget deficit.

The first understanding was reasonably successful in terms of raising the required funding. However, it failed to fully address the concerns of all three parties. The second Tripartite Action Plan on Revenues, Expenditures and Donor Funding for the Palestinian Authority was a more participatory tripartite pact, with major inputs from the European Union, the IMF and the World Bank. Signed in April 1995 at the Paris AHLC meeting, the plan covered external budgetary support needs from April–December 1995, estimated at $136 million.

The Tripartite Action Plan spelled out a set of essential steps that each of the main partners to the peace process would have to take over the course of future months.[24] It represented a serious attempt by all the concerned parties to take special measures to address the longer-term budget problems of the PA, and the development and viability of the Palestinian economy. The three main parties also agreed to specific conditionality.

The Palestinians committed themselves to establishing a functioning tax collection system in the West Bank and Gaza Strip. The PA also undertook important fiscal discipline measures, namely the freezing of wages and containment of hiring within the confines of budget parameters. In addition, the PA agreed to centralize its fiscal revenues and expenditures under the Ministry of Finance. In this context, the IMF would offer technical assistance to the PA in budget, treasury and revenue administration. On the institutional side, the PA was asked to clarify the roles and competencies of the Palestinian Economic Council for Development and Reconstruction

(PECDAR), the ministries of Finance, Economy and Trade, and International Planning. This last measure is of particular significance, because the lack of clarity in the responsibilities of and interrelationships between economic ministries and entities has been a contributing factor to delays in aid coordination and budget administration.

The Israelis agreed to cooperate with the PA in establishing tax operations in the West Bank so that the limited transfer of authorities in the West Bank cities under "early empowerment" would proceed more smoothly than the earlier Gaza transfer. Israel also committed itself to ensuring timely tax transfers and value-added tax clearances to the PA (on account of transactions by Gazans). In addition, the government agreed to provide technical assistance and training to PA tax administrators. The Tripartite Action Plan also contained provisions for the government of Israel to make its best efforts to minimize the negative impact on the Palestinian people stemming from tighter security measures Israel also agreed to help speed the clearance of goods destined for the West Bank and Gaza through Israeli ports and customs.

For their part, donors consented to intensify their efforts to provide additional support for start-up and recurrent costs for the latter half of 1995, and to cover certain expenditures not met under the previous understanding. Donors were also urged to earmark 25 per cent of their 1995 assistance pledges to start-up and recurrent costs. In this context, the donors were also requested to release any uncommitted portion of their 1994 assistance pledges to the Holst Fund. In turn, donors expected that the AHLC Secretariat and the IMF would act as a surveillance mechanism in monitoring and reviewing Israeli and Palestinian performance towards the goals contained in the Tripartite Action Plan.[25] Donors also stated that the PA should make its best efforts to ensure that the need for donor support for start-up and recurrent costs would not go beyond 1995.

Thus, donors have responded to the unexpected large Palestinian budget deficits in an unprecedented fashion, contributing considerable sums of money towards helping solve the most immediate and central problems facing the PA. New channels were opened to expedite donor funds towards this end. The two main protagonists, the Israelis and the Palestinians, took important measures to facilitate tax collection and revenue clearances, enabling the PA to assume greater fiscal responsibility.

CONCLUSION

The quick economic boom in the West Bank and Gaza that many had expected and hoped for did not materialize. The delays in the political negotiations contributed to enlarging the PA budget deficits while slowing down the donor-supported infrastructure reconstruction programme. Donor resources and energies were shifted towards trying to meet the demands imposed by an acute budget crisis. Given the inherent regional political risks and the ongoing closure inside the still-occupied territories, the private sector is still reluctant to launch substantial investment projects. Thus, politics has provided the driving force, with economic developments following rather than leading. What has been witnessed is a reversal of original expectations: the economic situation has not provided the catalyst for popular public support for the peace process but, rather, progress on the economic side has become contingent on advances on the political side. On balance, however, the donors, Israeli technocrats and Palestinian officials responded quite well to the unexpected ballooning of the Palestinian budget deficit.

Looking towards the more distant future, any eventual transfer of the West Bank (and the remainder of the Gaza Strip) to the Palestinians will set the stage for a resolution of the budget problem and will help the key actors move forward on the investment programme. Until the final phase of negotiations is reached, the three parties can work together to achieve further improvements in the fiscal situation. The PA can exercise greater efforts towards fiscal restraint: the Israelis can exercise more flexibility with respect to the transfer of taxes to the PA. For their part, the donors should try to reallocate a greater proportion of their pledges to grant terms rather than loans. And the donors can keep up the pressure on the Israelis and the Palestinians to move forward in the peace process and support measures to alleviate and improve the overall economic situation, especially by bringing an end to the closure and by other means.

Over the next several years, a new phase is due to be launched as the Israeli–Palestinian negotiations over final status issues begin. Given the difficult political items on the agenda – borders, settlements, Jerusalem, the refugees, water ownership and, if possible, a new economic agreement – this phase is likely to be much more complicated than the previous ones.[26]

Political bargaining is likely to be rough and tumble, with both sides using confrontational and delaying tactics to grab maximum political advantage in obtaining a better deal. The hope remains that potential economic gains – attained by mutual cooperation rather than confrontation – might eventually serve to facilitate the political process. While recent experience has shown that economics has not proven to be the hoped-for locomotive in driving the peace process, it still remains to be seen whether the economics of peace can play a constructive, conciliatory role in the region over the longer term, as was the case in Europe half a century ago.

Notes

1. Reprinted from *Politique Etrangère* 60(3) (Autumn 1995), with slight revisions. With grateful acknowledgement to the French Institute for International Relations and its quarterly journal *Politique Etrangère* for reprinting rights. We

would like to thank, without incriminating, Messrs Nigel Roberts and Ali Khadr for their helpful comments. The views expressed here reflect solely those of the authors and not those of the World Bank or its Board of Directors.

2. See also "Gaza/West Bank: Donors to Meet to Map Out Investment Plans", *Middle East Economic Digest*, 23 June 1995, p. 11.
3. World Bank, *Developing the Occupied Territories: An Investment in Peace*, six volumes (Washington DC: World Bank, 1993).
4. Samir Abdallah, "The Palestinian Public Sector", *Economic Research Forum Newsletter* 2(2) (1994); George Abed and Abdelali Tazi, "Laying the Foundation: A Fiscal System for Palestinian Autonomy", *Finance and Development* 31(3) (September 1994), pp. 14–17.
5. *Near East Economic Progress Report*, nos 1 and 2 (1994), Institute for Social and Economic Policy in the Middle East, Harvard University, Cambridge, Mass.
6. The leakage essentially represents tariff revenues paid by Palestinians for goods imported from third countries and entering through Israeli ports, and value-added tax balances on trade with Israel. It is impossible to estimate this figure with any degree of precision because of data limitations. In particular, trade between Israel and the occupied territories, and Palestinian imports from third countries can be estimated at best using partial information available. In addition, trade patterns are expected to undergo some changes as a result of the latest Economic Protocol and the opening of new trade routes with Jordan and Egypt. See World Bank, 1993, *op. cit.*
7. It was assumed that authority would be transferred to Gaza and Jericho and to the West Bank in five economic areas in April 1994. The transition of the vast remainder of the West Bank into the structure of the autonomy government was projected for July 1994; it appears to have been largely offset by Oslo II and by the advent of the Netanyahu government.
8. See also Ruba Husary, "Donor Funding for the Palestinian Budget", *Peace Economics Newsletter* (Supported by *Peace Media* – a programme of the European Union), 2nd quarter, 1995.
9. For analyses and different views on the Economic Protocol, see Sharif S. Elmusa and Mahmud El-Jaafari, "Power and Trade: The Israeli–Palestinian Economic Protocol", *Journal of Palestine Studies* 24(2) (Winter 1995); Ishac Diwan and Michael Walton, "Palestine between Israel and Jordan: The Economics of an Uneasy Triangle", *Beirut Review* 8 (Fall 1994), pp. 21–44; and Ephraim Kleinman, "The Economic Provisions of the Agreement between Israel and the PLO", Working Paper no. 300, Hebrew University, Jerusalem, February 1995.
10. In the context of the "early empowerment" phase, several economic functions were transferred in a handful of West Bank cities, but these entailed an essentially balanced local budget, and transitory losses were small.
11. Fiscal arrangements are similar to those existing in Israel where tax collection reaches 38 per cent of GDP. World Bank, 1993, *op. cit.* Also see Chapter 2 of J.W. Wright, Jr. (ed.), *the Political Economy of Middle East Peace: The Impact of Competing Trade Agendas*, (London: Routledge, 1999).
12. Kleinman, *op. cit.* Conversely, some Israeli businesses lose because of greater competition, but Israeli politicians advance in their goal of achieving participation in a regional forum.
13. World Bank, 1993, *op. cit.*
14. It has been already widely reported that the PA imposes additional *ad hoc* tariffs on the Gaza border when the budget situation worsens.
15. Diwan and Walton, "Palestine between Israel and Jordan", *op. cit.*

16. See also Geir Ovensen, "The Border Closure and its Effects on the Labour Market and the Palestinian Household Economy", in *The Economy of Peace in the Middle East*, Maisonneuve et Larose, 1995.
17. Kleinman, *op. cit.*
18. Consultative Group meetings bring together donors and recipients, and provide a forum where the parties can discuss aid coordination issues, as well as medium- to longer-term strategic development issues. Chaired by the World Bank, these fora have been an important component of the Bank's aid coordination efforts in many countries for nearly 40 years.
19. The Johan Jurgen Holst Fund was named after the late Norwegian Foreign Minister, who was instrumental in bringing about the Oslo peace accord between the Israelis and the Palestinians.
20. Major donors to the Palestinian police force include the European Union, Norway and the United States.
21. Donors also contributed assistance in kind: namely, goods and equipment for the police through the Committee for International Assistance to the Palestinian Police (COPP), which is chaired by the government of Norway.
22. Following the signing of the Declaration of Principles, the Ad Hoc Liaison Committee (AHLC) was created in November 1993 as a special aid coordination mechanism for the West Bank and Gaza Strip. The core membership includes Canada, the European Union, Japan, Norway, Russia, Saudi Arabia and the United States. Associate members include Egypt, Israel, Jordan, the PLO, Tunisia and the United Nations.
23. The Tripartite Understanding was signed at the November 1994 AHLC meeting. Donors made pledges of $102 million, and an additional $23 million for employment generation programmes.
24. See also Economist Intelligence Unit, "Israel and the Occupied Territories", Country Report, 2nd quarter, 1995.
25. The AHLC is responsible for a performance review process to oversee the implementation of this Action Plan, including: (1) the role given to the IMF to monitor the Palestinian budget; (2) the AHLC Secretariat to follow up on donor contributions and to implement the public investment programme; and (3) local aid coordination set up to oversee on a continuing basis the implementation of the Action Plan by the PA, Israel and the donors.
26. Samir Abdallah, "The Middle East Peace Process: Multilateral Conflict Resolution through Bilateral Negotiations"; and George Abed, "Economic Prospects for Palestine", both papers presented at the Economic Research Forum/World Bank conference on strategic visions for the Middle East and North Africa held in Tunis, June 1995.

11 The (Very) Political Economy of the West Bank and Gaza: What Lessons Should We Learn about Peace-building and Development Assistance?

Rex Brynen

INTRODUCTION

On 18–19 October 1995 representatives of the Palestinian Authority (PA), Israel, the World Bank, 29 donor states and ten international organizations met in Paris. The purpose of the meeting: to develop a renewed programme of development assistance for the West Bank and Gaza Strip, in the wake of the Taba (Oslo II) agreement between Israel and the PA calling for Israeli redeployment, Palestinian elections and an extension of Palestinian authority in the West Bank. The timing and focus of that meeting underscored the close connection that has existed from the outset between the Palestinian–Israeli peace process and international financial assistance. During the first such meeting, held in Washington in October 1993, donors pledged some $2.1 billion over five years in support of the Oslo agreement. The pledges, now totalling $2.5 billion, were intended to foster Palestinian economic and social development in the West Bank and Gaza and support the emergence of a Palestinian administrative infrastructure. Politically the assistance effort aimed at strengthening the Palestinian Authority and at creating tangible benefits from "peace" for Palestinians in the West Bank and Gaza, thereby generating popular support for the political process.

The international economic assistance programme has been much criticized. Much of this discussion has been directed at the bureaucratic inefficiencies of donor agencies, the types of projects supported, inefficiencies and even corruption within the Palestinian Authority and the "squeezing out" of Palestinian and international non-governmental organizations (NGOs). To this are added the negative effects of Israeli closure of the territories, the economic costs of which have frequently outweighed any benefits gained from external assistance. Indeed, in 1994 the gross national product per capita of the West Bank and Gaza actually fell by 1.2 per cent; in 1995 this figure declined by 8.5 per cent. No recent changes have been found and reversal of these trends is unlikely under the current circumstances; at least this seems to be the consensus of the contributors to this collection.[1]

It is essential to recognize, however, that economic assistance to the West Bank and Gaza has been and remains a profoundly *political* exercise which has economic implications. The delivery of economic aid has been shaped by the bureaucratic processes and domestic politics of donor states, as well as by relations between donors. It has been deeply affected by the politics of Palestinian (proto-) state-building and regime consolidation. Finally, the assistance effort has been closely tied to the ebb and flow of the overall Palestinian–Israeli negotiating process, and has occasionally found itself derailed by issues arising from political difficulties therein.

AHLC, CG, JLC AND LACC: A PRIMER ON THE ASSISTANCE PROGRAMME

The economic assistance programme for the West Bank and Gaza – involving more than three dozen countries and international organizations, not to mention individual Palestinian ministries, NGOs and others – is a complex one, not least because the donors ultimately retain control of their own aid programmes. Before assessing the performance of international aid efforts in the West Bank and Gaza, therefore, it is useful to first identify the players involved.

The major aid donors are the United States and the European Union, followed by Japan and Saudi Arabia (see Table 11.1). The bulk of US assistance ($375 million) is disbursed through the United States Agency for International Development (USAID), with $125 million to be allocated in the form of private sector guarantees administered by the Overseas Private Investment Corporation (OPIC). Similarly, approximately half of the $600 million in multilateral assistance pledged by the European Union is in the form of loans and guarantees from the European Investment Bank.

One major complaint regarding the aid process has been the slow pace of delivery: aid pledges have not always been committed to specific projects, and the actual disbursement of funds in the West Bank and Gaza has lagged still further (see Table 11.2). Overall, approximately one-third of assistance pledged have been in the form of grants, with the remainder as concessional loans or guarantees. About half of all support has been directed towards budget support and technical assistance, and the other half to investment projects.

Table 11.1 Donor pledges until July 1995 (US$ million)

	Grants	*Loans*	*Total*
European Union	300	0	300
European Investment Bank	0	300	300
United States	375	125	500
World Bank/IDA/IFC	0	210	210
Japan	200	0	200
Saudi Arabia	200	0	200
Norway	150	0	150
Italy	80	0	80
Israel	25	50	75
Turkey	2	50	52
Germany	52	0	52
Netherlands	50	0	50
Denmark	43	0	43
AFSED	40	0	40
Sweden	40	0	40
Others	295	15	310
Total	1 852	750	2 602

Note: For text concerning these contributions see *Journal of Palestine Studies*, vol. 24, no. 4 (Summer 1995), pp. 143–6.

Table 11.2 Donor commitments and disbursements (US$ million)

		1994		*1995*	*1996–98*
Pledges		802		735	1075
Commitments		761		626	
Disbursements	(October)	250	(July)	214	
	(December)	409	(December)	479	

The channelling of large amounts of development assistance to the West Bank and Gaza Strip in a relatively short period of time, as well as the overriding political imperative of the peace process, have presented both donors and the regional parties with new and often unanticipated challenges. Indeed, in the first year of the economic assistance programme, widespread complaints were heard about the slowness and inappropriateness of the aid effort. As a consequence, structures and programmes underwent significant modification over time in an attempt to improve the pace of programme delivery, to target aid more effectively, and to enhance coordination and local responsiveness.

At the outset, two major structures were established to provide overall external direction to the aid effort: the Ad Hoc Liaison Committee (AHLC) and the Consultative Group (CG). The Consultative Group is a typical World Bank mechanism used to coordinate donor programmes. It includes both aid officials and technical experts, and in the Palestinian case has generally been used to win support (and funding) for detailed assistance plans. By contrast, the AHLC is smaller (consisting of the United States, Russia, the European Union, Japan, Canada, Saudi Arabia and Norway, with Israel, the PA, Egypt, Jordan, Tunisia and the United Nations as associate members), meets less frequently, and often at a more senior level of political representation. Technically at least, it reports to the steering committee of the multilateral track of the Middle East peace process. It has acted as a sort of political steering committee, responsible for the overall guidelines and policies of the aid process. The chair of the AHLC is held by Norway, with all decisions reached by consensus. In additional to formal meetings of the AHLC and CG, much of the real work of these groups is done in advance, through informal meetings of the major participants, with the United States, the European Union and the World Bank, as well as Israel and the PA, playing the most influential roles.

Within this overall structure, a number of substructures have been formed (see Figure 11.1). During the initial implementation of the Gaza–Jericho agreement in the spring of 1994, a Coordinating Committee for Assistance to the Palestinian Police (aptly named COPP) was established, with Norway acting as chair, to secure and coordinate donor pledges of police funds and equipment. In November 1994 the AHLC decided to establish a Local Aid Coordination Committee (LACC) in the territories, which would facilitate coordination on the ground among the major aid agencies and with the PA. The LACC, co-chaired by Norway, the World Bank and the United Nations, has met at least once per month since January 1995, with approximately 30 local donor representatives in attendance. In turn, the LACC has established 12 thematic Sectoral Working Groups (SWGs), each with one or more PA ministries as "gavel holder", a donor as "shepherd" and a United Nations agency as "secretariat": agriculture (Spain/UNDP); transport and communications (France/UNDP); education (France/UNICEF); public works/employment (Sweden/UNDP and ILO); environment (Netherlands/UNRWA and UNSCO); health (Italy/WHO); institution- and capacity-building (EU/World Bank and UNSCO); infrastructure and housing (Germany/World Bank and UNSCO); police (Norway/UNSCO); private sector and trade (US/World Bank and UNDP); public finance (US/World Bank and IMF); and tourism (Spain/UNDP).

In November 1994 the AHLC also decided to establish a Joint Liaison Committee (JLC), consisting of the Palestinian Authority ("gavel holder"), Israel, the United States, the European Union, the United Nations, the

Figure 11.1 Organizational schema of assistance programme

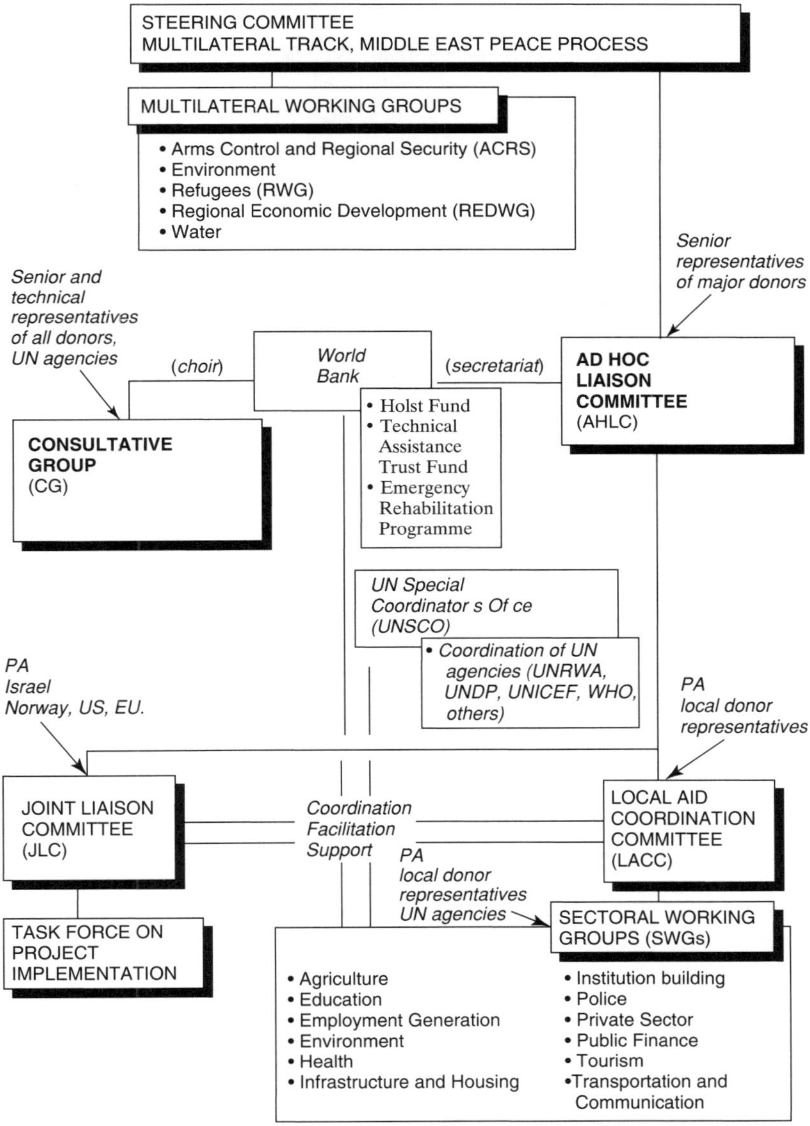

World Bank ("secretariat") and Norway ("shepherd"), to deal with significant obstacles in the way of the prompt and effective delivery of assistance, as well as reviewing Palestinian budgetary performance, revenue generation and priorities for technical assistance. The JLC has met once or more per month since May 1995. It is the forum within which implementation of the Tripartite Action Plan on Revenues, Expenditures and Donor Funding for the Palestinian Authority (TAP) is monitored. The TAP, signed by the PA, Israel and Norway (as the AHLC chair) in April 1995, contains specific commitments by the parties in such areas as tax clearances, PA fiscal and expenditure policy, and continuing budgetary support by donors.[2]

As is clear from this discussion, the World Bank has been of central importance in the assistance process. The Bank acts as Secretariat for AHLC, and in that capacity facilitates meetings and helps to track donor assistance. The Bank also acts as chair for the Consultative Group. It has assumed a major role in assessing economic conditions and in developing (in association with the Palestinian Authority) packages for projects for donor support. The first such package – the Emergency Assistance Programme (EAP) for the occupied territories – was presented by the Bank to the first Consultative Group meeting in December 1993. Based on a larger six-volume study prepared earlier by the Bank and released to coincide with the signing of the Declaration of Principles, the EAP identified sectoral needs and priorities totalling $1.2 billion through 1994–96.[3] The Bank also developed a more detailed aid programme of its own, the $128 million Emergency Rehabilitation Programme (ERP), involving 117 smaller projects throughout the West Bank and Gaza Strip. Of the $88 million pledged for the ERP, some has been provided by donors (notably Saudi Arabia, Denmark and Switzerland), while the World Bank has itself provided $30 million of its own through its associated aid agency, the International Development Association (IDA). Outside the ERP, some support for private-sector investment is to be provided through loans offered by the World Bank-affiliated International Finance Corporation.

Finally, the World Bank is responsible for managing the $25 million Technical Assistance Trust Fund (TATF) and the Johan Jurgen Holst Peace Fund (or Holst Fund). The TATF – now largely exhausted – has financed technical assistance, particularly to assist in the development of nascent Palestinian technical and administrative infrastructures. The Holst Fund is used to support the start-up and recurrent costs of the Palestinian Authority.[4] Because Palestinian tax receipts are still not sufficient to cover recurrent costs – and because the Palestinian Authority would grind to a halt were civil-service salaries and administrative costs to remain unpaid for any length of time – the Holst Fund has been of critical importance. It has also been chronically short of funds, forcing the World Bank and Norway to play the frequent role of emergency fund-raisers.

A number of other United Nations agencies are also important players, acting as the conduit for up to $100 million of funds committed for 1994. The most important have been the United Nations Development Programme (UNDP, which has acted as a conduit and implementing agency for a number of aid projects), the United Nations Relief and Works Agency (UNRWA, which has by far the most developed infrastructure and capacity of any aid/relief agency in the territories, and which plays a particularly important role in Gaza), and the International Monetary Fund (IMF, which assists in monitoring and strengthening PA fiscal management). A variety of other UN agencies are active in the territories, including UNICEF, the World Health Organization, the International Labour Organization, UNESCO and others. The United Nations Special Coordinator Office (UNSCO) acts to coordinate these and to facilitate cooperation between the United Nations, the Palestinian Authority, Israel and donors. Norwegian diplomat Terje Rød Larsen, who played a major role in the original secret Oslo negotiations, was appointed to the position by the UN Secretary-General in 1994.

The Palestinian counterpart to the World Bank is the Palestinian Economic Council for Development and Reconstruction (PECDAR), established in 1994 to track donor assistance, channel it into specific projects and generally act as the Palestinian Authority's interface with the donor community. PECDAR is chaired by Farouq Qaddoumi, with Ahmad Qurei (Abu Ala) serving as Director-General. With the subsequent establishment of Palestinian economic ministries – specifically the Ministries of Planning and International Cooperation (first headed by Nabil Shaath), Finance (then by Muhammad Zuhdi al-Nashashibi) and Economy (then by Ahmad Qurai) – these, as well as functional ministries, the Office of the President and existing municipal governments have all played important roles in the aid process. The Palestinian Authority has now drawn up its own $1.3 billion investment and development framework for 1995–98, the Palestinian Public Investment Programme (PPIP).

Upon the signing of the Taba (Oslo II) agreement on the extension of Palestinian Authority in the West Bank, both the peace process and the donor effort entered a new stage. In addition to the PPIP, and in consultation with both the Palestinians and the donors, the World Bank and United Nations produced the seven-volume study *Putting Peace to Work*, consisting of development strategies and $450 million in UN project proposals. Drawing upon unfunded core projects in the PPIP, and incorporating both the lessons learned from the EAP and the directions identified in *Putting Peace to Work*, the Palestinian Authority and the World Bank presented to donors at the October 1995 Consultative Group meeting a priority list of 16 projects (totalling $552 million) for future funding.[5] A special ministerial-level donor meeting centring on this same package of initiatives was subsequently held in January 1996.

INTERNATIONAL DONORS: SLOW TO RESPOND?

As mentioned above, one of the most frequent criticisms heard of the assistance programme for the West Bank and Gaza Strip has been its slowness. Since 1994 the Palestinian Authority complained that "the international community is moving very, very slowly", and charged that the delays were a form of political pressure.[6] Indeed, when Palestinian security forces first deployed to Gaza in May 1994, PLO negotiator Nabil Shaath was forced to privately borrow some of the required monies. Overall, of the $807 million pledged by donors for 1994, $773 million was committed to projects but only $407 million was actually disbursed (with much of this occurring in the final quarter of the year). Although small amounts of aid did flow quickly through discretionary embassy accounts (of which the Canada Fund is one of the best examples), larger aid projects were subject to bureaucratic processes that often entailed lengthy planning, proposal, assessment and procurement procedures, and particular evaluations required by donor priorities in such areas as the environment, gender and private-sector development. Moreover, many donors were particularly wary of funding continuing PA administrative costs or public make-work programmes, seeing these as a potentially never-ending drain on donor resources which were both economically unproductive and unsustainable, and which ran counter to the general free-market ethos of contemporary development assistance.

Such attitudes and processes reflected a decade of criticism of Western agencies for wasteful or inappropriate aid programmes – and, consequently, a desire by donors to spend funds carefully in support of long-term initiatives. However, these same attitudes and processes often proved poorly suited to the political realities of peace-building in Palestine, which required the rapid delivery of assistance in such a way as to strengthen the ongoing diplomatic process. This tension often expressed itself in a cultural clash between the *realpolitik* of foreign ministry officials in the donor states, and the commitment of their aid counterparts to careful and sustainable development. Thus, while State Department officials could often be heard to complain about the slowness and inappropriateness of USAID programmes in the territories, many USAID officials complained that they were being diverted from real, sustainable development: "How do you plan, develop, and do something of quality if you are under [constant political] pressure?"[7] On top of this, initial donor agency assumptions were often "very facile", underestimating the political and economic difficulties that lay ahead.[8] Israel's establishment of closure in the occupied territories and the institutional growing pains of the PA, for example, were largely unanticipated.

The delivery of international assistance was also complicated by legal restrictions. In the United States, congressional suspicion of the Palestine

Liberation Organization meant that the assistance programme was subject to periodic congressional review and a legislative requirement for periodic certification by the State Department of the Palestinian compliance with the Oslo agreement.[9] US legislation also prohibits direct American assistance to the Palestinian Authority and mandates USAID support for the establishment of cross-border industrial parks (despite a preexisting legislative ban on USAID projects that might result in competition with US manufacturers). Indeed, the requirement for congressional aid authorization has rendered the USAID budget a battleground for those in Congress who are critical of both foreign aid and the Palestinian–Israeli peace process.[10] Another major donor, Japan, found itself bound by domestic legislation that limited its assistance to international organizations and recognized states (thus excluding the PA). In the case of almost all donors, legal restrictions prevented most aid agencies from providing direct assistance to the Palestinian police force.

It is important to recognize, of course, that PA criticism of the pace of assistance has been, in part, politically motivated. By criticizing donors, the PA both diverts attention from its own shortcomings and exerts pressures for accelerated disbursements. Donors observe that support for Palestinian recurrent costs, transmitted through the Holst Fund, was delivered in a timely fashion and indeed represented a large share of 1994 disbursements. In the case of investment and rehabilitation projects, however, engineering cycles could only be compressed to a limited extent.

Moreover, one should not underestimate the institutional challenge of rapidly expanding aid programmes from around $200 million per year in the early 1990s[11] to four times that amount. New staff had to be hired and new projects identified. At the outset of the assistance programme most aid agencies had an existing "stable" of projects and local contacts. In many cases, therefore, the initial tendency was simply to do more of the same rather than to re-think aid priorities. Yet this itself was problematic, as earlier aid programmes had often been heavily dependent on small NGO projects and could not easily be "scaled up". In the case of the US, for example, pre-Oslo aid had been limited, and (for domestic political reasons) largely channelled through a limited group of US private voluntary organizations rather than administered directly. As a result, with the expansion of its programme for the territories, USAID had to rapidly expand its infrastructure on the ground, with bureaucratic and political struggles arising over such issues as staffing levels, location (Jerusalem versus Tel Aviv) and line authority.

Economic assistance for the Palestinians in the West Bank and Gaza has been heavily shaped not only by the legacies of earlier assistance but also by particular national priorities. Despite the formation by donors of a high-level Ad Hoc Liaison Committee (AHLC) and Consultative Group (CG) structure, there has been little real coordination (or even communication) among donors at the local level. Virtually all donors have been driven by a desire to become involved in projects that would maximize their political visibility and credit. There has also been significant political competition between the United States and the European Union, with the latter feeling that its status as the leading donor entitled it to a larger role in both the aid effort and the broader peace process.

Further compounding these difficulties has been some commercial competition among funders for projects that might be thought to have some longer-term economic (or political-economic) benefit. Some aid is tied, and procurement guidelines may mandate preferences for suppliers from the donor country. Finally, some countries (notably the United States and European Union) have allocated a significant portion of their economic assistance in the form of loans, risk insurance or export and investment guarantees, which have proven difficult to deliver. The result of all this has been a significant mismatch between the sectoral goals identified by the Palestinians and World Bank in the EAP (as well as inconsistent incentive structures) and the actual distribution of aid funds by donors.[12]

By late 1994 the assistance programme seemed to be in a state of crisis. Assistance was said to be slow in arriving and poorly targeted.[13] Armed attacks against Israel by Palestinian opposition groups and growing tensions between the PA and Hamas in particular signalled a deteriorating political situation. Most importantly, the Israeli institutionalization of closure in the territories – imposed both in response to armed attacks, and as a way of pressuring the PA – began to cause severe economic damage to the Palestinian population.

As a result, both multilateral and bilateral programmes were revamped. At its third meeting in November 1994 the AHLC endorsed the establishment of a Local Aid Coordination Committee (LACC) to facilitate aid coordination among donors on the ground in Palestine. At its subsequent meeting in Brussels in April 1995, the AHLC activated a high-level, locally-based Joint Liaison Committee as a way of facilitating the resolution of major bottlenecks and obstacles between the PA, Israel and donors. Donors recognized the political importance of "quick disbursing job creation projects",[14] and at the local level the various LACC sectoral working groups focused greater attention on the actual number of "person working days" generated by each project.[15] Ironically – and despite donors' considerable distaste for providing budgetary support – the Holst Fund has proven to be the most effective means of quick disbursement, while Palestinian police, civil service and public works expenditures have been the most successful form of local job-creation.[16] Some donors also looked to new mechanisms for communicating to Palestinians the benefits of the peace process. One of the most successful examples of this has been a series of new public areas in Gaza. With their highly visible green spaces and playground equipment, these have been hugely successful psychological indicators of positive change associated with peace.

In addition to these moves, the World Bank significantly revamped its aid distribution structure in order to speed the delivery of assistance. The most important aspect of this was the devolution of decision-making authority from the headquarters in Washington to the then resident representative in the occupied territories, Odin Knudsen. Although the move faced some bureaucratic resistance at the World Bank, it clearly served to improve response time, facilitate contacts with the PA, Israel and local donor missions, and enabled the World Bank to play a more proactive role in resolving obstacles on the ground. Knudsen assumed these tasks with inventiveness and vigour. Much the same could be said about the United Nations Special Coordinator, Terje Larsen, and his office. Reporting directly to the Secretary General, and with a budget (fiscal year 1995) of $3.1 million and a staff of over 30 persons,[17] UNSCO has a played a major role in not only coordinating UN efforts (its formal mandate), but also in acting as an effective diplomatic intermediary and an energetic "helpful fixer" on the ground. Indeed, very considerable synergy has existed between Knudsen's abilities as project-oriented problem-solver, and Larsen's political and diplomatic skills.

Donors have also shown varying degrees of procedural adaptation to the requirements of peace-building. The Japanese, unable to provide funds directly to the PA, have channelled assistance through UN agencies instead. The EU, although still rather bureaucratic in its aid process, recognized the value of supporting the emerging structures of Palestinian administration and consequently has targeted a large proportion of its aid at the PA and local municipalities. A number of countries have found ways of circumventing restrictions on assistance: Germany, for example, ultimately used commodity donations ("office supplies and toilet paper" in the words of one aid official) as a way of supporting recurrent administrative costs. Similarly, international funding for police salaries is "laundered" through UNRWA, while UNSCO has helped to coordinate technical assistance and equipment donations.[18]

The largest single donor restructuring took place within USAID, which under State Department and White House pressure reviewed and then revamped its programme in late 1994. As a result, previous long-term institution-building projects in the health and housing sectors were cut back significantly, as was support for private voluntary organizations; instead, more rapid job-creation projects were supported in the areas of municipal public works, micro-enterprise and a Gaza waste/storm-water project. In the process, many of the usual themes of USAID assistance were downgraded to allow for a clearer focus on the most politically-effective projects, and the project process speeded up.[19] Increased use was made of UN agencies, particularly UNRWA with its well-developed capabilities in the West Bank and

Gaza. All this was a painful bureaucratic process: in the words of one senior US official, there was "blood on the floor" at USAID when the reprogramming occurred: "a lot of people did not see the train coming and got smacked".[20]

PALESTINIAN CHALLENGES

The Performance of the Palestinian Authority

Although the donors have taken much of the heat for the slowness of the aid process, much of the blame could also be laid at the feet of the PA. Constructing a Palestinian administration from scratch was, of course, a daunting task: the PA lacked both resources and expertise. Even when the latter existed in the diaspora, many Palestinian professionals were understandably unwilling (or simply could not afford) to uproot themselves and work under difficult and uncertain conditions in the occupied territories. Above and beyond this, however, the emerging PA faced serious problems of institutionalization. The senior leadership, and Arafat in particular, seemed unwilling to create meaningful structures or clarify decision-making authority. Appointments to administrative and technical units were driven by political favouritism and nepotism. Some Palestinian officials engage in influence peddling, and some agents for external private sector interests are too willing to offer commissions or bribes. Emerging bureaucratic structures have become personal and political power bases, enmeshed in competition with one another and with preexisting civil and political institutions.

One manifestation of this problem was an unclear demarcation of authority between the remnants of the PLO's Tunis-based bureaucracy and the emerging power centres in the PA. In one memorable case, this led to the simultaneous announcement in Tunis and Gaza of a contract for long-distance telephone services – to two *different* companies. Tensions were also evident in the internal squabbling that accompanied the formation of PECDAR: the senior leadership of this agency was clearly appointed by Arafat on political grounds, sparking protests by economists and technocrats. Later, the establishment of three separate (and competitive) PA economic ministries raised questions about PECDAR's future role as well as the locus of economic authority. This was accentuated by political rivalries between Nabil Shaath (Minister of Planning) and Ahmad Qurai (Minister of Economy and Director-General of PECDAR, who periodically threatened to resign).

Donor meetings were sometimes preceded by disputes over which minister would represent the PA, while in early 1995 the World Bank also encountered some initial difficulties in getting PECDAR and the Ministry of Planning to agree on a new common set of project proposals. Finally – and not surprisingly, given Arafat's neopatrimonial[21] style of political management – the Office of the President has retained a role in a great many projects and economic decisions. Economic aid has clearly been used to advance the political (and sometimes financial) interests of the Gaza-based Fateh, as well as to pursue other objectives.[22] Surrounding the President are a bevy of assistants, advisors and shady hangers-on, all of whom claim some influence, or *wasta*, and who largely serve to further cloud economic accountability.[23]

Systemic weaknesses and confusion generated by weak Palestinian institutionalization have inhibited the ability of the PA to formulate and implement economic policy. They have also severely slowed the delivery of assistance and its subsequent distribution. In almost all cases, aid agencies have been required to demonstrate, and hence required from the PA, a fairly demanding level of accountability and transparency in the disbursement of economic assistance. Indeed, the PA found itself subject to audit, with a portion of its expenditures reviewed by the accounting firm of Touche-Ross Saba, and its revenue-collection process overseen by the International Monetary Fund.[24] In the absence of solid project proposals and sufficient procedural guarantees, funds were simply not released: many harried aid officials were reluctant to undertake what they saw as Palestinian responsibilities. Moreover, faced with unclear lines of economic authority, donors frequently pursued the path of least resistance, arranging whichever projects seemed easiest with whatever level or branch of Palestinian authority or society seemed most amenable – further complicating economic planning.[25]

These sorts of issues often became bound up with a second major issue of PA-donor contention: recurrent costs and Palestinian revenue generation. As noted earlier, despite the establishment of the Holst Fund for this purpose, donors have been reluctant to finance the continuing administrative costs of the PA, hoping that these would be financed through Palestinian taxation. Indeed, the Holst Fund has periodically run dry, resulting in delays in the payment of PA salaries, and urgent appeals by the World Bank and others (Norway and the United States) for new donations or the prompt delivery of earlier pledges. There has also been concern over the potentially runaway expansion of the PA bureaucracy (particularly given the tendency of the PA to use public sector employment as a political reward), and of financial accountability and transparency within the civil service.

The donors and the PA first achieved agreement on these sorts of issues at the November 1994 meeting of AHLC in the Understanding on Revenues, Expenditures and Donor Funding for the Palestinian Authority. Subsequently, the parties approved the broader Tripartite Action Plan in April 1995. In January 1996 a revised and extended TAP was signed at the ministerial-level Conference on Assistance to the Palestinian People. This provided a donor undertaking to finance a recurrent budget deficit of $75 million in 1996, on the understanding that the PA would balance its recurrent budget by 1997 and achieve a budgetary surplus in 1998 – hence obviating the need for any future donor assistance in this area.[26]

In general, Palestinian compliance with these agreements (monitored by the IMF, the World Bank, the Joint Liaison Committee and the AHLC) has been quite good. Indeed, overall there has been marked improvement in the functioning of PECDAR and various Palestinian ministries, with most donors now generally satisfied by the level of transparency and accountability. However, bureaucratic and political "turf" battles do remain a problem, particularly as the role of PECDAR is eclipsed by the PA's regular ministries. There is also some donor concern that the PA may be operating a "shadow budget", outside their knowledge.[27]

Whither NGOs?

The focus of post-Oslo international economic aid efforts, together with the establishment of the Palestinian Authority, has put a severe squeeze on both Palestinian NGOs (of which some 850–1200 operate in the West Bank and Gaza) and international private voluntary organizations (PVOs), of which approximately 200 are active.[28] In the early 1990s, the Palestinian NGO sector received approximately $170–240 million from the PLO and international donors. As a consequence first of the Gulf War and later the redirection of most aid funds to the PA following the Declaration of Principles, this amount has fallen to roughly $60–90 million. Many development projects are simply too large for PVOs and NGOs to effectively bid on or participate in. NGOs themselves show poor coordination and have yet to find an effective formula for representation with the donor coordination framework. Finally, the PA has attempted to bring Palestinian NGOs under an increasing degree of control, partly as a natural process of extending state authority into various social policy sectors, and partly for more cynical purposes of strengthening its political sway.[29] Given the cost-efficiency, flexibility and innovation shown by much of the NGO sector – as well as its broader contribution to a pluralistic Palestinian society – its weakening is a source of concern (see Chapter 12 in this volume for a discussion of Arab NGOs).

Unusually, the World Bank – which, as an institution, has historically been suspicious of NGO activity – has proposed the establishment of a $16 million NGO trust fund to supplement existing funding sources. Such a fund might not only strengthen NGO and PVO activities, but also enable the Bank to tap new donor resources. The proposal faces some challenges: the PA might be expected to be less than enthusiastic about the existence of an independent pipeline of resources to local NGOs, while donors may be unwilling to contribute to an anonymous fund when they can gain a higher political profile by directly financing PVOs and NGOs. However, the proposal received approval in principle from the PA and was included in the list of core projects presented to donors for consideration in their meetings of October 1995 (Consultative Group) and January 1996 (Ministerial Conference on Economic Assistance to the Palestinian People).

THE PRIVATE SECTOR

The character of the Palestinian private sector, distorted by years of "de-development" under Israeli occupation, has also played a role in shaping international aid efforts.[30] The construction sector in particular has suffered from weaknesses of both quality and capacity, as well as the material interruptions caused by continued border closures. Consequently, private sector firms were poorly equipped to tackle some of the larger projects proposed by donors. Recognizing this, the World Bank had designed its own Emergency Rehabilitation Project for the occupied territories around a variety of small- to medium-scale local projects. While this made better use of small-scale construction capacity, projects also proved too small and scattered to attract the bids of larger regional and international contractors. Today, contractor capacity has expanded somewhat (as has its quality), and more projects are designed more mindful of local capacity, the importance of local labour inputs and the potential contributions of external contractors.

Broader private sector growth has also been hampered by the weaknesses of local infrastructure in such areas as transportation, communication and energy. Moreover, the legal and regulatory context, based on a complicated amalgam of Turkish, British, Jordanian, Egyptian, Israeli and PA regulations, "is far from ideal, characterised by numerous regulatory hurdles and a lack of legal transparency which increases the burden, risk and confusion involved in doing business."[31] This is compounded by both weak local infrastructure and political and economic uncertainty.[32] As noted earlier here and in other chapters, such factors have hindered the provision of external investment-financing and loan guarantees. The local banking sector is underdeveloped – particularly in providing venture capital – and equally cautious (see Chapter 7 in this volume for more on Palestinian banking). Finally, it is not clear that the West Bank and Gaza offer obvious comparative economic advantages for foreign investment, especially given competition from Israel and Jordan. Although a few substantial Palestinian holding companies (notably PADICO, with $200 million in capital) have been active, and despite extensive real estate speculation in Gaza, Ramallah and elsewhere, Palestinian expatriate investment has still not reached hoped-for levels. A Palestinian investment law enacted by the PA in April 1995 sought to attract external investors by offering tax exemptions of up to five years,[33] but it does little to resolve the more fundamental impediments to private-sector development.

In order to redress this lack of private-sector investment, the PA has held high-profile meetings with Palestinian entrepreneurs, while the World Bank invited representatives of the Arab Bank to participate in the October 1995 CG meeting. More substantially, some initial efforts were made to regularize commercial codes, a task that the PA has committed to undertake under the terms of the Tripartite Action Plan. One version of the TAP also called for the establishment of three industrial estates by March 1996. The current list of Palestinian Public Investment Programme projects being considered by the donor community include major transportation and energy infrastructure projects, as well as proposals for the establishment of local and transborder industrial estates, technical assistance in the legal and regulatory field, and a guarantee fund for investments to be operated through the World Bank's Multilateral Investment Guarantee Agency.

ISRAELI POLICY

Just as the limitations of Israeli occupation determine the social, political and economic imperatives facing Palestinian planners, so too has Israeli policy had profound effects on the process of economic and development assistance to the Palestinians. The Palestinian economy remains closely entwined with the Israeli economy, with the former's dependency on the latter reflected in the lengthy provisions of the economic protocol signed by the PA and Israel in Paris in April 1994.[34]

This dependence has also been underscored by the serious economic disruption caused by the ongoing Israeli border closures. The closure has prevented thousands of Palestinian workers from reaching jobs in Israel, from moving freely between the territories and the external borders of Egypt and Jordan, and, for most Palestinians who live outside the East Jerusalem area, from entering or transiting the city. During periods of "internal closure", Palestinians are prevented from reaching even neighbouring towns and villages. The institution of closure overall has blocked Palestinian producers from exporting their products and interrupted the import of necessary goods and supplies, including building materials needed for development and investment projects. The closure has also hampered the mobility of aid workers and officials, especially as a result of the difficulties surrounding mobility in and out of East Jerusalem. Palestinian sources have estimated the immediate economic costs of the closure at $3 million per day, and perhaps double that if other costs are included.[35] By mid-May 1995 World Bank officials declared Gaza's exports (particularly the citrus sector) to be in a state of "complete collapse", while construction had ground to "a complete standstill".[36] In February 1996 Arafat complained that Israel during the previous 15 months had sealed off the crossing points to and from Israel for some 247 days, devastating the Palestinian economy.[37]

Because of the economic, political and human damage wrought by continued border closure Israel has found itself under international pressure to put an end to the practice.[38] Both the Israeli security services and cabinet recognize the disruptive effects of closures.[39] However, with polls showing that over 85 per cent of Israelis support it, the Israeli government has faced intense domestic pressure to continue with this policy, especially when it is intensified in connection with attacks inside Israel carried out by Palestinian opposition groups.[40] A number of "work-arounds" have been found for particular problems associated with border closures: for example, by arranging to have goods moved between Israeli ports and the Gaza Strip (and vice versa) in specially-guarded convoys.[41] At best, however, these are band-aid mechanisms for dealing with an intolerable situation.

Apart from this important structural issue, there have been a number of other Israeli policies which have undercut the international assistance effort. One of these was the initially slow pace of Israeli tax clearances to the PA under the terms of the Gaza–Jericho agreement. The PA also complained about the rate at which Israel transferred tax records and other economic data and the formats in which some data were received. For this reason, the Oslo II agreement included a re-write of Article VI of the earlier Protocol on Economic Relations, detailing with greater specificity the process for value added tax clearances between the two parties. Clearances now appear to be proceeding better, but there remain a number of smaller but recurrent irritations. Both donors and the PA have complained about the sclerotic rate of some Israeli customs procedures, which can leave imported materials languishing on Israeli docksides for weeks or months. Similar problems have been encountered in securing the necessary visas and other documents for foreign experts working on development projects.[42] The establishment of the Joint Liaison Committee – which allows both donors and the PA to raise such irritants directly with senior Israeli officials, and in so doing also flag them for the attention of AHLC – has eased these problems somewhat. Under the January 1996 version of the Tripartite Action Plan, Israel committed itself to facilitating the movement of project staff and PA officials, and expediting the movement of goods in, out, within and between the West Bank and Gaza.

Development Assistance and Palestinian–Israeli Negotiations

In many cases it has not been entirely clear whether many of the sorts of problems identified above stem from bureaucratic inertia or from deliberate

Israeli policy. Border closures, for example, have often been condemned by PA officials as an Israeli means of exerting pressure to force Palestinian concessions at the negotiating table. Similar suspicion has been voiced about the smaller problems as well. One case in point was the slowness with which the Israeli telephone company Bezeq responded to PECDAR's requests for telephone lines. These were not installed until December 1994, forcing PECDAR staff to depend on a limited number of UNDP-financed cellular telephones in the meantime. Some put this down simply to Bezeq's legendary lethargy. There is good reason to believe, however, that the delay signalled Israel's disapproval of PECDAR's location on the fringes of the Jerusalem municipal boundary.

The latter possibility is indicative of the extent to which the economic aid effort has been caught up in the broader Palestinian–Israeli negotiating process. In this, Jerusalem has often figured prominently. The initial formation of PECDAR was delayed, for example, by reference in its original charter to Jerusalem as its headquarters.[43] In September 1994 a meeting of the Consultative Group collapsed when the PA included some East Jerusalem projects among their proposals to donors. Resolution of that particular dispute required active Norwegian mediation, concluding in a joint declaration by Arafat and Peres on 13 September 1994, the first anniversary of the Oslo signing, in which they undertook not to raise disputed issues with donor countries. In the summer of 1995, leaked documents showing apparent covert PECDAR assistance for projects within East Jerusalem was used by the Israeli opposition and their US supporters to try to slow or halt the aid process.[44] Both Israeli government and opposition leaders have complained vociferously about the location of Palestinian research institutes and quasi-governmental offices within Jerusalem, resulting in an Israeli crackdown (and a subsequent Israeli–PA compromise on the issue) in August 1995.[45]

CONCLUSION

The Consultative Group, donors and the PA alike express the view that, after a slow and shaky start, the international economic assistance effort has largely been put back on track. Despite an estimated drop in real GNP per capita of 8.5 per cent in 1995 and an unemployment rate of around 23 per cent (much higher in Gaza), some indicators suggest that economic conditions could begin to improve in the occupied territories, depending of course on the future of the closure. Poll results showing relatively little dissatisfaction with donor assistance are encouraging,[46] and donor disbursement has indeed accelerated.[47] The PA has addressed many of the problems of transparency and financial accountability that slowed earlier aid delivery, although problems of muddled economic authority still remain. The PA has also shown, according to donors, "notable capability in improving the fiscal situation and implementation capacity".[48] A pipeline of projects at various stages of preparation is now well-established, and future project implementation promises to be more timely than in the past.

Many donors have also targeted their programmes more effectively, recognizing the value of high-profile projects, the importance of maximizing local job-creation, the constraints imposed by local contractor capacity and technical expertise, and the importance of sustainable infrastructure. The restructuring of USAID – the initial efforts of which were particularly poorly conceived – is the most striking example of the difficult adjustments that this has sometimes required. Even bank-type financing (investment guarantees, trade credits, risk insurance and so forth or mortgage lending, as Wright points out above), has thus far proven itself woefully ill-suited to supporting development in an unstable context of peace-building, and has begun to show greater flexibility. In the aftermath of Oslo II, donors and the PA have signalled their intention to shift some of the focus of the assistance effort. In particular, emergency rehabilitation projects will increasingly be complemented by efforts to expand longer-term capacity through new investment. Greater emphasis is to be placed on sustainability and encouragement of the private sector (both micro-enterprises and larger-scale projects). The PA itself is now playing, with support from the World Bank and UN agencies, a more proactive role in setting project priorities. Finally, donors will continue their efforts to wean the PA from continuing external budgetary support, although this goal may still be some distance away.

How successful all of this will ultimately be remains to be seen. Legitimate concern continues to be expressed about the efficacy and probity of the Palestinian Authority, as well as regarding the health of the NGO sector (and, in the larger sense, the general health of Palestinian civil society). Moreover, the strategic political and economic goals of donors – reshaped by bureaucratic processes, the PA and local conditions – are not always translated into practical realities on the ground. Finally, the Israeli closure in the occupied territories remains, in tandem with the threat of Palestinian rejectionist violence: collectively, they could easily smother the fragile progress made by the aid process since mid-1995.

Still, as Terje Larsen noted, "[in 1994] I called the donor effort a failure…but now donors are moving speedily".[49] Reflecting this, the January 1996 Ministerial Conference on Assistance to the Palestinian People announced that $1365 million would be mobilized between January 1996 and March 1997 to support the core projects of the Palestinian Public Investment Programme ($550 million) as well as other priority initiatives.[50] Clearly, international assistance is now playing its primary peace-building role in a substantial way and has started to address longer-term development concerns too. Indeed, experiences in the West Bank and Gaza – regarding bottlenecks and institutional constraints and the importance of flexibility and realism; the key contribution of the Holst Fund as an effective conduit for timely budgetary support; the valuable role of UNSCO and the World Bank as coordinators and "helpful fixers" (a role facilitated by the devolution of World Bank authority into the field); the importance of external diplomatic engagement (notably by the United States, the European Union and Norway); and the establishment of local liaison (JLC) and coordination (LACC) mechanisms – may hold out valuable lessons for multilateral peace-building and aid efforts in Bosnia, Rwanda and elsewhere.

Notes

1. Palestinian Authority, Ministry of Finance, *West Bank and Gaza Strip: Recent Fiscal and Macroeconomic Developments and Prospects* (Gaza: October 1995). These aggregate factors mask a disproportionate economic decline in Gaza. It should also be noted that economic recession and closure had gripped the territories prior to the 1993 Declaration of Principles, with GNP per capita growth at –9.8 per cent and –13.3 per cent in 1991 and 1992 respectively. On the squeezing out of Palestinian NGOs, see Dennis Sullivan's chapter in J.W. Wright, Jr. (ed.), *Structural Flaws in the Middle East Peace Process* (London: Macmillan, 1999).
2. Specifically, Israel undertook to expedite tax clearances to the PA, ease the passage of goods and establish a corridor for safe passage between the West Bank and Gaza Strip; the PA undertook to clarify authority and contact persons within its ministries, develop a unified commercial code, maintain budgeted limits on hiring and implement IMF recommendations on tax administration so as to eliminate the need for external budgetary support; and donors agreed to accelerate the release of uncommitted aid funds and maintain budget support through the end of 1995. The making of donor budgetary support contingent on Palestinian revenue generation was the most important part of the agreement. Text in *Journal of Palestine Studies* 24(4) (Summer 1995), pp. 143–6.
3. World Bank, *Developing the Occupied Territories: An Investment in Peace* (Washington, DC: International Bank for Reconstruction and Development, 1994), comprising six volumes on the economy, private sector development, agriculture, infrastructure, human resources and social policy; World Bank, *Emergency Assistance Program for the Occupied Territories* (Washington DC: World Bank, 1994).
4. As of October 1995, the Holst Fund had disbursed some $148 million to the PA. To that point, the largest contributors to the Holst Fund had been the United States ($40 million) and Kuwait ($21 million).
5. The PPIP projects presented by the PA and World Bank to the October 1995 meeting included some unfunded projects from the earlier Emergency Rehabilitation Programme, as well as major projects in the areas of water, sewage and drainage; electricity supply and distribution; road upgrading; a Gaza coastal parkway; a Gaza harbour; municipal infrastructure rehabilitation; housing development; schools upgrading; medical infrastructure; support for local and cross-border industrial estates; technical assistance in the area of private sector regulation; support for the establishment of a Palestinian mone-

tary authority; and trust funds for NGOs and for Palestinian expatriate experts. Substantial portions of the sewage, housing, medical and education components of this grew out of United Nations project proposals described in *Putting Peace to Work*.

6. Nabil Shaath in *Reuters World Report*, 5 June 1994; Yasser Arafat in *Reuters World Report*, 15 November 1994.
7. Interview with USAID official, December 1994. In USAID, as in a number of other aid agencies, many officials were particularly perturbed by pressures to donate to the Holst Fund. Since Holst supported the unproductive and recurrent costs of Palestinian administration, this was seen as a particularly inefficient mechanism for development. Foreign Ministry officials, by contrast, were more likely to see Holst as a political imperative.
8. Interview with World Bank official, January 1995.
9. PLO Commitments Compliance Act of 1993 (Public Law 101-246), and the Middle East Peace Facilitation Act of 1994 (Public Law 103-246). The text of the State Department's periodic certifications can be found in the documents section of the *Journal of Palestine Studies*, cited in note 20.
10. A.M. Rosenthal, "Aid, Congress and a Mother-in-Law", *New York Times*, 12 June 1995. Draft legislation introduced by Senator Alfonse D'Amato and Representative Michael Forbes in June 1995 sought to place greater restrictions on aid to the Palestinians. At times foreign aid has also been held hostage to other domestic political battles: in the fall of 1995, necessary congressional legislation was delayed not only by opposition by some members of Congress, but also by unrelated legislative battles over issues ranging from abortion to the State Department reorganisation plan.
11. United Nations Development Project, *1993 Compendium of External Assistance to the Occupied Palestinian Territories* (Jerusalem: UNDP, 1993).
12. The European Union allocated half of its assistance through the European Investment Bank (EIB); the United States allocated $125 million of its support to the Overseas Private Investment Corporation (OPIC); and $70 million was offered through the multilateral International Finance Corporation. However, it soon became clear that few projects in the occupied territories were sound enough to meet conservative bank standards; consequently by October 1995 only about 10 per cent ($67 million) of pledged loan and guarantee financing had been committed. In the case of OPIC, only one project – a Gaza-based concrete factory – had been financed by December 1995 (the US Trade Development Agency has been more forthcoming, supporting six major feasibility studies as well as several other studies). In the United States, this led to growing criticism of OPIC by State Department and USAID officials, as well as by NGOs. In Europe, the EU presidency committed itself to accelerating the disbursement of EIB funds. Interviews, Washington DC, July 1995; *Reuters World Report*, 11 September 1995; *Building Blocks* 1(4) (October–December) 1995. In addition, there was and is considerable firm, NGO, and even PA ministerial competition concerning the distribution and profit mechanisms that should be used to direct aid flows. See J.W. Wright, Jr. (ed.), *The Political-Economy of Middle East Peace: The Impact of Competing Trade Agendas* (London: Routledge, 1999).
13. According to UN Special Coordinator Terje Larsen, "Looking back at donor efforts until October 1 [1994], we see that the priorities had been wrong, the time schedule had been wrong". *Reuters World Report*, 16 January 1995. Larsen's criticisms may have also reflected an effort to carve out a larger role for UNSCO.

14. Tripartite Action Plan for the Palestinian Authority, in *Journal of Palestine Studies* 24(4) (Summer 1995), p. 145.
15. The impact of this is disputed: some aid officials assert that it has had a major impact on project design, while others suggest that the commitment to employment generation is largely rhetorical, and job-creation figures are little more than "back of the envelope" calculations intended to justify pre-existing projects.
16. As of January 1995, the PA employed some 25 000 police and approximately 45 000 civil servants. The local impact of this is quite significant: given an average household size of six or more, public sector employment alone helps to sustain over 420 000 persons.
17. As of July 1995 these included 14 international staff (seven of them professionals), and 17 local staff.
18. Commodity donations can still be problematic, as international support for the Palestinian police has shown. Thus, while the police have been able to obtain (for example) large numbers of vehicles, donor restrictions have meant that they have not been able to secure handguns and remain very short of riot-control equipment – thus forcing them to rely on assault rifles for policing and crowd control. Similarly, much of the communications equipment donated to date works on incompatible frequencies or on frequencies that have not been cleared for PA usage.
19. Indicative of this sharper focus on political requirements were the comments of one Western aid official regarding the downgrading of gender equality as an aid priority in the West Bank and Gaza Strip: "It isn't that gender is unimportant, but for the moment it is the unemployed young men that we have to worry about." Interview, Tel Aviv, July 1995.
20. Interview, Tel Aviv July 1995.
21. Rex Brynen, "Neopatrimonial Dimensions of Palestinian Politics", *Journal of Palestine Studies* 25(1) (Autumn 1995).
22. *Possible* evidence of this was released by United States Senator D'Amato during his attempts to restrict aid to the Palestinians. While the authenticity of these alleged PECDAR documents is uncertain, they do appear to show funds being channelled to Fateh loyalists and used to strengthen Palestinian institutions in and around East Jerusalem (neither of which, after all, would be terribly surprising). *Congressional Record*, 104th Congress, 1995, pp. S14008–14013.
23. Virtually all Western aid officials can recount a similar story: the approach of a business agent, seeking donor co-financing or other support, brandishing a letter of authorization from some PA official or another. Generally it is doubtful on what authority the letter has been issued and by what process it has been obtained – and there are almost always several other versions of the letter (issued by the same official or others) in circulation. Attempts to clarify the situation are rarely successful.
24. Touche-Ross Saba acts as the agent of the World Bank, assuring that the disbursements from the Holst Fund are appropriately allocated.
25. One collective beneficiary of this has been Palestinian universities and research groups, which are better able to mount project proposals and meet accounting requirements. While most projects have been worthwhile, there has also been a growth in "rentier scholarship" by researchers pursuing the lure of peace process funds.
26. *Tripartite Action Plan on Revenues, Expenditures and Donor Funding for the Palestinian Authority*, January 1996. The PA also undertook to further

strengthen its fiscal apparatus and accounting and to restrain police and civil service hiring in keeping with its 1996 budget.

27. Certainly, the PA has financed additional security personnel in this way. Donor concern about a "shadow budget" stems not only from questions of probity, but also (and perhaps more so) because of domestic political sensitivities in donor countries – particularly within the US Congress.
28. World Bank and UNDP estimates. Also see Dennis Sullivan's chapter in J.W. Wright, Jr. (ed.), *Structural Flaws in the Middle East Peace Process* (London: Macmillan, 1999). Sara Roy's chapter in this volume also addressed this issue, but with reference to alternative providers.
29. See, for example, the degree of state control proposed in the PA *Draft Law Concerning Charitable Societies, Social Bodies and Private Institutions*, in *Palestine Report* 1(22) (27 October 1995). The obverse of PA efforts to exert greater control, however, is the resistance of many NGOs (particularly those associated with opposition factions) to the legitimate establishment of state authority in areas such as health and education.
30. Sara Roy, *The Gaza Strip: The Political Economy of De-Development* (Washington DC: Institute for Palestine Studies, 1995).
31. Israel–Palestine Center for Research and Information, *The Legal Structure for Foreign Investment in the West Bank and Gaza Strip*, Commercial Law Report, series 1, October 1994: Introduction.
32. One survey of Palestinian, Israeli and international investors found that corruption and prohibitions on the free movement of goods and people were the most frequently cited concerns, followed by inadequacy of the local power supply and the transferability of capital.
33. See the overview in *Building Blocks* 1(4) (October–December 1995).
34. Protocol on Economic Relations, Paris, 29 April 1994. This was subsequently included as Annex IV of the 4 May 1994 Agreement on the Gaza Strip and the Jericho Area (the Cairo agreement), and – with modifications – as Annex V of the 28 September 1995 Israeli–Palestinian Interim Agreement on the West Bank and the Gaza Strip (Oslo II).
35. Nabil Shaath, quoted in *al-Ittihad*, Abu Dhabi, 10 December 1995, in *Foreign Broadcast Information Service,* 94–245.
36. Interviews, Washington DC and Gaza, June–July 1995.
37. *Reuters World Report*, 3 February 1996.
38. The European Union, for example, had initially called for the TAP to include a compensation clause whereby Israel would reimburse the PA for the economic damage caused by the closure.
39. *Ma'ariv*, 5 May 1995, via *Israel Information Service* gopher.
40. *Associated Press*, 20 October 1994.
41. The number of trucks in such convoys had grown to an average of 165 per day by October 1995.
42. Western aid officials note that despite official encouragement of the aid process, they continue to experience "a lot of problems" with such items as visas for technical experts and outside contractors, customs clearances, value-added-tax refunds, restrictions on mobility from the closure and so forth. Interviews, Tel Aviv and Gaza, July 1995.
43. Article 1.3 of PECDAR's bylaws noted that "The Council shall have its main office in Jerusalem..." *Al-nizam al-asasi lil-majlis al-iqtisadi al-filastini lil-tanmiya wa al-i'mar* [The Basic Organisation of the Palestinian Council for Development and Reconstruction] (Tunis: May 1994).
44. *International Herald Tribune*, 1–2 July 1995, p. 8.

45. On the proliferation of semi-official Palestinian establishments – complete with "mug-shots" of the offices concerned – see *Peace Watch, Peace Watch Report: Institutions of the Palestinian Authority in Jerusalem*, 14 March 1995.
46. *United Press International*, 3 November 1995. In a June 1995 survey, only 8.8 per cent of Palestinians who expressed a moderate or negative attitude regarding the performance of the PA cited donor aid as a reason. Moreover, the performance of the PA was rated "poor" by only 5.2 per cent in the case of education, 14.2 per cent in health, 16.5 per cent regarding PECDAR, and 23.2 per cent in the case of the taxation authorities. However, 30 per cent rated Arafat's overall handling of the economy as "poor". *JMCC Press Service*, 21 June 1995.
47. World Bank press release, 19 October 1995. However, the World Bank's claim that almost $500 million was disbursed in the first ten months of 1995, compared with $250 million during 1994, seems at odds with other data.
48. *United Press International*, 19 October 1995.
49. *Reuters World Report*, 26 October 1995.
50. *Final Communiqué of the Ministerial Conference on Economic Assistance to the Palestinian People*, Paris, 9 January 1996; *Reuters World Report*, 9 January 1996. The figure of $1365 million is inflated, however, since it combines the overlapping categories of undisbursed funds and commitment to the PPIP.

12 Civil Society Organizations in the Middle East: Can they Facilitate Socio-Economic Development during a Time of Transition?

Peter Gubser

INTRODUCTION

The subject of this chapter is civil society in Middle Eastern socio-economic development. Before delving into the substance of civil society, development and the peace process, it is helpful to define the key terms and put them in their context. Initially, I examine the concept of civil society in general; then I look at one of its key components in some detail, non-governmental organizations (NGOs).

Jean L. Cohen and Andrew Arato in their seminal work *Civil Society and Political Theory* define "civil society" as "...a sphere of social interaction between economy and state, composed above all of the intimate sphere (especially the family), the sphere of associations (especially voluntary associations), social movements, and forms of public communication." On the one hand, they distinguish civil society from political society (parties, parliament, and so on) and economic society (organizations of production, partnerships, and so forth). On the other hand, they insist that the elements of civil society are not of the informal type but only those that are institutionalized or in the process of being so. Finally, Cohen and Arato:

> ...stress that under liberal democracies, it would be a mistake to see civil society in opposition to the economy and state by definition. ...[These] notions of economic and political society refer to mediating spheres through which civil society can gain influence over political-administrative and economic processes. An antagonistic relation of civil society, or its actors, to the economy or the state arises only when these meditations fail

> or when the institutions of economic and political society serve to insulate decision making and decision makers from the influence of social organizations, initiatives, and forms of public discussion.[1]

Taking the subject from a slightly different perspective, Mustapha K. al-Sayyid of Cairo University lays down three minimal conditions that must be met before it can be said that civil society exists:

> the presence of formal organizations of various types among different social groups and classes; an ethic of tolerance and acceptance by the majority of minority legitimate rights, no matter how such minorities are defined; and limitations on arbitrary exercise of state authority. Undoubtedly, such criteria are not met entirely in any society, nor is it conceivable to find a society in which all three conditions are totally missing. It is safe to assume, however, that these conditions are largely met in liberal democracies.[2]

Both studies agree on the position and place of civil society. Al-Sayyid however would differ with Cohen and Arato on an important point: he asserts that it is a contradiction to say that a civil society can exist where a distinct degree of tolerance is not present or where state authority is oppressive. His is a more value-laden or normative definition of civil society. Cohen and Arato (and this writer) are not in agreement with that definition. They contend that elements of civil society can still be present in an intolerant or oppressive environment, but that they have entered into an antagonistic relationship with the state or economy rather than in a cooperative or mediating relationship with them.

As for NGOs, both studies would agree that NGOs may exist irrespective of whether or not society is civil. Also, neither is asserting that a state should establish a *laissez faire* environment for NGOs. They would both likely agree with John Keane when he states:

> Democratization is neither the outright enemy nor the unconditional friend of state power. It requires the state to govern civil society neither too much nor too little, [because] while a more democratic order cannot be built *through* state power, it cannot be built *without* state power.[3]

From a slightly different perspective, this view of government partly meets one of al-Sayyid's criteria that society has to be tolerant. As such, the state can help in promoting an environment of tolerance, but it cannot guarantee it. This means that the state is not necessarily just a hindrance or even a neutral force with respect to the existence of civil society, but that the state can contribute positively to its existence.

THE SPECIFIC ROLE OF NON-GOVERNMENTAL ORGANIZATIONS

Having looked at the broader concept of civil society, it is appropriate to turn to one of its important components: the vast array of unofficial citizen associations of virtually all possible types, grouped under the general heading of non-governmental organizations. NGOs are formal associations of people found in each of the various classes of society. They include local community, regional and national groups that bring people together to render services, solve community problems, observe religious beliefs, cultivate social, political and cultural pursuits, and communicate ideas or advocate policies in the local, regional, national and transnational arenas. Community service oriented NGOs, for instance, combine people's energies to resolve problems in the fields of medical care, job creation, assistance for the poor, education and rehabilitation of the handicapped, to name a few. They may also focus on socio-political and socio-economic subjects such as human and civil rights, population, health and nutrition, the environment, and many, many others including business associations, jurist societies, etc.

But the role of NGOs is more than just the function or ideals each pursues. They also contribute mightily to society as a whole. First, because many work at the grassroots, they are often in a propitious position to reach those afflicted with poverty, the deprived of nation, region and village. Thus, they play a significant role in social and economic development. They are also part of the essential social safety net that every country needs. Second, as people-oriented organizations, they help give structure to civil society, as well as to society in general. In addition to family, they provide additional loci to which people can relate at the ground-level, participate in, and benefit from. As formal organizations they help the society produce leadership not only for civil society but also for the higher economic and political arenas.

Third, as an essential element of civil society, NGOs help to develop and sustain democratic development and popular participation. One cannot argue that NGOs or civil society groups are capable of producing democracy by themselves. However, the existence of civil society is necessarily associated with the existence of democracy. We are not aware of any democracy with success over time that has not also enjoyed a flourishing civil society.

NON-GOVERNMENTAL ORGANIZATIONS AND THE MIDDLE EAST PEACE PROCESS

Having given sufficient attention to theory and definition, let us now turn to the state of civil society and NGOs in particular during the "antepax" years –

that is, the period before 1993 when the Palestine Liberation Organization and Israel signed the Declaration of Principles, catapulting the regional peace process into an entirely new phase. Subsequently I look at the role of NGOs in Middle Eastern socio-economic development as the region gradually transits to peace. With respect to each period, civil society and NGOs are considered in terms of the above definitions: civil society as part of the larger society (that is, inclusive of the political and economic components), the NGOs as a major part of civil society, and NGOs in tolerant societies with a liberal state, NGOs in confrontation with the state or the economy. Their emerging role in transnational human concerns is also reviewed.

During the Ottoman period, the Middle East contained a thin layer of civil society sandwiched in between the state – a military-fiscal apparatus imposed by conquest – and a primordially fragmented society. The thin civil society consisted of *awqaf* (Islamic trusts), *sufi* orders, churches and synagogues, guilds in urban areas and occasional water associations in the rural regions.[4] The twentieth century, especially the last two to three decades, has witnessed a rapid growth of civil society, especially NGOs, in most countries. However, each set of NGOs and the other components of civil society have had profoundly different environments in which they have had to operate and, thus, quite different experiences. To limit the scope of this survey, I characterize the state of NGOs only in the following countries: Egypt, Israel, Jordan, Lebanon, Palestine (West Bank and Gaza Strip) and Syria.

Egypt has a rich array of NGOs from social clubs to charities, religious groups to professional associations, and from cultural centres to advocacy organizations. Since Egypt is such a large country, the NGOs number not in the hundreds but in the thousands. That being said, do they constitute a recognizable portion of civil society? Due to state constraints on many organizations, sometimes even their registration, as well as on freedom of expression in general, one must conclude that a portion of civil society is in confrontation with the state. Al-Sayyid goes even further, in concluding that the requisites for civil society do not exist.[5]

Syria falls into the same category as Egypt, perhaps even more so. While civil organizations certainly exist there, many are associated with the state or the ruling party and therefore are not truly non-governmental. As quasi-official institutions, these associations necessarily fall outside our standard definition of what types of entities constitute civil society. And, as in Egypt, there are limitations on the registration of NGOs as well as generalized constraints on freedom of expression.[6]

Israel, Jordan and Lebanon have civil societies that are similar to one another, but with a uniqueness particular to their own societies. The Zionists formed a plethora of NGOs in the early part of this century, some of which evolved into organs of the Israeli state after its establishment in 1948. It has been said that Israel was built on the back of the *kibbutzim*, its unique form of cooperatives. Since Israel's establishment, the state has been largely tolerant of its own (Israeli) NGOs and often delivers services through them. In the last decade or so, Israeli NGOs have enjoyed considerable growth in their reach and variety. Likewise, the Arabs in Israel have begun to articulate a form of civil society, subject, however, to some official restraints as they establish numerous village charities, clubs, newspapers and other associations, some of which have taken on a national character.

In Jordan a large variety of NGOs participate in that country's vibrant civil society. While Jordanian NGOs have been active both locally and nationally for years, they have experienced exponential growth during the last 15 years or so. While the social and economic need and desire for more NGOs is certainly a contributing factor, the democratic opening of the country during the last decade has contributed as well. In the continuum of relations with the state, from all reports the Jordanian NGOs would fall on Cohen and Arato's liberal democracy end as opposed to the confrontational one.

Lebanese NGOs operate in a virtual *laissez faire* atmosphere. Hundreds of them existed prior to the civil war, which began in 1975. Indeed, they dominated many functions often performed by the state in neighbouring countries, such as the provision of education and medical care, for example. During the civil war with the virtual collapse of the state, most of the country's social services fell to them. Realizing the ability of NGOs to reach people at the grassroots level, many political factions sought to form their own service organizations. Some of these will survive the end of the civil war; others will probably fall by the wayside. There are reports that the Lebanese government is considering passage of a law restricting NGO activities. This action, if it were to occur, would be a major step backwards.

Palestinian NGOs are the heroes of the military occupation and *Intifada*. Prior to 1967, under Jordanian administration, the West Bank had flourishing charities, clubs, Arab women's unions, and other associations, as in Jordan proper. In the Gaza Strip, however, the number of NGOs was much more limited among the largely refugee population under Egyptian administration. In the 30 years subsequent to 1967, under the Israeli occupation, the Palestinian NGOs multiplied and came to play an indispensable role in the provision of many essential civilian services as well as constituting forums where people could come together to resolve societal and economic problems. All of this was undertaken despite a relatively hostile state atmosphere. While constraints on NGOs have varied over the years, the relationship was largely confrontational. Registration of new NGOs was frequently problematic, and the activities of existing civil organizations were often constrained. Instead, during the early 1980s the Israeli military government tried to foster its own Palestinian groups, subservient to itself: namely, the much-despised Village Leagues. And during the first months of the *Intifada* the military government outlawed the popular committees, a new form of civil organization that provided social cohesion for the uprising and, hence, gained considerable popularity among Palestinians during that time.

While the contrast is not absolute, there is a major difference in attitude towards Palestinian NGOs on the part of Likud governments as compared to that of Labour governments. The Likud, including Netanyahu's regime, has tended to put more constraints and obstacles in front of the NGOs than has Labour. Many Palestinian NGOs have nevertheless maintained strong external relations: they have received financial and technical assistance from Jordan, other Arab countries and international NGOs. Also, as in Lebanon, political factions have understood the value of NGOs. Accordingly, the various Palestinian factions formed some of their own and attempted to take over the leadership of others. Despite or perhaps because of this fact, Palestinian NGOs flourished, especially during the last decade and a half. In a changed context, they must now chart a new future.

As we have demonstrated, civil society in general and NGOs in particular have contributed to the improvement of the larger society in virtually every country, especially in countries whose national governments do not severely constrain their activities. Civil organizations have existed in a variety of different atmospheres, but nevertheless they are important players. Their absence or containment would make each country a lesser place.

What might they contribute in this period of transition to peace? What is their role during this critical time? A simple answer is that they should continue doing what they are doing. It is valuable and important. They contribute to the larger society and should sustain their activities. That being said, there are special challenges and opportunities which they must confront during this transition period.

Before turning to these, however, it is necessary to say a word about the focus of the world community during this period, especially as it pertains to the Middle East peace process. Suffice it to say, although some players pay attention to NGO roles and interests, their focus is mostly on governments and national economies. From the newspapers and journals as well as many conferences, one would think these are the only societal sectors involved in the peace process. In a way, this is natural. It is governments that are signing treaties and making peace with each other. It is the economies that are going to have to make structural changes so that they will be able to relate to each other in a context of peace rather than conflict. The World Bank, the multilateral organizations and the donor states for the most part relate to governments. Indeed the World Bank's development plan for the West Bank and Gaza is largely government-focused and economy-intensive. Civil society groups in the Middle East, including the region's NGOs, are given a backseat or no seat at all in these plans.

This approach is not sufficient. Peace is not just political agreements between states or adjustments in economies. Rather it is fundamentally, in the final analysis, a process of reconciliation, or the establishment of goodwill and mutually beneficial relations between peoples. This being said, how are the peoples involved except through their governments and economies? The response, naturally, is that they are not, and therefore that civil society, including the NGOs, must be somehow integrated into the process. Indeed, if this peace is to succeed the people must be part of the process.

To focus this part of the discussion[7] I suggest that involvement of the NGO sector in the peace process be divided into three components: (1) promotion of confidence-building for peace and stability; (2) fostering sustainable development and open political systems; and (3) encouraging regional cooperation and integration. With respect to each of these components, the recommendations found below are based upon the needs of the process and the capabilities of the NGOs and other elements of civil society. Also, each section is not exhaustive but rather suggestive of what might be done. With respect to each area of activity, an NGO, for instance, might play the role of facilitator, communicator or implementer. An NGO might relate to fellow NGOs in other countries or work in partnership with one or more governments. Or it may seek to influence those governments in various ways. There is a myriad of potential patterns, the limits of which are only in people's minds. Now let us turn to the three components in detail.

Promotion of Confidence-building for Peace and Stability

In view of past hostilities and continuing tensions among diverse political, economic, national, ethnic, linguistic and religious groups in the region, initiatives that break down suspicion and promote dialogue between diverse groups will be mandatory for building a sustainable peace and crucial for socio-economic development. Attention should be paid to the efforts of NGOs in the region, including peace groups, religious institutions, human rights groups, labour unions, professional organizations, and others, in order to facilitate dialogue between diverse groups.

The objective would be to encourage the various peoples in the region to live together in harmony and mutually supportive communities, in recognition that citizens' groups can help in the process of people-to-people communication. This might involve instituting measures designed to facilitate reconciliation and mutual cooperation, such as:

(1) the design of new educational curricula in the region based on less stereotyped images of the people of each country;
(2) the introduction of living–learning experiences, such as Israeli–Palestinian–Jordanian summer camps for children;
(3) joint education, research and study projects in the occupied territories, other Arab countries, Israel and abroad; and

(4) joint teacher-training projects, medical exchanges and vocational projects.

Support of Sustainable Development Initiatives within the Countries of the Region

One of the most serious impediments to building sustainable peace and stability in the Middle East is the economic despair and hopelessness of so many of its people (as Brynen also illustrates above). According to World Bank data, one out of four people live in poverty, and only 55 per cent of adults are literate, partly as a result of low female literacy (45 per cent) associated with the low economic and social status of women in much of the region. One out of five children is underweight, and infant mortality is 52 per 1000 live births. Eighty-four per cent of people have access to safe water, but only 62 per cent have access to sanitation. On average, women in the Middle East bear 4.9 children, more that in all other developing regions except sub-Saharan Africa. Yet, despite all this, only 13 per cent of all foreign economic aid to the region is spent on basic education, primary health care, safe drinking water, sanitation, nutrition and family planning.

With respect to the subject of this section, I suggest that civil society and the NGOs continue doing what they are doing, and that governments and international donors help them by providing the means, funding and policy environment for them to do so. With that note, there are several initiatives that can be instituted by non-governmental organizations at the grassroots level. One is support for human resource development, such as basic education, child survival activities, primary health care and family planning, especially in the form of education and information for women. Consideration should also be given to supporting secondary, university and technical education in the non-governmental sectors. Second, I suggest an intensification of institution-building aimed at strengthening civil society by increasing the problem-solving capacity of community groups and other civil institutions.

Third, the growth of such vibrant groups and institutions should be encouraged and that they should be allowed to develop in freedom. Thus it is also important that a suitable political environment, meaning open and accessible political systems, be created in order to allow civil society to operate and develop freely, with independence. Although this is important for civil societies everywhere, a special note is warranted with respect to the West Bank and Gaza Strip. While the Palestinian civil society under occupation has survived a difficult period, its future environment is unknown. The Palestinian Authority has the opportunity to promote openness and political tolerance in this sector of Palestinian society and to construct a relatively liberal and democratic environment, though subject to Israeli limitations.

The development community should strongly urge the Palestinian Authority to opt for this model for the sake of preserving what has been a positive and flourishing civil society, as well as its potential future contribution to Palestinian economic and political development.

Finally, support should be provided for small businesses, young entrepreneurs and small farmers, and for essential services necessary to spur job creation and increase the economic potential of local communities. To promote this goal, the donor community should support a variety of initiatives with defined objectives, including:

(1) the provision of credit to small enterprises or and farmers through various indigenous institutions, including co-operatives;
(2) stimulating the adoption of improved, environmentally-sound production, quality control, packaging, marketing and management practices; and
(3) support for the growth of associations to serve as effective advocates of just and sustainable development.

Also, for the private sector to serve the people and be successful, there must be a policy framework in which small businesses can function without undue government interference or market concentration: namely, a legal and regulatory environment that supports private and community initiative and which protects the public interest in areas such as health, safety and the environment. Particularly constraining to entrepreneurial activities are perceived barriers to entry, restrictions on the movement of people and goods, and insecurity about property rights. Additionally, a legal system that protects personal rights as well as property rights must also be put in place. Some countries in the Middle East have made great progress in assuring this policy context. Others have not. Accordingly, the international donor community should enter into policy dialogue with countries in the latter category.

Support of Initiatives to Strengthen National Economies and Encourage Regional Economic Integration

Successful development as well as sustainable peace depend on regional cooperation to develop a basis for a shared existence, stimulate economic growth and protect the natural resource base. Regional cooperation is important both as a means for solving regional problems and in itself, as a process by which the states and peoples in the region can learn to work together in mutually supportive ways.

The Arab–Israeli conflict has had a devastating economic impact in much of the region. In addition to diverting resources to military purposes, the conflict has generated a myriad of economic restrictions and regulations including the Arab boycott, closed borders and other actions that have prevented or distorted economic relations within the region. The peace process provides an opportunity both for stimulating increased trade and other economic relationships, and for integrating the region economically in the larger sense.

Economists point out that the assets of countries in the Middle East region complement each other in terms of availability of capital and labour, agricultural and manufacturing capacity, and natural resource endowment. These complementary endowments offer important opportunities for the more efficient use of resources, expansion of regional markets, joint production enterprises and environmental conservation activities. Many activities under this category may be only appropriate for governments or the private sector. In some areas, however, civil society and NGOs in particular, ranging from the community to the national level, can play a very positive role.

One possibility may be to support regional development institutions, as determined by the countries in the region. This support might take the form of strengthening existing institutions (such as the Arab Fund for Economic and Social Development) or creating a regional development bank, as well as providing resources for development activities undertaken by those institutions. A regional development institution could serve both as a mechanism for mobilizing and channelling external resources to the region, and as a locus in which countries in the region could work together to solve regional development problems. Interested NGOs could play an advocacy role with respect to this possibility.

A second possibility is to support regional infrastructure initiatives, such as water resource development and management, electric power grids, highways, ports and communications systems. There is broad agreement that water resource development and management must be a top regional priority. In a region where most countries already suffer from water scarcity and where the population is expected to double in the next 30 years, sustainable economic development and long-term political stability are both closely linked to availability of water. Financial and technical resources will be needed for initiatives to increase the supply of water, as will diplomatic encouragement of regional agreements to regulate water use. Other regional infrastructure initiatives would also serve to link more closely the countries of the region. These issues are not only of interest to governments and businesses, but also to the development and advocacy NGOs, some of which are already engaged in many of these areas.

A third possibility is to support the development of regional trading and labour exchange blocs (like that of the Benelux involving Belgium, the Netherlands and Luxembourg). The peace process may open up the possibility of lifting restrictions and encouraging the free flow of trade, capital and labour across borders in the Middle East. In view of the fact that the region's economies complement each other in important respects, working towards the Benelux model offers important opportunities for economically strengthening both the region as a whole and the national economies of individual countries. NGOs will be interested to make certain that human-level concerns are addressed so that the people are not just rolled over by economic interests. Conversely, NGOs can play a beneficial role in helping educate the people about the benefits of free trade.

Finally, the donor community might decide to support activities aimed at protecting natural resources. The Middle East has the lowest proportion of arable land (4.5 per cent of total land area) of any region of the world. It also has the smallest forest area (4 per cent of total land area), yet it suffers from the highest annual rate of deforestation of any region. It has the least amount of renewable water resources per person of any region, yet it withdraws 68 per cent of its renewable fresh water resources annually, again more than any other region. Tensions in the Middle East have resulted in intense competition over natural resources with no integrated management of natural resources or conservation planning. Joint action is sorely needed to protect and manage dwindling resources, especially water; to combat desertification; to fight pollution of air and water; to address population pressures; and to protect the animal and plant life of the region. NGOs with an environmental, population or development brief are interested in this area. Indeed, most NGOs are concerned in one way or another with this set of issues.

CONCLUSION

Civil society, including its wide spectrum of associations and organizations, can and do make a major contribution to the overall society in normal times of slow evolution. In this current period of transition to peace and the acute need for development, their role will be especially valuable. Not only can they make the peace and development processes easier and more friendly for the people, but they can also influence these processes and help them to evolve into a better kind of peace and development that actually benefits people. In a complementary manner, civil society can be instrumental in ensuring that the process goes in the right direction, that it not be dependent on any particular regime or on a single political personality or leader.

That is, with the involvement of civil society, the process has a broader base and thus a greater possibility of succeeding. One may think it is idealistic, but civil society in general, and the voluntary associations that form an important part of it in particular, have proved in the past that they improve lives and will continue to do so in the future. Finally, the absence of civil institutions and the networks they provide would lead to serious breakage in the economic links that might promote national and regional trade and other forms of interaction. Thus, the corresponding lack of freedom to establish and sustain civil organizations and their resulting networks could pose serious economic and political impediments to Middle East peace.

Notes

1. Jean L. Cohen and Andrew Arato, *Civil Society and Political Theory* (Cambridge, Mass.: MIT Press, 1992) ix–xi.
2. Mustapha K. al-Sayyid, "A Civil Society in Egypt?", *Middle East Journal* 47(2) (Spring 1993), p. 230.
3. John Keane, *Democracy and Civil Society* (London: Verso, 1988); p. 23, emphasis in original.
4. Raymond A. Hinnebusch, "State and Civil Society in Syria", *Middle East Journal* 47(2) (Spring 1993), p. 244.
5. Al-Sayyid, *op. cit.*, p. 140.
6. Hinnebusch, *op. cit.*, p. 243–57.
7. This discussion is influenced by a document prepared by the Coalition to Rethink US Aid in the Middle East, entitled *Toward a Safer Future for the Children of Abraham: A Proposal for Restructuring U.S. Aid to the Middle East*, January 1995. The author is a member of the Coalition and participated in writing the proposal.

13 From Front State to Backyard? Syria and the Risks of Regional Peace[1]

Volker Perthes

INTRODUCTION

Since the beginning of the current phase of the Arab–Israeli peace process in October 1991, Syria's official attitude towards the conflict with Israel and towards Israel itself has gradually been adjusted. In the media, Israel is now usually referred to by its name, rather than as "the enemy" or "the Zionist entity", and President Hafez El-Assad is now called the "hero of liberation and peace". The negotiations between Israel and the Palestinians and Israel and the Jordanians, and their results, have been widely covered, if critically commented upon. Regional peace is expected at some point, and the Syrian leadership is eager to make it clear to international and domestic opinion alike that it is politically prepared to make peace with Israel. At the same time, Damascus has left no doubt as to its unwillingness to compromise on Syrian essentials, especially the demand that Israel fully withdraw from the occupied Golan Heights as well as from southern Lebanon, and that no symbol of occupation remain. If peace cannot be made on Syria's terms, Damascus prefers the status quo.[2]

So far, by simply stating its demands for a peace treaty and waiting for the other side to move in its direction, the Syrian leadership fared considerably well. During the reign of Israel's Labour party from 1992 to 1996 the Israeli leadership has incrementally revised its negotiation position *vis-à-vis* the Syrians. Even before the assassination of Prime Minister Rabin, the Israeli government had by and large come to accept the fact that without a full withdrawal from the Golan there will be no peace with Syria. By early 1996, as the election of Prime Minister Netanyahu approached, the territorial dispute still to be solved at the negotiation table had in principle been reduced to a few square kilometres. The difference was between the international border of 1923 (agreed upon by Britain and France as the Mandatory powers over Palestine and Syria, respectively) and the front-line separating Syrian and Israeli forces prior to the June 1967 war. Israel had shelved its demands, raised in the first round of discussions between the Israeli and Syrian chiefs of staff in December 1994, that Syria dismiss substantial parts of its standing forces and that Israel be allowed to maintain Israeli-manned early warning stations on Syrian territory, even after a general withdrawal from the Golan.

Thus, by declaring its willingness, in principle, to conclude a peace treaty with Israel and discuss reasonable security arrangements, while at the same time not rushing for such a treaty and actually refusing to speak seriously about the content of future bilateral relations, Syria won, at least initially, substantial concessions from the Israeli side. Going it slow, however, was more than just a tactical maneuver for the Syrian leadership which, in contrast to its Israeli counterparts, was not feeling the pressure of election dates. The Syrian side, to the contrary, needed to win time; that is, for domestic reasons it could not plunge into peace with Israel too fast.

Syria's political readiness to contemplate peace has been evident since 1991. Economically, however, and probably culturally, Syria is not yet prepared for the challenges of peace and the new division of labour a settlement will bring about in the Middle East. Rather, the transition from a regional state of war to a regional state of peace could, at least in the short and middle term, create problems that might outweigh the gains of such a settlement. For a long time, Syria, by virtue of its strategic front-line position in the Arab–Israeli conflict, has been able to harvest what might be called a war dividend. With the recent changes in the Middle East at large, this is now much less so. However, in the event of a comprehensive regional peace down the road, the peace dividend which will accrue to the region will be unequally divided, and Syria will not expect to receive its fair share. Moreover, whether Syria will gain a peace dividend or not will depend on more than a treaty with Israel (see Chapter 6 for more on the Syrian peace-time budgetary dividend).

SYRIA'S WAR DIVIDEND

Syria is one of the few countries which has been able to combine large military expenditures with a comparatively high level of non-military public expenditures. The severe economic crisis with which the country had to cope during the 1980s resulted primarily from misguided economic and development policies – in particular, a statist import-substituting industrialization process that neglected agriculture – not from high defence spending.[3] Since the mid-1980s the government has embarked on a cautious, home-made economic reform programme which has led to the reduction of state control over production, foreign trade and consumption, increased the scope of the private sector, and given more importance to market principles. However, the government has also sought to control the reform process and prevent any loss of political power, thus making reforms limited and selective and subjecting them to a logic of political control rather than economic rationality. The ability of the Assad government to sustain control and limit reform is, to some extent, the result of its having been able to ensure a considerable inflow of foreign revenues.

Rather than being burdened by defence expenditures, Syria has been able to benefit from its strategic and regional position since the 1973 war. As one of the leading confrontation states with Israel – since 1979 the primary confrontation state – and as a country that has developed a potential for limited interference in the Arab regional system, Syria has long been supported with massive financial aid from the more wealthy Arab countries. At the same time the Syrian government has managed to pay only a fraction of its armaments bill. Most of Syria's arms imports have been financed by its Arab allies – mainly the states of the Gulf Cooperation Council (GCC) and Libya – or were financed by the Soviet Union on a concessionary loan basis.[4]

Syrian arms purchases totalled some $21 billion for the 1980s alone.[5] This arms buildup has led to an estimated $11 billion military debt to the former Soviet Union. Syria, however, always regarded Soviet arms shipments as political rather than commercial ventures, since hardware deliveries were linked to Soviet security guarantees. Russia, as the successor state to the Soviet Union, has been neither able nor willing to extend these guarantees, and the Syrian government has therefore shown little inclination to commit itself to a full repayment of its debt. The Russian government will be fortunate if it succeeds in securing repayment of more than 10 or 15 per cent of what Damascus officially owes for Soviet arms shipments. Syria may even manage to secure Arab Gulf funding for such a limited repayment.[6]

With arms deliveries largely financed from abroad, only Syria's current military expenditures, as reflected in the official defence budget, have had to be covered from domestic sources. Although high,[7] these expenditures can be considered a necessary investment to make maximal use of the country's location in order to earn a war dividend, namely financial transfers for non-military expenditures which Syria's regional partners have put at the disposal of the Syrian government because of, and only because of, Syria's strategic regional position and military credibility (as Looney points out in Chapter 6).

It is significant that some 85–90 per cent of all non-military financial aid that Syria has received since the early 1970s has come from regional sources. Between 1973 and 1978, official Arab aid to Syria averaged close to $600 million per annum. The Baghdad summit of 1978, called by the Arab states to oppose the Egyptian–Israeli Camp David accords, pledged a $1.8 billion annual grant to Syria for a ten-year period. A substantial portion of this promised aid materialized in the first years after the summit: net Arab assistance jumped to an annual average of almost $1.6 billion during the 1979–81 period, declining thereafter to an average of $670 million until 1987, and to near zero in 1988 and 1989.[8] The decrease after 1981 was primarily due to political factors, namely Syria's support for Iran during the Iraq–Iran war. Diminishing funds from Arab sources were to a large extent replaced by

Iranian grants in the form of free and concessional oil deliveries which, conservatively estimated, may have been worth between $300–800 million per annum by 1986. Thereafter, Iranian assistance decreased, reaching a low of less than $50 million in 1990 before being terminated altogether.[9]

Thus, by the end of the 1980s aid flows to Syria from virtually all sources had diminished. Moreover, substantial repayments on loans from Western sources, international organizations and Arab agencies were coming due. In 1989 Syria's debt-service actually exceeded incoming revenues. Only with the 1990–91 Gulf conflict did aid flows to Syria increase again. Arab Gulf aid alone was estimated at $1.5 billion for the 1991–92 period, while net total non-military financial assistance in the early 1990s totalled around $600–700 million per annum.[10]

Compared to the early 1980s, annual aid of around $700 million does not seem very impressive. One has to consider, however, that international and particularly Arab funds shrank enormously after the decrease in oil prices in the early 1980s.[11] During the first half of the 1990s Syria may actually have received some 20–25 per cent of total Arab financial assistance. Even given Syrian economic indicators, aid inflows remain substantial, equalling approximately 4–5 per cent of GNP. If foreign assistance is of considerably less importance to Syria today than it was in the late 1970s and early 1980s, when it ranged around 10 per cent of GNP, it is high in comparison to other middle-income countries in the region.[12] Moreover, aid has remained the main source of finance for public investments. As economic assistance amounts to more than half of Syria's projected development or investment budgets, it can still be assumed that the foreign exchange portion of public investments is all but completely covered from external sources.

To establish how much of the funding that Syria has received from regional sources actually represents money provided because of Syria's strategic position in the Middle East conflict, one might compare aid flows to Syria with similar flows to structurally-similar Arab states that are not confrontation states, such as Tunisia or Morocco.[13] Equal criteria applied, Syria could, at best, have received between one-and-a-half to two times more in the way of regional financial assistance than Tunisia, and not more than half as much as Morocco. In fact, in the 1973–89 period, Tunisia received some $530 million in Arab non-military aid, while Morocco received $3.7 billion. Syria, in contrast, received some $12 billion in Arab non-military aid and approximately another $12 billion from Iran. On the basis of this comparison, Syria's war dividend can be estimated at about $12–13 billion.[14]

THE CHALLENGES OF PEACE

Syria's war dividend has been dependent on changing regional alignments. When Egypt left the Arab front in 1979, Arab support for Syria reached unprecedented heights. However, Syria's pro-Iranian stance during the Iraq–Iran war reduced Arab aid flows. Its pro-Saudi stance during the second Gulf war, its establishment together with Egypt of a loose alliance with the GCC states, initially embodied in the (now defunct) Damascus Declaration of March 1991, and its participation in ongoing bilateral Middle East peace talks, have all led to a resumption of Arab Gulf aid. The Syrian government has made considerable efforts in the past two years to diversify its sources of funds, mainly by increasing oil production and exports and by trying to stabilize its relationship with the GCC countries. To the extent that these attempts were successful, they have also reached their limits. It is highly unlikely, for instance, that Syria will be able to increase its portion of Arab Gulf aid beyond the 20 or 25 per cent which it has received in recent years. And, in any event, oil price fluctuations in the late 1990s make it more likely that the overall level of GCC aid will continue to decline.

From the perspective of the Syrian government, the situation of "no war, no peace" which has prevailed, with notable exceptions, between Syria and Israel since 1973 has been most beneficial. Even in the current state of affairs it provides the regime with both political and economic advantages. For one, it has furthered the government's nationalist credentials and legitimacy, both domestically and in the wider Arab world, while simultaneously enhancing Syria's international stature. Consider, for instance, that the Syrian President, Hafez El-Assad, has never had to travel to the United States to meet with his American counterparts, instead making them come to Damascus or meeting with them on neutral territory. It is hardly imaginable that any other head of state in the Third World could have allowed himself such liberties.

Second, the "no war, no peace" situation has secured external economic assistance for Syria without endangering its economic infrastructure. Moreover, any full-scale war with Israel would almost certainly lead to a Syrian defeat – the 1982 war in Lebanon made this clear – thus the ambiguity of "no war, no peace" continues to allow Assad to avoid putting the Syrian armed forces at unnecessary risk. When Syria agreed to join the US-sponsored Middle East peace talks in 1991, its leadership knew very well that among the potentially disastrous alternatives to a peaceful solution of the Arab–Israeli conflict was another war with Israel. And given that the great powers had developed an interest of their own in pacifying the Middle East, the indefinite continuation of the "no war, no peace" situation became increasingly untenable.

Damascus has been prepared to enter negotiations for a peaceful settlement of the Arab–Israeli conflict since 1974. It is today prepared to conclude a peace treaty with Israel if its core conditions – principally a full withdrawal of Israeli forces and settlers from the Golan Heights – are met. Syria's objective is not as much the conclusion of a peace treaty or a quick resolution of the conflict with Israel as it is avoidance of the next war. As for peace itself –

or "full peace" to employ a now much used expression – the Syrians are not in a hurry. Rather, they need time to prepare for such a "full peace" and for the economic, technological, intellectual and political challenges it will entail.

Syrian policy-makers were caught by surprise when sudden progress on the Israeli–Palestinian track became evident in mid-1993. Still, by September 1994 when Israel and Jordan concluded their peace treaty, and by September 1995 when the Oslo II agreement was signed, organized internal attempts at evaluating the impact that regional peace would have on Syria's economic environment were strikingly absent on the Syrian scene. No studies, let alone plans for economic responses, were undertaken or commissioned, whether in the government, the ruling Ba'th party, Syrian universities, or even chambers of commerce and industry, on the economic repercussions peace would have for Syria. Official rhetoric remained restricted to warnings against normalization with Israel and accusations against those Arab brethren who actively sought to prepare for a new Middle East that would include the Israelis.[15] Neither the media nor other public forums debated the questions and challenges Syria would have to face after a peace treaty. The matter was not yet a topic of discussion.

This apparent inertia was only partly motivated by politics. Syrian officials tried to justify the absence of a Syrian debate on a future Middle East by arguing that the outcome of the peace negotiations must not be predetermined.[16] As a result, Syria did not take part in the multilateral peace negotiations and was wary of efforts, such as international study groups, that in their format virtually replicated the multilateral approach.

Other factors were of greater importance in the absence of debate and planning in Syria. The authoritarian nature of the system did not, in practice, allow anyone but President Assad to take as important a decision as the preparation for peace with Israel or even to open a public debate over the issue.[17] Moreover, there were objective, if often hidden and unconscious, fears on the part of Syrian policy-makers, officials, academics and even members of the private sector, about the challenges of a new and pacified Middle East. These resembled, to a large extent, the fears of Arab public opinion in general: fears of further disunion and fragmentation in the Arab world, of an Israeli-dominated Israeli–Palestinian–Jordanian economic union, of Israeli cultural and economic hegemony, and of Arab economic dependence on Israel.[18]

In Syria, such fears were, and remain, even more pronounced than in other Arab countries. Syria's major gain from a peace treaty with Israel, the return of the Golan Heights, will be of greater national-political than economic benefit. Several thousand Syrian refugee families from the Golan, now crowding into Damascus, will probably resettle on the Heights and once again resume farming activities. Others, particularly from the second and third generations of refugees, are likely to sell or lease their land to agricultural entrepreneurs. Thus the Golan, once regained, may contribute to increasing Syria's fruit and vegetable exports. It is of little economic value, however, when compared to what Egypt gained in 1975 and 1979 when it disengaged from, and eventually made peace with, Israel: namely the reopening of the Suez Canal and the return of the occupied Sinai oil fields. At the same time, a return of the Golan, an end to the "no war, no peace" situation between Syria and Israel, and a comprehensive settlement of the Arab–Israeli conflict, would deprive Syria of the strategic position it now holds in the regional balance of power. Peace is likely to reduce Syria's political weight; the aid which the country has been attracting from the regional system will most probably decrease or, at best, remain steady, and its political system could subsequently be threatened.

This is why it does not seem as if Syria, in the short term at least, will be able to obtain a fair share of any "peace dividend" which is expected for the region if peace comes about. The fact that even international agencies expect Israel to reap more economic benefit from regional peace than the Arab states[19] can only increase Syrian and Arab anxieties and suspicions.

WHAT PEACE DIVIDEND FOR SYRIA?

International observers and agencies expect that three mechanisms will provide economic benefits to the Middle East in the event of a general peace settlement: intra-regional trade and cooperation in a new Middle East that would integrate Israel and reduce trade barriers; investments from regional and international sources which a pacified and integrated Middle East would attract; increased competition would enhance consumer choice; and reduced military expenditures and the freeing of resources for development efforts.[20]

Intra-regional Cooperation

At the centre of most scenarios of a future Middle East is what can be called the Middle Eastern regional market. Such a regional market would, in principle, permit the exchange of goods and services between states, irrespective of whether or not this will eventually lead to the establishment of regional or sub-regional free trade agreements. As things stand today, Syria may well find itself at the losing end of such a development. In the short term, the threat to Syria from the integration of Israel's more advanced and cost-effective economy into the regional economic system comes not so much from direct competition in Syria's domestic market as from regional competition and the likely changes this will provoke in the economic geography of the Middle East.

Syria does not have to fear a flood of Israeli products in its domestic market. Israeli industry undoubtedly offers a range of comparatively advanced industrial products which neither Syria nor other Arab states produce, but they are not always price competitive. Moreover, Syrian consumers in the foreseeable future will probably prefer to buy such goods from Europe or Japan. Only certain categories of Israeli products, such as irrigation equipment, might have a promising future in the Syrian market. Nothing will prevent Syria from continuing to protect its own industries and agriculture against competition or to conclude preferential trade arrangements with Arab countries such as Lebanon and Jordan, and possibly with a future Palestinian state, providing them with favoured access to the Syrian market for their agricultural and industrial products when domestic Syrian supplies are insufficient.

There is little doubt that opportunities for the Syrian economy will improve once regional trade relations are normalized. Among the first economic sectors to profit from peace and the new linkages in the Middle East will be the tourism sectors of the Arab Mashreq (eastern) states, among them Syria's lively tourist industry.[21] As regards the exchange of goods, Israel may in a future peace scenario prove to be of as limited interest for Syrian producers as Syria is for Israel's industries. Syria could, in theory, supply Israel with oil and natural gas; a pipeline project from the Syrian oil fields to the north of Israel would no doubt make sense in terms of purely economic considerations. It is unlikely, however, that Israel would wish any time soon to depend on fuel deliveries from its staunchest former enemy.

Syria could gain a reasonable share of the Palestinian market, political conditions there permitting. Historically, geographic Palestine was the most important export market for Syrian agriculture and industry. The Palestinian entity would probably like to offer reasonable market opportunities for Syrian products, particularly cheap manufactured mass consumer goods. At the same time, however, Syrian exporters are likely to lose market shares in the Arab Gulf states in the event of peace. Here, Israeli competition is likely to directly threaten Syria's largely successful attempts over the last few years to penetrate regional markets with its fruits and vegetables.

From the Syrian perspective, what is most alarming is the fear that Damascus could lose ground as a result of regionwide infrastructural developments which would make Israel, the Palestinian Authority and Jordan the centrepiece of a realigned Mashreq (eastern) sub-region. Recent studies conducted by the World Bank and other institutions tend to view the reconstruction of the Beirut port and the Beirut–Damascus highway as low-priority projects. At the same time, these studies predict that the main communication lines in a post-peace Middle East region will start from or lead to Israel, with Haifa becoming the main regional port; that the main east–west connections will all emanate from Israel rather than Lebanon; and that a reopened Tapline may probably terminate in Haifa rather than Sidon.[22] Such developments would pose a real threat to Syrian (and Lebanese) transit trade and reduce economic and political opportunities for services and industry that usually accompany transit functions.

In the longer term, Syrian businesspersons and industrialists are likely to adapt to a new regional setting and find niches for their services and products. Syrians have often, and rightly so, stated that Syria's economic future lies in a regionally integrated economy. From a Syrian perspective, however, peace with Israel is not the only important condition for such integration. Of similar importance to Syria is whether a stable framework for cooperation with the countries of the GCC can be established, and whether, or how, Iraq will be reintegrated into the region. Syria could potentially challenge some of the adverse results of Israel's entry into the Middle East economy by reestablishing economic links with an Iraq whose regional isolation has ended.

From the late 1970s, when Syrian–Iraqi relations temporarily improved, until 1982 when trade relations between the two countries were almost completely severed, Iraq was Syria's single largest Arab trading partner, absorbing up to 30 per cent of its regional exports. For Syria, all plans and scenarios for regional infrastructural development and integration must take the Iraqi dimension into account. To the extent that the new Middle East market might be an Israeli–Palestinian–Jordanian affair, Syria risks finding itself at its fringes; with Iraq included, the Syrian role would undoubtedly be much more pivotal. For instance, a railway connection linking Damascus with Baghdad, Basra and the Gulf, with an extension from Beirut to Damascus, could become as important for Syria as the projected coastal highway along the eastern Mediterranean coast. For the time being, however, political considerations, namely the political divide between Damascus and Baghdad, and the US and Baghdad, are likely to weigh heavier than economic rationality.

Regional and International Investment

It is generally expected that regional stability and peace in the Middle East would encourage the inflow of foreign capital and help return private capital that has fled the region in the past decades. Capital flight from Syria has been particularly high: the savings of Syrian residents abroad have been estimated at some $26 billion, almost twice as much as the net inflow of Arab non-military assistance to Syria over the past two decades. There is no doubt, therefore, that a partial reversal of capital flight from Syria could promote economic growth and could potentially alleviate the most serious of the problems Syria faces in the years to come, namely, that it must provide employment for an extremely young and rapidly growing population.[23]

The Syrian government, in the course of the cautious economic liberalization programme which it has been pursuing since the mid-1980s, has expended considerable effort to attract local, expatriate and foreign investments. As a result, capital that was taken out of Syria may now re-enter under the label of "expatriate capital". Under the provisions of Law No. 10 (an investment law issued in 1991), Syrian and foreign investors alike are offered far-reaching incentives and guarantees such as exemption from customs duties and foreign exchange regulations, and tax holidays of up to seven years.

There doubtless exist investment opportunities in Syria. Up-stream food production, textiles processing, Syria's traditional industries, could be further developed with foreign capital and become successful export industries. The same applies to some of the local metal-working industries. Even larger investment projects such as factories for the assembly of cars, pickups or light trucks could make sense in a country like Syria, particularly if the regional market becomes easily accessible. Local metal-working and plastic-producing establishments could, with an injection of capital, easily extend their product range and supply parts for such industries. Generally, Syria's very-small-scale private industrial sector is capital-poor and would benefit a great deal if foreign and expatriate investments were allowed in the banking sector, thereby making money available for private industrial development.[24]

Some difficulties remain, however, as regards Syria's prospects to attract foreign investment and even expatriate capital. Given that Eastern Europe, with its high comparative advantage, is a strong competitor for investment, there is no abundance of international capital-seeking investment opportunities in the Middle East. Syria in particular, except for its oil sector – the only sector of the national economy where multinational companies are already operating – is not at present exceptionally interesting for investors. In a regional economy after a peace settlement, Syria will have to compete for investment with Lebanon, Jordan, Israel and the Palestinian Authority, and the banking systems in the neighbouring Arab states are more developed than in Syria. The Syrian government, for its part, has still not permitted private banks, the services provided by public-sector banks are notoriously poor, and talk about a reform of the banking sector and the establishment of mixed public-private banks has been stalled as has the debate about opening a stock exchange.

Similarly, physical infrastructures such as the electricity and telecommunications networks are in a much better state in Israel and Jordan than in Syria, while Lebanon is pursuing an ambitious infrastructure reconstruction programme in order to regain its position as a services centre in the Middle East. Lebanon, Jordan, Israel and the Palestinian territories all offer better vocational training and university education than Syria does, and they produce more and better qualified technical and administrative local personnel in practically all sectors. Moreover, none of these countries has as inflexible a bureaucracy as have the Syrians.

Political conditions in Syria do not especially favour the government's endeavors to attract foreign and expatriate investments. While authoritarian government as such does not necessarily discourage potential investors, the absence of rule of law, the lack of an independent judiciary and doubts about Syria's internal stability do. Until now, the Syrian government has not been accountable to anyone but itself. Therefore, neither a local entrepreneur nor a foreign investor would be unable to sue the government or any official authority in case of a business conflict; nor could they take legal measures if their property were seized, or worse, if their personal freedom were threatened by any of Syria's internal security agencies. This is why a majority of Syrian entrepreneurs, even those whose closeness to official circles has helped them attain quasi-monopolistic control over certain sectors of the economy, keep most, if not all, of their liquid assets outside the country. This is also why expatriates or residents who redirect some of their foreign assets to Syria often seek speculative and quick-return ventures rather than long-term investments that would tie their capital to the restrictive regime.

This tendency is further supported by feelings of uncertainty and uneasiness regarding the political future of Syria. While there are many reasons to expect that the transition from the Assad government to a successor may come about rather smoothly,[25] no one can guarantee it. The state that Hafez El-Assad has built since his takeover of power in 1970 is strong, with tight economic and political control and very limited social autonomy; moreover, institutions are weak and may only begin to fulfill their roles once this powerful leader is gone. At present, confidence in the state and its institutions is low, as is the confidence of entrepreneurs, potential investors and other social groups in the ability of state institutions to manage a major regime crisis such as the death of the president. Even in the event that his son succeeds him, people are dubious about his abilities to both maintain control and minimize resistance to the major economic and political reforms the new Middle East order seems to be demanding.

Military Expenditure

Despite the fact that optimistic scenarios of a future Middle East at peace have envisaged substantial cuts in military budgets and a redirection of public expenditures from defence to development, one should not realistically expect this any time soon, even if an agreement is signed. This applies particularly to Israel and Syria. It is notable that even Israeli economists – as opposed to representatives of the military – do not expect, let alone demand, a reduction of military expenditures in the foreseeable future.[26] Regional peace, if it does occur, will most probably not translate into an immediate regional drive towards disarmament. All parties – with Jordan and the Palestinian Authority most probably providing significant exceptions – will remain on their guard and maintain a high level of military preparedness. Syria in particular will remain suspicious not only of Israel, but also of its neighbours Turkey and Iraq.

Even if there is peace between Syria and Israel, this will not automatically lead to a reduction of defence and external security expenditures. If the Golan is returned to Syria and demilitarized, expensive early-warning systems will likely be installed in place of tanks and gun batteries on both sides of the border. If, in the long run, the Middle East should become a zone free of weapons of mass destruction, Syria for its part may feel compelled to exchange its comparatively cheap arsenal of chemical weapons for more expensive and technically advanced armaments.

It must also be remembered that the Syrian military budget has already been reduced in the early 1990s, mainly in response to economic constraints. Official figures may exaggerate budget cuts, but they reflect a genuine tendency. In addition, active military manpower has remained stagnant over the last decade, with thousands of conscripts whom the armed forces could not absorb being channelled into the police forces. Syria's military leadership may therefore find that the armed forces have already sacrificed more than they should. However, on the one hand, one can still imagine the Syrian authorities reducing the length of military service and making further cuts in numbers of troops in the aftermath of any future peace treaty in order to streamline their military budget. On the other hand, the military and police services provide Syrians with a social employment safety net; the government will have to consider that the number of unemployed youth will increase in inverse proportion to the number of conscripts released from the armed services.

In regard to military hardware, the Syrian armed forces by all international standards are in urgent need of modernization. Not only does most of Syria's military technology date from the 1960s, 1970s and, at best, the early 1980s, but a considerable number of its tanks, guns and jets have been cannibalized, and most of its air force is virtually grounded for lack of spare parts. Syria's military capability is therefore far less impressive than internationally-available figures would suggest.[27] From the Syrian point of view, if a modicum of military credibility and preparedness are to be maintained, then peace should in no way imply a further reduction in defence spending.

For these reasons, Syrian arms expenditures are likely to remain relatively high, certainly not dropping below the 25 per cent mark in the national budget. In the foreseeable future, the GCC countries may still be prepared to provide some funding to Syria and even to finance a modernization of the Syrian armed forces. And, should Assad die, the Gulf states may provide his son with additional short-term political–military assistance as they have pledged to do for King Abdullah of Jordan. Subsequently, however, Arab funding for Syrian defence spending may decrease, and Syria would then have to cover the costs of arms imports or a considerable portion of them from internal resources. Domestic power equations and the position of the military in the Syrian political system will determine whether such a development will entail increased defence expenditures, or, conversely, lead to a substantial cutback in military spending and a reduction in the privileges of the military elite.

CONCLUSION: A POLITICAL PEACE DIVIDEND?

It thus seems that Syria will not, in the short term, receive substantial economic gains from any peace settlement. Also, Syria will lose much of its international weight if the Arab–Israeli conflict is finally settled. The strategic rent-seeking or war dividends which the country has so far been able to increase would disappear. Even some alternative inflows of Arab aid that might be obtained and maintained over time would not suffice to compensate for domestic economic mismanagement and lack of reform. In regard to Western sources of finance, Syria cannot and does not expect that the United States, in the aftermath of a Syrian–Israeli peace treaty, would begin supporting the Syrian government with American grants as it has been supporting its Egyptian counterpart since Camp David. If Washington were at all to commit itself financially to stabilize peace between Syria and Israel, such commitments would most likely be directed towards the strengthening of Israel's defence after an Israeli withdrawal from the Golan Heights, and to finance the presence of American troops there if the two countries request such a deployment. Economically, Syria is looking to Europe rather than to the United States, and Syria might, in the medium term, decide that serious economic reforms should be pursued in the next couple of years.

Given these realities, Syria is not in a hurry to sign a peace treaty with Israel and open its borders to its erstwhile enemy. It is notable in this regard that even Syria's economic liberals are not demanding that the peace process be speeded up. Their priority is for internal economic reform to put the Syrian house in order, and then perhaps to confront the political risks of peace.[28] Otherwise, if regional peace were to occur with Syria unprepared for its challenges, the country could be pushed from its front-line regional diplomatic status to a much less comfortable backyard position.

At the same time, a peace agreement would be likely to alter Syria's domestic variables. If the external confrontation loses importance, it will become increasingly difficult to justify the maintenance of Syria's authoritarian rule, the privileges granted to the military and the general militarization of public life. Notably, many Syrians would expect a political more than an economic peace dividend, hoping that peace might bring about a reduction in the political power of the security apparatus, a restoration of respect for the law, and an increase in government accountability and public space.[29] Such hopes may, for the immediate future at least, exceed reality. One should not expect the Syrian military to forgo its strong position even if the state of war between Israel and Syria is eventually terminated.

Most likely, Syria's military and security apparatus will remain a strong corporate actor that will ward off attempts to reduce its privileges beyond a certain threshold and maintain a veto power, for some time at least, over Syria's political future. Popular expectations of declining military and security influence, however, reflect a de-legitimation of the Middle Eastern security state which Syria has so much represented, and whose era might well, in time, come to an end. Only then, it seems, when the present authoritarian system gives way to a more democratic, less-militarized state (whose government may still have to take the corporate interests of the military into consideration) will Syria be able to pursue all the necessary reforms, to make use of its human capital reserves and innovative forces, and thus to begin to constructively deal with the challenges of a new regional environment.

Notes

1. An earlier version of this chapter was published in *Beirut Review* 8 (Fall 1994).
2. Cf. President Assad's interview in Egypt's *Al-Ahram*, 11 October 1995.
3. Volker Perthes, "The Syrian Economy in the 1980s", *Middle East Journal* 46 (1992), 37–58; Rizkallah Hilan, "The Effects on Economic Development in Syria of a Just and Long-Lasting Peace", in Stanley Fischer, Dani Rodrik and Elias Tuma (eds), *The Economics of Middle East Peace: Views from the Region* (Cambridge, Mass, and London: MIT Press, 1993) p. 64.
4. Cf. Patrick Clawson, *Unaffordable Ambitions: Syria's Military Build-Up and Economic Crisis* (Washington, DC: Washington Institute for Near East Policy, 1989); Volker Perthes, "Syrian", in Veronika Buttner and Joachim Krause (eds), *Rustung statt Entwicklung? Sicherheitspolitik, Militarausgaben und Rustungskontrolle in der Dritten Welt* (Baden-Baden: Nomos, 1995).
5. United States Arms Control and Disarmament Agency (ACDA), *World Military Expenditures and Arms Transfers* (Washington, DC: 1990).
6. Cf. *Al-Hayat*, 11 February 1995.
7. Military expenditure, as reported in Syrian budgets, ranged around 35 per cent of the total from the early 1970s to 1978, increased to peaks of around 40 per cent in the years until 1987 and has since dropped again to some 30–35 per cent. See International Monetary Fund, *Government Finance Statistics*, Washington DC, various years.
8. OECD Development Assistance Committee, Development Cooperation, Paris, various years; Pierre van den Boogaerde, *Financial Assistance from Arab Countries and Arab Regional Institutions* (Washington DC: International Monetary Fund, 1991).
9. On Iranian oil deliveries to 1987 see Clawson, *Unaffordable Ambitions*, *op. cit*: p. 55. Syria's 1990 budget was the last one listing an entry under the title "Grants and Assistance", which used to stand for the Iranian oil gift.

10. World Bank, *World Development Report,* (1995); OECD, *Development Cooperation,* (1995); *Le Monde*, 5 January 1993; *Al-Hayat*, 13 October 1993.
11. Official aid flows from Arab OPEC states decreased from more than \$9.5 billion in 1980, to a low of less than \$1.5 billion in 1989. During the year of the Gulf crisis in 1990 the Gulf states increased their aid to over \$6 billion; in 1991, however, aid was again reduced to \$2.7 billion. See World Bank, *World Development Report*, 1993, table 19.
12. A notable exception is Jordan which traditionally has been highly dependent on foreign aid flows. See World Bank, *World Development Report*, various issues; Boogaerde, *Financial Assistance*: p. 81 as cited in Note 8.
13. Syria, Tunisia and Morocco are all considered middle-income developing countries. The population of Syria amounted to about 12 million in 1990 (1980: 8.7 million); Tunisia about 8 million (1980: 7 million); and Morocco 25 million (1980: 20 million). Per capita GDP in 1980 was estimated at \$1340 for Syria, \$1310 for Tunisia and \$900 for Morocco; in 1991 at \$1160 for Syria, \$1500 for Tunisia and \$1030 for Morocco. Source: *World Development Report*, various issues.
14. The magnitude of this amount becomes clear in comparison to the non-military debt which Syria accumulated over (mostly) the same period, amounting to only some \$5 billion. Looney takes a different approach to analyzing the costs and benefits of Syria's military expenditures; see Chapter 6 in this volume.
15. For example, Riyad Muhammad Bilqis, "*Al-muqata'a al-'arabiyya li isra'il: silah 'arabi mashru' yanbaghi altamasuk bih*" (The Arab boycott of Israel: a legitimate Arab weapon that must be maintained), *Tishrin*, Damascus, 19 April 1994.
16. The example of neighbouring Lebanon, however, which has followed Syria in staying away from the multilateral talks, but which is nevertheless conducting a lively debate on and preparing itself economically for a post-peace Middle Eastern environment, shows that the boycott of the multilaterals need not imply an absence of planning and preparation for expected regional changes.
17. On the political system cf. Raymond A. Hinnebusch, *Authoritarian Power and State Formation in Báthist Syria, Army, Party, and Peasant* (Boulder: Westview, 1990); Volker Perthes, *The Political Economy of Syria under Asad* (London: I.B. Tauris, 1995).
18. These fears have been analysed by Ghassan Salame, "*Afkar awwaliyya 'an al-souq al-sharq al-awsati*" (Preliminary ideas about the Middle Eastern market), and partly represented by Mahmoud Abd al-Fadil, "*Mashari' al-tartibat al-iqtisadiyya al-sharq awsatiyya: al-tasawwurat, al-mahadhir, ashkal al-muwajaha*" (Projects for Middle Eastern economic arrangements; scenarios, precautions, forms of confrontation), both in *Al-tahaddiyyat "al-sharq awsatiyya" al-jadida wal-watan al-'arabi* (The new "Middle Eastern" challenges and the Arab homeland) (Beirut: Centre for Arab Unity Studies, 1994).
19. Commission of the European Communities, *Die Kunfigen Beziehungen und die Kunfrige Zusammenarbeit Zwischen der Gemeinschaft und dem Nahen Osten*, Brussels, 8 September 1993, p. 23. Assuming that regional peace will come about and intra-regional cooperation will increase, the report foresees that per capita GDP will grow by 59 per cent in Israel, but only by 16 per cent in the Arab Mashreq until the year 2010.
20. In this sense, see Commission of the European Communities, *Die Kunftigen Beziehungen* (1994); Ishac Diwan and Lyn Squire, "Economic Development and Cooperation in The Middle East and North Africa", World Bank Discussion Paper Series: Middle East and North Africa, no. 9, Washington DC, November 1993. It is notable that some Israeli scholars are less optimistic than

international agencies with regard to the regionwide economic prospects of peace. See for example Eliyahu Kanovsky, "Assessing the Mideast Peace Economic Dividend", Security and Policy Studies no. 15, Begin and Sadat Centre for Strategic Studies, Ramat Gan, Israel, March 1994. Six Israeli authors also make contributions to J.W. Wright, Jr. (ed.), *The Political Economy of Middle East Peace: The Impact of Competing Trade Agendas* (London: Routledge, 1999). Four of the six conclude that the promised dividend from peace is unlikely to be high enough to overcome profits made from "Israel's Impermanent War Economy" and from "Economic Discrimination in Israel". See the contributions made to this volume by Noah Lewin-Epstein, Moshe Semoynov, Shemson Bichlor, Jonathan Nitzen, and also Shaul Gabbay and Amy Stien.

21. For an optimistic assessment of the opportunities for Middle Eastern tourism in an economy of peace, see Axel J. Halbach (ed.), *Perspektiven regionaler Wirtshaftskooperation im Nahen Osten Empirishe Analyse der Wirtschaftsbeziehungen von dem Hintergrund einer umfassende Friedensregelung* (Munich: Ifso Institute für Wirtschaftsforschung, 1994), pp. 161–71.
22. World Bank, "A Note on Priority Regional Infrastructure Projects", Paper prepared at the request of the Multilateral Working Group on Regional Economic Development, Washington DC, October 1993, cited in *Al-Hayat*, 4 November 1993.
23. Conservatively estimated, some 250 000 job seekers will enter the Syrian labour market annually during the coming decade. This is based on the assumption that the annual net increase of the labour force equals about 60 per cent of the increase of the number of persons under 15 years of age, which implies that there will be no significant increase in female participation in the labour force. For more detail see Perthes, *The Political Economy of Syria under Asad*, *op. cit.*, pp. 62–5.
24. On the structure of Syria's private sector, see Volker Perthes, "The Syrian Private Industrial and Commercial Sectors and the State", *International Journal of Middle East Studies* 24 (1992), pp. 207–30.
25. For more detail see Perthes, *The Political Economy of Syria under Asad*, *op. cit.*, pp. 267–71.
26. See, for instance, the interview with Israel's Central Bank governor, Jacob Frendel, in *Das Parlament*, 29 April 1994; and Kanovsky, "Assessing the Mideast Peace Economic Dividend", *op. cit.*, p. 11f. (Also see, Nitzer and Bichlor, "The Impermanent War Economy," as cited in n. 20.)
27. According to the International Institute for Strategic Studies (IISS), Syria has some 4600 main battle tanks and 639 combat aircraft. Military experts doubt that more than half of these are actually operational. See IISS, *The Military Balance, 1992–1993* (London: Brassey's, 1992).
28. See Juzif Samaha, "*Suriya: al-ihtimam bi-l-i 'ala qa'adatay al-tajahul wal-thiqqa bil-nafs*" (Syria: Concern with National Preparation on the Bases of Ignoring and Self-Confidence), *Al-Hayat*, 7 August 1995.
29. This view is well-expressed by Hilan, "The Effects on Economic Development in Syria of a Just and Long-Lasting Peace". *op. cit.*

Epilogue: Critical Questions and Alternative Scenarios

William Stoltzfus

When I agreed to write this epilogue, I made it clear that my comments and observations would be personal. Having been listed in *The Arabists*[1] as one of the "hard core" supporters for changing US policies towards the Middle East region – a somewhat inaccurate designation I share with Richard Parker and Talcott Seelye, among others – I want to point out that my role the last 20 years has been only that of an observer of the developing diplomatic dialogue between Americans, Arabs and Israelis. My statements here grow out of lectures I gave with J.W. Wright, Jr. at Yale and Rutgers Universities.[2] These lectures combined the insights I have acquired as an American Ambassador to the region, but I have no official role in current diplomatic initiatives.

That said, however, I do not think there is much that is subtle about the current US administration's approach to the Middle East in particular or to the Islamic world in general. Nor is there much that is balanced or sophisticated about the American media's approach to Arab–Israeli affairs, nor is there evidence among the American public at large of an in-depth understanding of the political and economic situation in the Middle East. In each case, the opinions expressed are naive and based mainly on conjecture and the selective use of information provided by special interest groups. The resulting, rather skewed presentation of events has created much political and social distance between Americans and Arabs, and it has even affected the way Arab and Muslim Americans are treated inside the United States.[3]

I see three primary excuses for the American position *vis-à-vis* Arab and mostly Muslim countries. First, Americans tend to see themselves as being superior to other peoples on both social and moral grounds. This perception contradicts evidence that people in the Arab world are endowed with the same basic personality traits and support ethical systems similar to those espoused by Westerners and indeed by human civilization at large.[4] Second, Americans feel that they are a long way from the rest of the world, and they are politically self-centered; this remains the case despite the fact that technology is producing an ever-shrinking world. Nonetheless America's ability to exert a large degree of control over international communications technology adds to the problem; in some cases America misinforms the world. Third, the United States is currently the world's major power; there is simply too much on Washington's agenda to have time for nuance or for digesting too much information; the result is a dangerous level of superficiality in research and policy formulation at the governmental level.

To understand the scenarios these positions create, one must differentiate between stated American policies, which might include the promotion of democratic governance, free trade and economic development for Third World nations, and American interests, the factors around which US diplomacy really centres; Washington seems too willing to selectively sacrifice global policies if they impinge on its perceived interests within a particular region. I do not aim to pass judgement on the ethics of this fact, but it is naive to believe that this is less than the true state of affairs. Global policies include promoting democracy, freedom and human rights; upholding the international rule of law among nations and peoples through the United Nations Security Council; reducing trade barriers; and promoting an environmental agenda to combat the dangerous trends that threaten to destroy the Earth.

Current US interests in the Middle East region, however, centre around quite different priorities, such as: protecting American hegemony over the Gulf oil region, including the dual containment of Iraq and Iran to prevent them from becoming too powerful; reducing tensions in the Arab–Israeli theatre, part of which involves the promotion of a direct political process between Israel, the Arab states and the Palestinians that bypasses the UN Security Council and its resolutions; preventing civil violence and military offensives if at all possible, especially if they are waged against either the Gulf oil monarchies or Israeli interests; and finally, the reduction or elimination of chemical, biological and nuclear weaponry in those nations the US has judged to harbour adversarial intentions towards either itself or allied governments.

These specific interests have historically been driven by Cold War fears about Soviet penetration into the Middle East region through infiltration of individual Arab states. In addition, the scenarios they have created have reflected the perceived need to dominate the geopolitical situation in the Middle East by way of American political and military support for successive Israeli governments in the Arab–Israeli conflict. Since the 1970s several economic items have been added to the list of US interests: an ensured continuous access to Arab oil at low prices; the desires of American industry for access to oil-rich commercial markets; and, finally, the goal of sustaining American jobs via military exports to America's biggest clients, the pro-American Arab governments and the Israelis. These are all examples of situations where short-term American regional interests have come into conflict with general policy objectives at the global level and have consequently fostered regional disputes rather than alleviated them.

It is also true that American economic policies have often come into conflict with – and have usually lost out to – perceived political-strategic interests. Consider that the US economy was threatened by a short-term oil embargo in the early 1970s, waged mainly by Arab states, resulted from Arab frustration over continued US support for Israel. During the 1980s, several hundred American lives were needlessly sacrificed in Lebanon as a consequence of the Israeli invasion and occupation of that country. All this time, Israel routinely topped the United Nations' list of leading human-rights abusers, occupying Arab territory contrary to UN Security Council resolutions, preventing Palestinians from returning to their country, and excluding those who remained under occupation from both the political and free market processes. In 1991, the United States led a war coalition against Iraq as a means of both protecting American oil interests and asserting the renewed policy of alliance with Israel through the post-war peace process. Since 1979 Washington has spent billions of dollars to keep Egypt and Israel at peace; potentially billions more will be pledged to bolster other aspects of the Arab–Israeli peace process – some $400 million at Wye alone.

Most characteristic of the American position is that Washington has too often considered only Israeli interests in formulating its policy objectives because such support improves the political standing of individual politicians with important domestic elite and electoral blocs. In the face of these interests, and in conflict with American policy at the global level, the US has continually endorsed scenarios that have led not to peace but rather towards further inflammation of the political atmosphere in the region. This means radical change is required in US policy; the first step would be to engage in a serious effort aimed at the identification of the real problems that exist in the Middle East. For the enforced maintenance of the regional situation in its current state is only good for those who see the age-old solution to conflict – "might makes right" – as appropriate, a dwindling group of people to be sure. A *status quo* that must constantly be enforced against the majority of the people in the region at whatever cost can only benefit those who are powerful enough to impose their will on the less powerful, and to do so through repression and forms of violence.

Among those who have suffered most have been the Palestinian refugees who remain in political exile in Jordan, Syria and Lebanon, and those Palestinians living in equally intolerable conditions under occupation in the West Bank and Gaza Strip. The powerful may find it difficult to see themselves as repressive, or to recognize that American values might be in conflict with American actions, but from the Arab point of view the Western great-power exercise of control in the region has been at the very least oppressive.

Along the economic dimension, the need to understand the ways in which resource inequities might lay the groundwork for future conflict make this book extremely important reading. Once diplomatic initiatives are completed and left to the administrators and technocrats for implementation, it will be the remaining economic realities that will ultimately determine the fate of regional peace. And, it is at this point when competing trade agendas will most affect either the delivery or debilitation of implementation plans and processes.[5] If American economic assistance is merely meant to bolster Israeli interests while thwarting the Palestinian aspiration to ultimately achieve full national independence, and if the Palestinian standard of living continues its precipitous free-fall in conjunction with the peace process, it will be Hamas and the Islamist opposition regionwide – rather than the Arab and Israeli supporters of the peace process – who will come into the forefront of the Middle East in the historical sense. If American military and economic assistance in the Arab countries is geared only towards keeping friendly client governments in power, but not at helping the vast and growing populations of those countries, then it will be peace – and America's long-term interests – that will ultimately suffer.

If, however, international assistance programmes promote Israeli–Palestinian cooperation in banking, manufacturing and participation in global markets, and if they encourage Palestinian economic independence, then Palestinians will be able to earn a living, both Palestinian and Israeli exports will flourish, and economic growth will be sustainable on both sides of the Green Line. It will also be important to encourage a higher degree of support for American trade interests in the region, not only so that US companies can profit from this exchange, but also because they have great abilities to produce jobs and transfer needed capital, technologies and training to the West Bank and Gaza as well as to other parts of the region. This will apply particularly to countries such as Lebanon – my former home – which is currently undergoing a massive reconstruction effort but where American trade interests are still inexplicably hindered by a long-obsolete US policy. In sum, I predict it will be economic interdependencies that will eventually sustain peace in the Middle East, once it has been achieved at the political level. The questions are: will Arab and Israeli governments and their peoples really be able and willing to work together, as equals? And, will Americans really help? Critical questions, indeed!

Notes

1. See Richard Parker's review of Robert D. Kaplan's *The Arabists: The Romance of the American Elite* (New York: Free Press, 1993), in *Journal of Palestine Studies* 24(1) (Autumn 1994), pp. 67–77.
2. Other quotes from these lectures can also be found in J.W. Wright, Jr, *Competing Trade Agendas in the Arab–Israeli Peace Process* (Abu Dhabi: Emirater Center for Strategic Studies and Research, 1998), and J.W. Wright, Jr, *The Political Economy of Middle East Peace: The Impact of Competing Trade Agendas* (London: Routledge, 1999).
3. J.W. Wright, Jr, "Social Distance, Discrimination, and Political Conflict: Arab-ethnics in America", *Journal of Intergroup Relations* 21(4) (Winter 1994–95), pp. 3–11.

4. Jennifer L. Hozik and J.W. Wright, Jr, "A Cross-Cultural Investigation of Personality Traits among Arab and American Business Students", *Social Behavior and Personality* 24(3) (1996), pp. 221–30; Jennifer L. Higgins, J.W. Wright, Jr and Katherine Paluighi, "Values Representations Among Arab and American Business Students", *Journal of Intergroup Relations* 22(4) Winter 1995–96), pp. 38–51.
5. See J.W. Wright, Jr., "Introduction," and Paul J. Findley, "Epilogue," in *Structural Flaws in the Middle East Peace Process* (London: Macmillan, 1999). Also see citations in n. 2 above.

Index